D1565839

Break-ins, Death Threats and the FBI:

The Covert War Against the Central America Movement

Break-ins, Death Threats and the FBI:

The Covert War Against the Central America Movement

Ross Gelbspan

South End Press
Boston

Cover design by Jane Carey
Text design and production by the South End Press collective
Printed in the U.S.A. on acid-free paper.
First edition, first printing

Library of Congress Cataloguing-in-Publication Data
Gelbspan, Ross
Break-ins, death threats and the FBI: the covert war against the Central America movement / Ross Gelbspan.
p. cm.
Includes index.
ISBN 0-89608-413-2 : $30.00. – ISBN 0-89608-412-4 : $14.00
1. United States. Federal Bureau of Investigation. 2. Committee in Solidarity with the People of El Salvador (U.S.) 3. Criminal investigation--United States--Case studies. 4. Political persecution--United States--Case studies. I. Title.
HV8144.F43G45 1991
364.1–dc20   91-129 CIP

South End Press, 116 Saint Botolph Street, Boston, MA 02115
99 98 97 96 95 94 93 92 91   1 2 3 4 5 6 7 8 9

Contents

Chart of Information Flow / vii

Acknowledgments / viii

Foreword by Frank J. Donner / x

Preface
On Frank Varelli and Other Sources / 1

1
Beginnings of a Secret War / 13

2
An Epidemic of Terrorism / 25

3
**The FBI's Sister City Program:
From Dallas to San Salvador / 35**

4
**Back Channel Partners:
The FBI and the National Guard / 47**

5
"Gilberto" and "The Doctor" / 61

6
**Allies in the Shadows:
The FBI's Private Network / 73**

v

7

The "Active Measures" Equation:
Advocacy + Propaganda = Terrorism / 85

8
An Album of Terrorists, An Underground of Spies / 97

9
The Decoy or the Duck / 105

10
The CIA at Home, the FBI Abroad / 121

11
An Explosion of Names / 135

12
The Heart of the Terror Network / 149

13
Passing the Torch: From the FBI to the NSC / 169

14
The FBI and Oliver North's "Private Network" / 183

15
An Epidemic of Terrorism: Continued / 197

16
Completing the Cover-Up / 209

Notes / 233

Index / 251

Chart of Information Flow

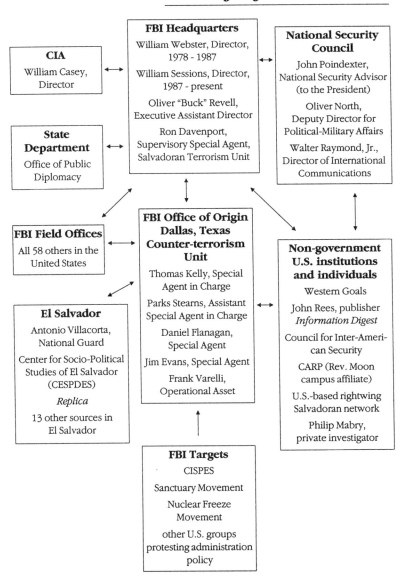

CIA
William Casey, Director

State Department
Office of Public Diplomacy

FBI Headquarters
William Webster, Director, 1978 - 1987
William Sessions, Director, 1987 - present
Oliver "Buck" Revell, Executive Assistant Director
Ron Davenport, Supervisory Special Agent, Salvadoran Terrorism Unit

National Security Council
John Poindexter, National Security Advisor (to the President)
Oliver North, Deputy Director for Political-Military Affairs
Walter Raymond, Jr., Director of International Communications

FBI Field Offices
All 58 others in the United States

FBI Office of Origin Dallas, Texas Counter-terrorism Unit
Thomas Kelly, Special Agent in Charge
Parks Stearns, Assistant Special Agent in Charge
Daniel Flanagan, Special Agent
Jim Evans, Special Agent
Frank Varelli, Operational Asset

Non-government U.S. institutions and individuals
Western Goals
John Rees, publisher *Information Digest*
Council for Inter-American Security
CARP (Rev. Moon campus affiliate)
U.S.-based rightwing Salvadoran network
Philip Mabry, private investigator

El Salvador
Antonio Villacorta, National Guard
Center for Socio-Political Studies of El Salvador (CESPDES)
Replica
13 other sources in El Salvador

FBI Targets
CISPES
Sanctuary Movement
Nuclear Freeze Movement
other U.S. groups protesting administration policy

Acknowledgments

So very many people helped make this book possible that merely to list their names, let alone acknowledge my debts to them, would take pages. My apologies, as well as my gratitude, go to all those who are not acknowledged by name here.

Any thanks must begin with Tottie, Thea and Joby, who contributed far more to this book than any family members should ever have to give. Numerous personal friends permitted me to secret copies of documents, tapes and computer disks with them—and provided safe phones and mailing addresses—during a period when our own phones were tapped and mail opened, and we lived in fairly constant fear of break-ins.

I am especially grateful to Lance Lindblom and the J. Roderick MacArthur Foundation for their financial help and their unswerving encouragement. Now that Mr. Lindblom has recovered his own FBI files, I can assure him he is in excellent company.

To John Roberts and the Board of the Civil Liberties Union of Massachusetts I owe a great gratitude for their institutional, as well as personal, support. I am especially indebted to Jeff McConnell for the hours he spent helping me pick through clues to sort out the mysterious patterns of activity that lay below the surface of the break-ins. Chip Berlet and Bob Greenberg were as generous with their own sources of information as they were with the time and thought they donated to this project.

Dan Alcorn was particularly helpful on several occasions in mediating my relationship with his client, Frank Varelli, as well as in his encouragement throughout. Thanks are due, as well, to Lindsay Mattison and Robert White for their financial support of Varelli and their intellectual support for this book early in the project.

Clearly I owe a great deal of gratitude to the people at the Center for Constitutional Rights—especially Ann Mari Buitrago, David Lerner, Adelita Medina and Alicia Fernandes, as well as Margaret and Michael Ratner—who opened their files and their recollections to me. Professor

Gary Marx was tremendously helpful in sorting through a disastrously disorganized early version of the manuscript and helping me focus and clarify the material.

Many, many colleagues at the *Boston Globe* were wonderfully supportive in their understanding of both the importance of the subject matter and the difficulty of the reporting. In particular, I will always be grateful to Kirk Scharfenberg for his role in shepherding a good portion of the material into the paper. Loie Hayes and other members of the South End Press collective have been relentless in their enthusiasm and encouragement and untiring in their editing help.

Finally, it is clear this book would not have been written—at least not in its current form—without the full cooperation of Frank Varelli. While he decided to withdraw from active participation in the project, due to lack of funding near the book's completion, it is my personal hope that at some point in the future he will be able to find in those portions of the book that deal with his story the vindication of his honor which he has so long sought.

—Ross Gelbspan,
January, 1991

Foreword

Break-ins, Death Threats and the FBI: The Covert War Against the Central America Movement raises the curtain on the Bureau's secret attempts to undermine and demonize the nationwide network of individuals and protest groups opposed to the Reagan Administration's Central America policies and programs. Ross Gelbspan demonstrates that the more than two hundred verified instances of break-ins, burglaries, death threats, harassment, and arson cannot be viewed, as many preferred, as a series of scattered horror stories, but must be recognized as unified by an overall plot to eliminate critics and opponents of Reagan's Central America initiatives.

An investigative reporter for the *Boston Globe,* Ross Gelbspan has won prominence for his exposés of political repression and invasions of protected freedoms. A tenacious hunter of clues to the Administration's complicity, Gelbspan has tracked down the principal operators in this assault. Most U.S. citizens are kept in the dark by a languid and frequently biased media. Our people remain largely ignorant with a nativist addiction to social amnesia, fueled by an "our country can do no wrong" orthodoxy and a callousness in responding to invasions of First Amendment freedoms. Thus, our responses to government-sponsored political repression range from disbelieving to indifferent to supportive.

Gelbspan's account of the FBI's role in this assault on dissent cannot be dismissed, as the Bureau has tried to do, by claims that the misconduct was self-inflicted or, in any event, too petty to warrant federal investigation. This book is not written with a conspiratorial mind-set characteristic of the ultra-right which Gelbspan exposes; he refrains from imputing to power-holders fantasized responsibility for politically motivated misconduct. His style is calm and measured, as are his conclusions concerning the extent of complicity of the Reagan Administration. Gelbspan's account draws on an awesome array of sources and establishes his commitment to the truth-is-bad-enough school of investigative journalism.

The core of the book deals with the wide-ranging assault on the Committee in Solidarity with the People of El Salvador (CISPES) by the FBI, concocted to destroy the group and silence its opposition to Reagan policy in Central America. Gelbspan's narrative is focused on the disclosures of an infiltrator who had gained access to CISPES leaders, Frank Varelli, surely one of the most fascinating of modern FBI undercover recruits. A Salvadoran former Baptist minister consumed by a passionate hatred of Communists, Varelli served the Bureau by forging a link between it and the Salvadoran National Guard, a nesting place for death squads. Most riveting is Gelbspan's account of how the FBI, with Varelli's invaluable assistance, progressively ratcheted CISPES up the national security threat scale from a non-violent foreign policy protest group, to an unregistered foreign agent, to an operative in a "Soviet active measures" campaign, to an agent of domestic terrorism in the service of Salvadoran revolutionaries, Cubans and/or Soviets.

Gelbspan's book cannot be viewed as merely another exposé of the FBI, an account of a dead past, a moment of excess never to be repeated. Right now the counter-subversive troops in Washington, D.C. are desperately searching for a new "negative reference group" to replace communism and its (invented) offshoots, terminally stricken by the end of the Cold War. But rescue may be in the right wing's sights: perhaps protesters against the Gulf War can be portrayed as fronting for any potential Middle Eastern terrorists in the United States.

—Frank J. Donner, author, *The Age of Surveillance: The Aims and Methods of America's Political Intelligence System* and *Protectors of Privilege: Political Repression in Urban America*

On Frank Varelli
and Other Sources

My involvement in this book began near the end of 1984. As a *Boston Globe* reporter, I covered two break-ins at the Old Cambridge Baptist Church in Cambridge, Massachusetts, which had recently joined the Sanctuary movement and which housed the offices of several Central America-oriented political groups. While the stories ran only a few paragraphs, I found the break-ins at the church very troubling.

In both cases, the intruders who ransacked the offices and rifled and apparently copied organizational files, left—untouched—cash, office equipment and other items of value. Since it was clear this was not a case of normal street crime, I wondered why these political groups had been targeted. At the time, I had little interest in —and less knowledge of—events in El Salvador, Guatemala and Nicaragua. But I had (and continue to have) an almost religious belief in the United States' bedrock committment to free speech and the sanctity of the democratic process. The break-ins, as inconsequential as they appeared, evoked an ominous premonition of a "brownshirt" type of political thuggery.

Over the next few years, I was appalled to learn that the break-ins in Cambridge were merely the early symptoms of a nationwide epidemic of such events. Over the next six years, Central America activists experienced nearly 200 incidents of harassment and intimidation, many involving such break-ins and thefts or rifling of files. Many of those reports came from the Movement Support Network of the Center for Constitutional Rights, which had set up a hotline for political groups to report various types of political harassment. A number of other reports of such harassments came to me from people who were aware of my reporting for the *Globe*. In the case of virtually all such reports, I

1

confirmed them personally, both through interviews with the victims and, wherever possible, interviews with investigating police officers.

While many of the victims felt virtually certain that the break-ins were the work of the FBI, which had established a track record for "black-bag jobs" in the 1960s, I was more prone to accept the Bureau's explanation that the FBI played no direct role in the break-ins. What did disturb me about the FBI, however, was its failure to investigate what surely constituted an interstate conspiracy to deprive political activists of their civil liberties. Time and again, the FBI declined to investigate the break-ins, saying they constituted sub-felony level burglaries which fell under the jurisdiction of local police and did not warrant the intervention of a federal enforcement agency. But local police, many of whom asserted their belief that the break-ins were political in nature, had neither the resources nor the inclination to devote serious time and personnel to low-level break-ins during a period when family violence, street crime and drug-related brutality were reaching alarming proportions.

Beginning in 1985, my assumptions about the involvement of the federal government in the harassments began to change. Reports surfaced of a number of public, overt activities by the FBI which seemed designed to harass and frighten political activists concerned with Central America. First came the reported interrogations by FBI agents of more than 100 American citizens who had traveled to Nicaragua. Later, we learned of the confiscation by Customs officials of personal diaries, books and newspapers from U.S. citizens returning from Central America. There were reports as well of Internal Revenue Service audits of low-budget political groups which seemed to have no explanation except for political motivations.

My convictions about the importance of this story were strengthened by the famous November 1986, Reagan-Meese press conference, and subsequent revelations, about a covert government operation, run out of the National Security Council, to provide illegal support to the Nicaraguan contras. We later learned that our allies in El Salvador played a key and, as yet, largely unexplored role in the covert contra-support operation.

As the cumulative revelations of the Iran-Contra affair indicated an increasingly extensive public-private apparatus that had contravened and undermined our constitutional form of government, I became more and more convinced that the break-ins, as well as the massive FBI investigation of Central America groups, represented the domestic side of a national scandal of which only the international aspects had been partially revealed to the public and the Congress.

That conviction was strengthened when I came to learn that the covert assault on political activists involved not only the FBI and the Salvadoran security forces, but also the CIA, the National Security Council and a range of private, right-wing groups—most of whom had been integrally involved in the secret contra operation.

What troubled me more, perhaps, than the clarifying picture of a well coordinated, multi-pronged assault on political dissenters was the apparent indifference of the press and the public to a brazen attack on the civil liberties of a significant segment of U.S. society. The implicit message in the lack of press attention was that there is nothing improper about widespread domestic surveillance. Equally disturbing was the tacit assumption that there is nothing newsworthy about the government condoning the harassment and intimidation of political dissenters. The attitude of many of my journalistic colleagues seemed to be a mix of deference to the overwhelming popularity of the President and indifference to an alarming threat to civil liberties. To this day, I am puzzled by the news judgment of peers who determined that a clear pattern of break-ins, thefts of files and death threats aimed at political dissenters is not a compelling subject of coverage.

So it was with eager anticipation that I attended a two-day hearing on the break-ins before the House Judiciary Subcommittee on Civil and Constitutional Rights in February 1987.

The star witness at that hearing was Frank Varelli, a naturalized Salvadoran-born U.S. citizen and a former employee of the FBI who had infiltrated the Dallas branch of one of the largest Central America groups, the Committee in Solidarity with the People of El Salvador (CISPES).

In his prepared statement to the House committee, Varelli alluded to a bizarre subterranean collaboration between the FBI and the Salvadoran National Guard designed to target U.S. liberal and left-wing activists as well as Salvadoran refugees. That collaboration involved the passing of names of both U.S. activists and Salvadorans between the FBI and the Salvadoran security forces and death squads. Varelli cited his role in preparing a Terrorist Photo Album for the FBI, which included entries on a former U.S. ambassador as well as several members of Congress. And he implicated his former case agent in the Dallas FBI office, Special Agent Daniel Flanagan, in the break-in of the apartment of a political activist in Texas. (That allegation was later denied by the FBI following an internal investigation by the Bureau.)

Varelli's testimony was effectively sabotaged—and his presentation discredited—by Rep. James Sensenbrenner, a conservative Republican member of the committee. During his testimony, Varelli told the Committee that "not once did I find, see, hear or observe any illegal conduct of any nature. The CISPES organization was peaceful, nonviolent, and devoted to changing the policies of the United States towards Central America by persuasion and education." But Sensenbrenner interrupted Varelli's testimony to produce a copy of a report—attributed to Varelli—which indicated that the group was plotting to assassinate President Reagan at the 1984 Republican Convention in Dallas. The production of that report effectively put an end to Varelli's testimony.

It was only later, after hearing Varelli's account of how a former right-wing colleague in Texas had altered the report on the colleague's word-processor—and after listening to tape recordings of Varelli's private briefing by Secret Service agents entrusted with the security of the convention—that I became convinced of the essential truth of the bulk of Varelli's testimony. (In fact, what Varelli reported to his FBI superiors was that CISPES was planning to disrupt the convention by some sort of street theater, such as blocking the President's motorcade and demonstrating against U.S. support for the government of El Salvador. His concern about the President's safety stemmed from a scenario in which armed terrorists, using the CISPES demonstration as a cover, might use the opportunity to launch an attack.)

Much of what he said in Congress, and what he elaborated in much greater detail in months of subsequent conversations with me, was confirmed in the winter of 1988-1989, when Varelli won the release of nearly 4,000 pages of his own FBI documents through a Freedom of Information Act (FOIA) lawsuit. Those documents showed that, with several minor exceptions, the tale he tried to tell to Congress was the truth. The documents also showed that Sensenbrenner was not alone in his effort to discredit Varelli. Embedded in his FBI papers were documents that indicated that the Bureau had, around the time Varelli went public, altered the results of his 1984 polygraph examination in order to convince Congressional investigators that his story was not to be taken seriously.

As a result of my reporting, I began, with the eager assistance of Varelli, to write a book on the assault on political liberties during the Reagan era. Over time, both Varelli and I experienced a number of the same type of harassments which were reported by political activists. Our phone calls were clearly overheard. On several occasions, when one of us hung up the phone, the other heard a tape recorder play back the conversation in speeded-up form. I began to receive unsolicited magazines sent to my address under an obscene variation of my name. On a couple of occasions, mail sent to me from sources around the country was opened and re-wrapped in plastic by the Post Office—with critical documents mysteriously removed.

The book that follows is admittedly incomplete in a number of areas. For one thing, neither the perpetrators—nor the coordinating hand—behind the string of break-ins has been conclusively identified. For another, the domestic surveillance role of Oliver North's network, both within and outside of the National Security Council, remains, except for a few teasing clues, shrouded in mystery.

Similarly, the full role of William Casey's (and now William Webster's) CIA remains a subject of speculation. It is clear that the Agency collaborated with the Salvadoran National Guard to provide the FBI with bogus evidence to trigger a nationwide investigation of Central America activists. The CIA, moreover, was authorized by an obscure 1982 presidential order to "request the FBI to collect foreign intelligence or support foreign intelligence requirements of other agencies within the Intelligence Community."[1] It is also clear that Casey instituted a domestic propaganda apparatus designed to counter the effectiveness of groups like the Nicaragua Network, the Inter-Religious Task Force on Central America, Witness for Peace and CISPES. In addition, large numbers of FBI documents released to both CISPES and Varelli were routed to or from the CIA.[2] There are other anecdotal clues from reliable sources of an ongoing relationship between members of the CIA and elements of a U.S.-based covert network of right-wing Salvadoran activists. The winter of 1989 and the spring of 1990 brought new evidence of the collaboration between U.S. State Department officials with the Salvadoran security forces in targeting U.S. religious activists in Central America. It also brought a new spate of break-ins. But the specifics of the Agency's role in setting in motion a massive investigation of U.S. citizens unfortunately remain hidden.

In short, this book does not pretend to be comprehensive. In that regard, it differs from most scholarly books on the FBI and other intelligence agencies which have been written years after the fact, when retired sources are willing to talk and documents are old enough to be declassified. By contrast, this account is a mosaic of known facts and obvious holes, written in real time as a product of investigative reporting. As such, it suffers from all the predictable shortcomings of that genre.

With that disclaimer in mind, some comments on the sources of information contained in the book are in order.

The accounts of harassments, interrogations, mail tampering, break-ins, audits, Customs seizures and the like have virtually all been confirmed. In the course of my reporting, I interviewed more than 70 victims of political harassments. While many of those episodes were brought to my attention by staff members of the Center for Constitutional Rights (CCR), I have, wherever possible, confirmed them through direct interviews with victims, local police and other relevant officials. In fact, the members of the CCR have been quite thorough and meticulous in their own confirmations of these episodes. But I mention my own confirmation of these stories to lay to rest accusations by both FBI officials and conservative activists that most victims' accounts are fabrications or that the break-ins and other harassments have been "self-inflicted." (Those accusations, which have made the rounds among political critics, were echoed last year by conservative Salvadorans and members of the U.S. intelligence community who suggested that the six Jesuits who were slain in San Salvador in 1989 were killed by the FMLN leftist rebels in order to sabotage continued U.S. support for the Salvadoran government.) In both cases, the accusations seem patently specious. In the case of the persecution of U.S. left-wing and liberal political targets of the FBI and its collaborators, I can guarantee they are false. The epidemic of covert, low-grade political terrorism which has swept through the country—and has continued into 1990—is all too real.

The second body of research from which the book is drawn includes 3,500 pages of FBI documents released to CISPES as a result of a protracted lawsuit by the Center for Constitutional Rights against an FBI which dragged its heels interminably before reluctantly releasing the heavily redacted documents. The third body of material includes about 4,000 separate pages of Frank Varelli's FBI documents concerning his role in various FBI investigations of political activists. Those documents were obtained through a successful FOIA lawsuit by Varelli's attorney, Daniel Alcorn.

In addition to his FOIA papers, Varelli has provided the author with hundreds of hours of interviews, some 40 tape recordings and a host of documents from El Salvador and the United States which illuminate and corroborate elements of his story. Several of Varelli's accounts of events involving officials in El Salvador were confirmed through discussions with his father, Col. Agustin Martinez Varela, former head of the Salvadoran Military Training Academy, former Director of the National Police of El Salvador, former Minister of the Interior of El Salvador and former Salvadoran Ambassador to Guatemala.

While the FBI files, a host of other documents, the tape recordings of conversations with the Secret Service, with other FBI agents, with members of CISPES and with his contact at the National Guard of El Salvador provide the factual armature on which to hang Varelli's portions of the book, a number of people have raised questions about his overall credibility.

The Roles of Frank Varelli

The roles of Frank Varelli—both in the FBI's campaign against Central America groups and as a central character in this book—are complex and multi-faceted. Initially viewed by the FBI as an intelligence analyst to help advise the Bureau in its investigations of Central American terrorism, he became, just a few months into his FBI employment, an "operational asset" through his infiltration of the CISPES chapter in Dallas. The FBI would later cast Varelli as a "mere informant" to dismiss his allegations of FBI misconduct on the ground that he was too marginal and insignificant a player to speak with authority about FBI policies and operations.

But his infiltration of CISPES was only one of the roles Varelli played.

In addition to establishing a back-channel of communication between the Bureau and a network of intelligence sources in El Salvador, Varelli also provided a great deal of the political and historical context that underlie the FBI's terrorism investigations. He identified various factions both in the U.S. and El Salvador for the Bureau, and provided the FBI with the Salvadoran intelligence community's version of the permutations and linkages between various radical and revolutionary groups in Central America and elsewhere. His acceptance by the Bureau as an expert in Central American terrorism peaked in 1983 when he was invited to address a gathering of elite FBI and CIA counter-terrorism officials at a special seminar at the FBI Academy in Quantico, Virginia.

Because of that special status, he was given access to far more information by his FBI superiors than would normally be furnished to an informant. As a result, he was much more knowledgeable about the overall outlines of the FBI's operations—as well as those of the CIA—than most "operational assets."

That knowledge was enhanced by his work in the Dallas Field Office which, from the outset of the investigation, was designated as the "Office of Origin." That means the Dallas Field Office—effectively Varelli and three superiors—was the central coordinating office that routed the flow of reports, queries and responses to and from other FBI field offices around the country as they became involved in the investigation of CISPES and other Central America peace groups. Through his work in the Office of Origin of the FBI's CISPES investigation, Varelli had a view of the FBI's counter-terrorism operations nationwide—again, a much more comprehensive view than had he worked, say, as a paid informant in another FBI field office.

Nevertheless, Varelli played no policy-making or supervisory role within the FBI. That fact becomes central to understanding the FBI's cover-up, in 1988, along with the help of the Senate Intelligence Committee, of the dimensions of the Bureau's assault against opponents of Reagan Administration foreign policies.

While the FBI tried to dismiss Varelli's allegations in 1987, saying that, as a mere informant, he was too insignificant to have an overview of FBI operations, the following year, FBI Director William Sessions would lay the blame for the entire five-year, nationwide investigation on the shoulders of one Frank Varelli.

The fact is that no single FBI agent—let alone a foreign-born contract asset—has the ability to persuade the Bureau to open anything larger than a limited, short-term preliminary investigation.

The direction, scope, intensity and duration of the FBI's campaign against political activists was dictated from the highest levels of the FBI's counter-terrorism and counter-intelligence apparatus. It was FBI policy makers in Washington who decided what information, procured by Varelli from his Salvadoran sources, was valid per se and what other information, while investigatively useless, could be exploited by the Bureau to justify its own domestic campaign.

When Director Sessions told the Congress that the Bureau did not learn until 1984 that Varelli's information was unreliable and that the Bureau had been led down the garden path by one FBI asset, he knew full well—as did Senate investigators—that the information used by the FBI to investigate CISPES and other groups did not originate with Varelli. Sessions must have known that FBI superiors in Washington, especially Supervisory Special Agent Ron Davenport and Executive Assistant Director Oliver "Buck" Revell, both encouraged the production of such material and approved the Bureau's exploitation of it for the FBI's own purposes.

The role of Frank Varelli as a character in this book is equally multi-faceted. For one thing, he provides a writing vehicle simply as a hands-on FBI employee who is able to provide highly detailed accounts of FBI operations which would otherwise never be known. For another, his account provides a revealing portrait of the thinking and motivations of other FBI agents with whom he worked. He also provides a strong and authentic voice for the thinking that has characterized the Salvadoran right wing. They are his people. Finally, as a veteran practitioner of disinformation and a close associate of the information director of the Salvadoran National Guard, he provides a revealing window on the information war that underlay the activities of right-wing operatives in El Salvador, as well as in the Reagan Administration, in their fight over what was essentially an informational war of conflicting realities.

Frank Varelli is a volatile, obsessive and extraordinarily intelligent man. He is also a most accomplished undercover actor as witnessed by his ability to insinuate himself into the leadership of the Dallas chapter of CISPES. His artistry was exploited by some sources inside the FBI who have portrayed Varelli as so diabolically clever as to successfully penetrate to the center of the Bureau's super-secret counter-terrorism apparatus on behalf of his Salvadoran masters. Personally, I do not believe Varelli intended at any point to betray the FBI. Rather, he saw his role with the Bureau as benefitting the anti-communist cause in both the United States and El Salvador. It was only after the revelation of his very significant role with the FBI through the release of FBI documents, when the Bureau was no longer able to dismiss him as an inconsequential informant, that the FBI began a whispering campaign, on total journalistic background of course.[3] There is no question that Varelli is obsessive in his anti-communism. He is also obsessive in his hatred of the FBI which, he believes, exploited him, dropped him, thwarted his attempts to recover funds that were illegally withheld from him, and, in 1988, laid the entire blame for the Bureau's nationwide five-year campaign at his feet. For this, he feels, his Salvadoran honor must be vindicated.

Other questions about his credibility come from his lionization, around the period he first went public, by several liberal and left-wing activists and writers. Intent on using Varelli's testimony to prove their negative suspicions about the FBI, they erroneously cast him as a political convert who had repented the error of his right-wing ways and had come to embrace the liberal position on both the FBI and Central America. Because he accepted funding for a period of time from a Texas member of the John Birch Society and, subsequently, from a liberal Washington-based think tank, the International Center for Development Policy, Varelli has also been portrayed as a man without principles who would say whatever he is paid to say.

Neither one of these characterizations—Varelli as a born-again liberal or Varelli as an unprincipled mercenary —is accurate.

In the more than two years that I knew Varelli, I did not detect one contradiction or inconsistency in his accounts. In several areas, particularly those involving the U.S.-based Salvadoran activists, he did, for a time, keep his accounts intentionally vague for obvious reasons of personal loyalty and physical security. And while he generally possesses an almost photographic memory, there were some areas in which he was uncertain of a specific detail. In those cases, he invariably acknowledged his uncertainty. Most of them were subsequently clarified when one of us discovered corroborating material in other documents.

The throughline of Frank Varelli's motivation is his virulent anti-communism, his bone-deep conviction of the truth of a world-wide conspiracy by the forces of communism to undermine and eventually triumph over the forces of capitalism. In some cases, that conviction has propelled him to exaggerate or overstate the "terrorist-communist" links of U.S. liberals and to participate in a campaign of disinformation. While knowingly false in some particulars, Varelli's anti-communist assertions fit the assumptions of those, like Varelli's former colleagues in the Salvadoran National Guard and the FBI, who saw themselves fighting a war against the forces of violence and chaos. But even in those cases of exaggeration, Varelli has been quite candid in identifying those portions of Salvadoran or FBI documents which contained deliberate instances of disinformation.

To this day, Varelli believes that CISPES, as well as a host of other U.S. left and liberal political groups, conceal deeply embedded links to the FMLN, the Cuban intelligence agency, the Palestine Liberation Organization, the Soviet Union and other "terrorist" forces around the world. As late as 1989, he believed that the reforms of Mikhail Gorbachev constituted a gigantic fraud, designed to lull the West into a false sense of security. That conviction comes from his own background with the Salvadoran military and intelligence agencies, his strong ties to intellectual leaders of that country's private right wing, and his personal attachment to right-wing Christian fundamentalism.

Not once during my entire association with Varelli did he ever portray himself as sympathetic to the Salvadoran or U.S. left. At no time during my association with him did he ever pretend to change his political stripes. He did, however, express his disillusionment with elements of the nativist U.S. right wing in which he was personally repulsed by expressions of racism, anti-Hispanic and anti-Semitic sentiment and the arrogance and exclusivity of U.S. white supremacist attitudes.

A few months prior to the completion of this book my collaboration with Varelli ended over the issue not of ideology but of money. Despite the fundamental opposition of our worldviews, and despite several subsequent efforts by Varelli to discredit the work, the parting was, for me, a sad one. We spent a great deal of time working with feverish intensity to complete a story both of us felt was worth great personal sacrifice to tell. Partnerships of that kind of intensity breed a peculiar kind of intimacy, a strong personal empathy and an "us versus them" kind of combat bond. While I regard his worldview as essentially paranoid and destructive in its simplicity, and his domestic espionage and disinformation skills as manifestations of a frightening strain of repressiveness, I have learned much from the man. My life is richer for our association.

Other key documentary and human sources of information for this book include, among other things, an internal police report on links between the Intelligence Division of the Los Angeles Police Department and the Western Goals Foundation, a manuscript and assorted other documents from the State Department's Office of Public Diplomacy, several documents unearthed in private legal actions, and interviews with a number of sources who worked in groups loosely categorized as part of the "FBI's private network" or in the private, contra-support network coordinated by Oliver North. Other points in the book are corroborated by newspaper and magazine articles and other published accounts which are identified at appropriate points in the text.

I am sending this small book out into the public arena with two hopes. One is that readers will be sensitized to the fragility of their personal and political freedoms. Won at terrible costs to countless patriots, they can be lost with the ease of a yawn.

The second is to add a small document to the depressingly persistent history of the FBI as a national political police force. The Bureau should be in the business of catching criminals. It should be removed, once and forever, from the business of monitoring citizens' political beliefs. As a federal police force engaged in the pursuit of inter-state crime, drug trafficking, fraud and violence, the FBI is a significant element in the defense of society. As a political police, mobilized to protect the interests of any political establishment, it is an affront to the basic rights of free speech and association and an insult to the letter and the spirit of the Constitution.

Beginnings of a Secret War

During the eight years of the Reagan Administration, members of the President's inner circle mobilized the federal law enforcement and intelligence apparatus in a massive campaign of surveillance, disruption, information suppression and character assassination which targeted citizens who opposed the administration's policies, especially in the area of Central America. This operation involved at least four federal agencies—the FBI, the CIA, the State Department and the National Security Council, in concert with a variety of private conservative groups and the security forces of a foreign government—in an effort to intimidate, terrorize, discredit and silence Administration opponents. The campaign not only drew upon the federal government's awesome intelligence and police powers, but, perhaps as significantly, it made full use of the government's instruments of information control to neutralize opposing viewpoints, to bury uncomfortable facts under an avalanche of rhetoric, and to alter the public's perception of domestic and international realities.

Driven by the anti-communist obsession of the Reagan Administration, the campaign ironically came to incorporate aspects of abuse of official power, intimidation, character assassination and official lying which U.S. citizens have traditionally associated with totalitarian regimes.

In a cynical exploition of the public's fear of terrorism, the Administration branded thousands of law-abiding policy dissenters as "terrorists." In order to discredit legitimate expressions of opposition by religious and political groups, it labeled them as "fronts" through which the Soviet Union and its allies were "manipulating" the American political process.

Perhaps the most troubling legacy of the administration's war on citizen activists was the embrace by the FBI, CIA, National Security

Council and State Department of a doctrine called "active measures," under which political dissenters can be labeled as "communist proxies" and investigated as "terrorists" simply because some of their opinions may conform to some positions held by the Soviet Union or another government which is considered hostile to the United States.

While elements of the FBI's probe of domestic political groups in the 1980s may have been discredited by subsequent revelations, the doctrine of "active measures" remains in force as a justification for investigating citizens—whose activities are not only legal but are specifically protected by the First Amendment to the Constitution—as terrorists. So categorized, an individual can become subjected to governmental surveillance, harassment and intimidation which is legitimized by an array of arcane regulations governing the federal law enforcement and intelligence apparatus; may become an instant suspect in the event of an outbreak of violence in the United States; can be denied any public- or private-sector job requiring a security clearance; and can, at any time, find his or her reputation in shambles. During the 1980s, the FBI's terrorism files swelled by more than 100,000 names, a large portion of whom were law-abiding activists who participated in demonstrations, contributed to political groups or subscribed to publications critical of Administration policies.

At the same time the Reagan White House was using the nation's intelligence and police powers to "neutralize" adversarial points of view, it was also, under cover of secrecy, pumping a stream of propaganda through the nation's libraries, universities and communications media into the public consciousness through writers and speakers who posed as "independent" experts, but who were, in fact, acting covertly on behalf of the governing Administration. That operation was apparently conceived by CIA director William Casey and directed by Walter Raymond, Jr., a long-time CIA propaganda expert who worked with Oliver North at the National Security Council and directed the covert domestic propaganda campaign through a little known office in the State Department.

The FBI - Death Squad Connection

The Administration, moreover, entered into an alliance with the Salvadoran security forces to pressure and intimidate liberal North American activists. Through its contacts with the Salvadoran National Guard, the CIA passed on forged and altered intelligence material to the FBI which used it as the basis for its investigations of liberal groups inside the United States.

This confluence of FBI and CIA operations, of foreign and domestic spies working against U.S. citizens, marks a distinct difference between the government's secret domestic war of the 1980s and the Bureau's earlier politically-motivated campaigns against civil rights, anti-Vietnam War, Black Liberation and American Indian groups in the 1960s and 1970s. The National Guard of El Salvador is one of the more repressive and terrorist police agencies in the world. While Salvadoran intelligence officials helped the Bureau target U.S. groups by providing falsified material to implicate them in illegal activities, the Bureau, in turn, entered into an intelligence-sharing relationship with Miami-based Salvadorans who had organized right-wing Salvadoran activists into a secret intelligence-gathering network inside the United States. That collaboration resulted in, among other things, the harassment and surveillance of left-wing Salvadorans who had fled to the United States.

In return, FBI agents used their access to records of the U.S. Immigration and Naturalization Service to provide the Salvadoran security forces with the names and flight numbers of Salvadoran refugees who had entered the U.S. illegally only to be denied asylum and deported back to El Salvador. Although their numbers cannot be verified, it seems clear that many of those refugees were met, surveilled and, in a number of cases, assassinated on their return.

In its broad efforts to capture public opinion and discredit dissent, the Administration also entered into a partnership with private right-wing propagandists, spies and provocateurs whose activities were protected from Congressional oversight, insulated from inquiries by the press and immune to disclosure under such laws as the Freedom of Information Act.

The government's official, overt campaign against its opponents included FBI interrogations of members of domestic political groups, as well as citizens who traveled to Nicaragua. It also involved the seizure by Customs officials of books, documents and personal papers by hundreds of U.S. travelers returning from Central America. It spawned a host of apparently politically motivated audits of such groups by the Internal Revenue Service, as well as hundreds of incidents of reported mail tampering. The investigations, moreover, involved the surveillance and compilation of FBI files on at least a dozen U.S. Senators and Congressmen who were opposed to Reagan foreign policies in the hemisphere.

Simultaneous with the official investigations of intelligence and law enforcement agents, political and religious activists around the country reported more than a hundred break-ins and thefts of files at their homes, offices and churches. In virtually all cases, lists of names and organizational material were stolen or copied while valuable items were left untouched. None of those break-ins—several of which involved the abductions and terrorizing of political activists, as well as arson attacks on at least two of their homes—have been solved. From the accumulated clues surrounding the episodes, it seems clear that the perpetrators might be found in a network of private, right-wing groups which worked in concert with the nation's law enforcement and intelligence agencies to terrorize policy opponents.

Early Warnings

Even before Ronald Reagan took office, it was apparent that the refinement of democracy through the free play of ideas was not a priority of his administration. Between his election and his inauguration, a transition team headed by his campaign manager, William Casey, was laying the groundwork for a massive domestic operation to stifle dissent and engineer the terms of the national debate over U.S. foreign policies.

In 1980, the conservative Heritage Foundation compiled a report which laid the groundwork for a number of Reagan-era governmental policies, particularly in the areas of intelligence-gathering and information controls. The report recommended the restoration of extraordinary powers to the intelligence agencies, many of which had been restricted by Congress following the inquiries into FBI and CIA abuses by the Church, Pike and Rockefeller committees in the mid-1970s. Those hearings yielded stunning revelations of assassinations abroad and spying at home by the CIA, as well as disruptive and illegal activities by the FBI's counterintelligence program (COINTELPRO), including forgeries and burglaries aimed at people involved in the Civil Rights and anti-Vietnam War movements.

The 1980 Heritage report recommended, for example, reinstating a much broader use of wiretaps and domestic spies and infiltrators as well as the reinstatement of burglaries as a tool for gaining intelligence on citizens suspected of "subversive" activities.

The Heritage report also recommended exploiting a political asset of the Reagan Administration. The new president's ideological rhetoric and ultra-conservative agenda provided tremendous encouragement for activists on the far right who had been excluded from the inner circles of power for three decades. In keeping with the President-elect's emphasis on privatizing some of the functions of government, the Heritage Foundation recommended that the intelligence agencies be permitted to contract secretly with private sources for intelligence-gathering and, moreover, be authorized to conceal the existence of such contracts.[1]

A year after the publication of the Heritage Foundation report, President Reagan ordered most of its recommendations into effect by way of a classified executive order. At the same time, the President ordered the Department of Justice to draft new and less restrictive FBI guidelines which were implemented two years later in 1983.

Shortly after taking office, the President further sought to bolster the morale of the FBI by pardoning two FBI officials who had authorized a series of break-ins against Civil Rights and anti-Vietnam War groups in the 1960s and early 1970s. Responding to requests by the American Civil Liberties Union and other groups that he forbid the Bureau from committing such "black-bag jobs" in the future, the President responded that it was not his intention to tie the Bureau's hands and that such a prohibition was unwarranted.[2]

Government By Secrecy

The Heritage report, which proved to be a partial blueprint for the Reagan transition team, also recommended a number of measures for controlling information, including severe restrictions on the Freedom of Information Act.[3] Using that report as a springboard, Administration officials instituted a series of measures designed to tighten the cloak of secrecy around the federal apparatus. Virtually all those measures were implemented through secret presidential orders which bypassed the processes of Congressional ratification.

As early as 1981, the President ordered the seizure of thousands of Cuban publications, claiming the import of such books and magazines violated an act prohibiting "trading with the enemy," although the material had been permitted to enter the country freely for 20 years. In 1982, he signed an order which dramatically increased the amount of federal documents which could be "classified" and withheld from public view. That same order authorized the "re-classification" of information which had previously been released into the public domain. That same year, the President signed the "Intelligence Identities Protection Act," which, while it purported to protect the identities of CIA agents, also threatened to subject anyone who exposed illegal activities by U.S. intelligence agents to up to 10 years in jail and $50,000 in fines. The act threatened to silence journalists and government "whistleblowers" who have traditionally served the country by exposing illegal intelligence abuses.

The following year, announcing that his presidential powers were being undermined by "leaks" from civil servants, the President announced an initiative to subject more than five million bureaucrats and one and a half million government contractors to random lie detector tests.[4] The unreliable nature of polygraphs aside, the use of the tests flew in the face of a report from the President's own Office of Information Security Oversight that the Administration had suffered only "between six and 10 significant leaks" in the first three years of the Reagan Presidency.[5] Around the same time, President Reagan signed an order requiring officials with access to certain categories of classified information to sign secrecy agreements which would require them to submit any speeches, books or articles to censorship boards for the rest of their lives.

Throughout the Reagan presidency, moreover, the State Department denied visas to scores of foreign speakers whose views were antithetical to the Administration, thus depriving the public of the right to hear from a range of foreign authors, experts and officials whose opinions were likely to challenge assumptions promoted by the Administration.[6]

The effect of these information restrictions was to intimidate civil servants into silence, to place off limits whole categories of information which were previously accessible to the public, and to marginalize, if not eliminate, viewpoints which the Administration wanted to keep outside the mainstream of political dialogue. It also fortified the wall of secrecy which protected a host of covert and, in some cases, illegal operations. Were it not for the exposure of the government's covert dealings with the Iranian government in a Lebanese newspaper, for instance, the Iran-Contra scandal may never have come into full public scrutiny. But even while that operation attracted a good deal of attention in the late 1980s, a veil of secrecy covered the domestic aspects of the Administration's Central America policies.

President Reagan's Central America position was initially presented in terms of a new set of foreign policy priorities: human rights, the guiding policy of the Carter administration, was to be subordinated to counter-terrorism—the new policy umbrella under which the administration would wage its fight against the advance of communism in all its forms. But despite the best efforts of the Reagan Administration, the controversy surrounding the United States' role in Central America grew into one of the most polarizing and inflammatory issues in the nation's political life.

Almost from the beginning of the 1980s, the controversy spawned a proliferation of grassroots political groups which supported the fight of the Salvadoran rebels, who had unified under the banner of the FMLN to oppose a government marked over the last fifty years by repression, death squads and institutionalized terrorism. At the same time, religious and political activists, moved by the plight of thousands of Salvadoran and Guatemalan refugees seeking safe haven in this country from the relentless violence in their homelands, began a movement that eventually grew to include more than 200 churches and synagogues around the country whose members worked to change the Administration's immigration policies and to provide sanctuary for the undocumented aliens.

Other groups formed to support the new Sandinista government of Nicaragua which was enjoying the widespread support of its citizens despite the escalating attacks from the United States—at first through trade embargoes and the mining of that country's harbors, and later through the CIA's creation and support of an armed opposition force popularly known as the Nicaraguan contras.

The Administration's activities gave rise to a third set of organizations which, beginning around 1986, set out to investigate and expose the covert and illegal policies which came to be known as part of "the Iran-Contra affair" and which threatened not only to destabilize the Sandinista regime in Nicaragua but to undermine and subvert the Constitution of the United States as well.

El Salvador: The Lightning Rod

In the earliest days of the administration, it was El Salvador, even more than Nicaragua, that most concerned Bill Casey, the new Director of Central Intelligence. Strategically, the value of the tiny, impoverished country lay in its access to the Pacific coast of Central America—from which the movements and communications of the Nicaraguan government could be monitored. But Casey attached even greater importance to the symbolic value of El Salvador, whose government was coming under attack from the insurgent FMLN rebel forces, threatening the stability of a country long dominated by ultra-conservative business and military interests. To Casey, a defeat in El Salvador would lead to a world-wide loss of prestige for the United States as well as a major victory for the Soviet Union and its support of "wars of national liberation."[7]

Traditionally, the level of interest of most U.S. citizens in Latin and Central America has been characterized by pervasive indifference. But during the 1980s, with the exception, perhaps, of the Nuclear Freeze movement which was more widespread but relatively short-lived, Central America became the lightning rod of U.S. politics.

The conflict over Central America policy reflected a profound schism within the U.S. political community which, in the 1980s, began to echo, albeit in a relatively non-violent fashion, the same kind of political polarization that had overwhelmed El Salvador.

Underlying the conflict over the Administration's Central America strategy was a profound and irreconcilable clash of worldviews. Where religious activists felt deeply moved by the flight of thousands of Salvadoran and Guatemalan refugees into the United States to escape the violence in their own countries, officials in the FBI and other intelligence agencies saw the mass influx as an ideal cover for the infiltration of left-wing terrorists into the United States.

Many political activists, saddened or angered by the escalating atrocities in El Salvador, opposed the flow of military aid from Washington to San Salvador that bolstered a repressive regime that maintained power through the terrorism of government security forces and unofficial death squads. By contrast, policy architects in the Reagan Administration believed they were supporting a moderate government which was El Salvador's only hope against a Moscow-driven communist guerrilla insurgency.

Later, many U.S. citizens spoke out in opposition to the Administration's escalating assaults on the Sandinista regime in Nicaragua, especially the creation and support of the contras, as provocative, anti-democratic and illegal. But to the national security and foreign policy architects in the Administration, the underlying objective in Central America was crystal clear: the neutralization of what President Reagan declared to be the growing threat of an international communist-terrorist conspiracy with links from Moscow to Bulgaria to the Middle East to Havana to Managua to San Salvador.[8]

It is this clash of worldviews that is central to understanding the context of the campaign against liberal and left-wing activists.

Active Measures and Privatized Intelligence

Three developments at the beginning of the Reagan presidency would prove critical to the Administration's war against dissenting citizens. The first was the commissioning of the FBI by the new President and his Director of Central Intelligence to take the lead in the fight against international as well as domestic terrorism. That charge was embodied in the 1981 executive order which governed the conduct of intelligence.

That order authorized the FBI to "conduct counterintelligence activities outside the United States in coordination with the CIA as required by procedures agreed upon by the Director of Central Intelligence and the Attorney General." The same order authorized the Bureau to "produce and disseminate foreign intelligence and counter-intelligence."[9] The international scope of the Bureau's new mandate would become more visible later in the decade when the FBI asserted its right to travel to foreign countries to arrest foreign nationals suspected of involvement in terrorist operations directed against U.S. citizens.

Early in his tenure as CIA Director, Bill Casey ordered two studies done by analysts within the Agency. One study, aimed at implementing the new executive order, recommended ways of breaking down barriers between the CIA, on the one hand, and the FBI and other intelligence agencies on the other. It is not known what that study recommended nor to what extent it was implemented.

The second development involved a newfound concern by Casey and others in the intelligence establishment with traditional Soviet attempts to influence the U.S. political process through a set of activities which, in the past, had been marginally successful, if at all. Despite a finding that the Soviets had been unable to ever significantly affect the decision-making process in the United States, Casey also ordered the CIA to produce a second study containing a set of recommendations to counteract Soviet "active measures." "Active measures" is a term used by the Soviets to denote "soft" propaganda and disinformation activities designed to promote Soviet interests in the political processes of other countries. The techniques include such time-honored tactics of political advocacy as propaganda, disinformation and manipulation of the media. The CIA study cited the recently formed Committee In Solidarity with the People of El Salvador (CISPES) as an "active measures" front group.[10] And in March of 1981, shortly after the completion of the CIA study, the FBI requested and won approval from the Justice Department to launch an investigation into CISPES on grounds it was representing a hostile power—the Salvadoran FMLN rebels—and, as such, had violated the Foreign Agents' Registration Act. That was the beginning of a massive FBI operation which targeted more than one thousand domestic political groups—and hundreds of thousands of citizens—opposed to the President's policies in Central America.

A third initiative promoted by Casey and others in the Reagan national security establishment involved the "privatization" of some of the government's intelligence-gathering functions.

A little-noticed but extremely important provision of the 1981 executive order authorized U.S. intelligence agencies "to enter into contracts or arrangements for the provision of goods or services with private companies or institutions in the United States and need not reveal the sponsorship of such contracts or arrangements for authorized intelligence purposes."[11]

During the Reagan presidency, the Administration enlisted the aid of a host of domestic conservative activist groups in its campaign against domestic political opponents. Many of those same organizations, together with a number of foreign intelligence and security forces, would eventually surface as players in the Administration's secret and illegal initiative to train, arm and support the Nicaraguan contras.

One of the earliest and most influential of these private conservative groups was the Western Goals Foundation, founded at the end of 1979 by Larry McDonald, U.S. Representative from Georgia and chairman of the John Birch Society. Western Goals' agenda included the creation of the largest private U.S. database of "subversives" in the U.S. in order to help the intelligence community root out domestic "terrorists" and augment the power of the FBI, which had been "crippled" in the previous decade by a "runaway" Congress. McDonald's partner in the operation was John Rees, a right-wing journalist, publisher since 1967 of a newsletter about the left, a consultant to police in Newark, Chicago, and Washington, D.C., and a paid informant of the FBI.

Much of the bogus allegations, character assassinations and red-baiting contained in Rees' newsletters and in Western Goals publications later turned up in the files of the FBI and other federal agencies, where it was used to open files on groups and individuals as "terrorist" threats or Soviet "fronts."

Similar material was recycled and generated by other private, conservative groups—the Council for Inter-American Security, Students for a Better America, the Young Americas Foundation and the Rev. Sun Myung Moon's organization, among others—until it became cited as gospel by conservative activists and commentators. Much of the material generated by those groups was also disseminated by an obscure division of the State Department, the Office of Latin American Public Diplomacy, which turned out to be the center of a secret CIA-conceived domestic disinformation and propaganda campaign designed to promote the Administration's Central America policies.

It was not until 1987 that the FBI's massive campaign against political dissenters surfaced briefly into public view with the Congressional testimony of Frank Varelli. Varelli, a former FBI employee, began to detail both the FBI's secret collaboration with Salvadoran security forces as well as its illegal assault on liberal activists in the United States before his testimony was sabotaged by conservatives in Congress who wanted to protect the reputation of the Reagan-era FBI.

The full scope and extent of the FBI's investigations into domestic political groups became publicly known in January, 1988, when attorneys at the Center for Constitutional Rights won a long and difficult Freedom of Information lawsuit, which the Bureau fought tenaciously, which resulted in the release of some 3,500 pages of FBI documents.

Defenders of the FBI point out that the Bureau's political neutralization campaign of the 1980s was less intrusive and more restrained than the COINTELPRO activities of the 1960s and early 1970s. But it is clear that the difference in degree reflected only the fact that the Central America movement never attained the breadth and impact of the radical movements of the 1960s. Had the issue of Central America attained the same proportions as those earlier movements, it seems evident that the Bureau's campaign would have intensified apace with the strength and influence of the dissenters.

Finally, there remains the mystery of the little-publicized epidemic of low-grade, domestic terrorism. It includes break-ins, death threats, and politically motivated arson attacks which have plagued hundreds of activists and organizations across the country for the past seven years. While the FBI has repeatedly denied any role in those activities, the Bureau has, at the same time, refused scores of requests to investigate what is clearly an interstate conspiracy to violate the civil liberties of the victims.

From 1984, when the first reports of mysterious political break-ins and death threats began to surface, the list of such episodes has continued to escalate. Nevertheless, the FBI has maintained they were all local crimes subject to the jurisdictions of local police. But America's urban police departments, overburdened by serious crime, have few resources to expend on solving crimes which, taken in isolation, seem insignificant as well as virtually impossible to solve, given the care and expertise of their perpetrators. Of nearly 200 political break-ins and thefts of files reported by Central America and Sanctuary activists, not one has been solved.

The following chapters will lay out what has been learned of a host of secret political operations by the FBI and other groups. But it should be borne in mind that the Administration's early groundwork in hiding a substantial portion of the government's operations behind a maze of regulations and laws designed to strengthen the wall of official secrecy was quite successful. So was its practice of privatizing some of those operations and putting them beyond the reach of conventional journalistic tools of inquiry. As a result, this picture of the multi-faceted assault on thousands of concerned citizens remains an approximation of the reality that haunted many U.S. citizens during the 1980s—and continues to haunt them as a still-persisting threat to their constitutionally-protected political liberties even as the Reagan Administration recedes into history.

An Epidemic Of Terrorism

It is difficult to date with precision the beginning of the extended campaign of official harassment and covert low-grade domestic terrorism that continued to the end of the Reagan Administration and beyond. The reporting of such incidents is not comprehensive. Except for a few veteran activists, most Americans are not comfortable telling others they are the subject of an FBI inquiry. Many mainstream church members and younger activists, as well as refugees from El Salvador and Guatemala, have been intimidated into silence. Other targets of harassment and intimidation, unaware of the systematic nature of such activities and believing their experiences to be isolated events, had no reason to go public with their stories.

But in piecing together scores of confirmed reports of both official harassments and secret, mysterious violations, there emerges the unmistakable picture of a deliberate, coordinated and extended campaign of political rape, in which the homes and workplaces of political activists have been invaded, their belongings stolen or trashed and their sense of security deeply violated.

It may have begun in 1982 when a New York woman returned from Nicaragua to learn that she was the subject of a sudden and inexplicable IRS audit.

Another clue surfaced in November 1983, when agents from the Milwaukee field office of the FBI began questioning members of two local Central America groups about their connections to terrorist organizations. Daisy Cubias, a Milwaukee woman who did volunteer work with the Ecumenical Refugee Council, told a newspaper reporter that FBI agents visited her once at her workplace and twice at her home. "They asked me if I knew that some members of CASC were in the Communist Party. They told me, 'You're going around with a bunch of terrorists and we want to help you keep clean.'"[1] Several months later,

25

following a query from a law professor at Marquette University on behalf of two Milwaukee-based Central America groups, Sen. Robert Kasten of Wisconsin asked the FBI about the interrogations. While the Bureau officially stonewalled the senator, an FBI teletype of March 29, 1984, referring to the inquiry, notes: "Milwaukee [field office] is not to divulge any information concerning this investigation or acknowledge the existence of this investigation to anyone outside the FBI."[2]

Others trace the campaign against activists to December 1983, when the Guatemala News and Information Center in Oakland, California, was the target of a break-in in which mailing lists and files were stolen while cash and office equipment were left untouched.

By 1984, the break-ins and harassments had surfaced into public view with sporadic notices in at least a few alternative and mainstream newspapers.

Sunday Morning Spooks

At 6 o'clock on a Sunday morning in late October of 1984, Ed Richardson, a member of the Sojourners religious community in Washington, D.C., which helped coordinate rallies by the anti-contra Pledge of Resistance group, stopped by the office on his way out of town. As he approached the building, he saw four men looking into the building, one of whom was carrying a camera. When one of the men asked whether this was the Sojourners office, Richardson said it was and asked whether he could help the men. Clearly uncomfortable, the four men edged away and scrambled into a nearby car, driving off with the tires squealing. The car bore a government license plate which was later traced to the super-secret National Security Agency. Joe Roos, editor of *Sojourners* magazine, explained later: "Since government agencies often exchange license plates, we are not certain that NSA agents were visiting us that morning. But it is clear we were subjects of government surveillance."[3]

The next month, on the night of Nov. 27, intruders broke into the office of three Central America political groups which were housed in the basement of the Old Cambridge Baptist Church, about two blocks from Harvard University. While valuable office equipment and a purse containing cash and credit cards were untouched, the thieves rifled files and desk drawers. The only item missing was the outgoing message tape for one of the groups' answering machines. The church had recently declared itself to be a part of the Sanctuary movement and granted safe haven to a Salvadoran union organizer who wore a bandana over her face in public and gave her name only as Estela.

About four weeks later, on the night of December 18, five offices in the church were ransacked. Again, items of value were left behind. Desk drawers and files were examined. On the same night, the Church of the Covenant in Boston—which had recently voted to support the Sanctuary effort—was broken into. Drawers were rifled and files examined, although a valuable camera was left in plain view.[4]

Almost a year later, on the night of December 5, 1985. the Old Cambridge Baptist Church was hit again. The door to the church administrator's office was broken open. Mail was ripped open and scattered along a counter. A drawer containing keys to other offices had been opened. In the church basement, the door to the Central America Solidarity Association was kicked in. File cabinets and desk drawers were opened and files and index cards were strewn about the office. The office of the New Institute of Central America, next door, was also broken into. Intruders rifled financial records and membership files. In addition, the door to the church sanctuary, which had been locked the night before, was found to be opened. On the night of the break-in, staff members of the church and the Central America organizations were at a reception, sponsored by CASA, to mark the opening of two films about Central America.

Monitoring Subversion in Maimi

In January, 1985, Edward Haase, a 32-year-old Kansas City-based radio journalist, arrived in Miami after spending two months in Nicaragua. As he moved through the Miami airport, a Customs official examined his belongings, which included personal diaries and a number of Nicaraguan newspapers. The Customs official told Haase: "We're checking for possible subversive material for the FBI. They want to talk to you." After a twenty minute wait, Haase was approached by an FBI agent from the Miami office.

He asked the journalist how long he had been in Nicaragua and what he had been doing. Haase explained he was a freelance journalist who had gone down to observe the elections. When he asked the agent what constituted subversive material, he was told: "Anything that advocates the violent overthrow of the U.S. government." Haase breathed a sigh of relief. "I thought, I'm fine. I'm not carrying anything like that here." Meanwhile, Customs officials were combing Haase's belongings—especially books, writings and printed material. After about three hours, Haase told the Customs officials he was concerned about missing his connecting flight to Kansas City. As the Customs official took him to an upper level of the airport to check on flight times, Haase saw the FBI agent, Jose Miranda, leaning over a Xerox machine copying his papers. He was subsequently given his material back and allowed to leave. On his return, Haase called the Center for Constitutional Rights. Attorney Michael Ratner contacted the Miami FBI office who said they copied Haase's material in order to disseminate it to the INS and other FBI field offices. The material included an address book that listed the names and phone numbers of Haase's friends and contacts. They had also copied his diary. "There was nothing special in it that disturbed me. But it feels like a tremendous violation of my person," he said later.

Haase said that the FBI later defended its activities, citing its mandate for foreign counter-intelligence. But, as in the case of the 100 or so other travelers subjected to Customs seizures, nothing illegal was discovered. "This might have been legitimate had the FBI had some prior evidence that the travelers were working on behalf of the Nicaraguan government. But no such evidence existed. This was harassment pure and simple. Even then, it didn't do what it set out to do—stop citizens from participating in work to prevent American intervention in Nicaragua," Haase said. "There was no evidence that any of us was acting as an agent of a foreign power. What we were doing was carrying out our responsibility as citizens of the United States, expressing our opinions and doing everything within the law to make this a better country. If we think our country is doing something wrong, it is a duty as an American to raise our voices." [5]

Intimidation in Detroit

By the mid 1980s, Sara Murray had become deeply involved in helping Salvadoran and Guatemalan refugees in the Detroit area. Her work with the Michigan Interfaith Committee on Central American Human Rights (MICAH) brought her a fair measure of visibility, as she lectured around the state and appeared occasionally on television and in local newspapers. But toward the end of 1984, it was becoming clear to Murray that her visibility was also beginning to put her at risk. It began with the mail. In January, Murray received a first class package which had been mailed from Adrian, Michigan, the previous October. In November 1984, she mailed 77 letters to various groups around the state—none of which were subsequently received. Issues of the MICAH newsletter, which were mailed regularly, were not received for several months. Then on a Saturday morning in March, 1985, Murray went into her office at MICAH to find that a number of files and clippings on Sanctuary matters had been stolen. At one point, Murray spoke to a small CISPES chapter about the progress of the Sanctuary campaign in the Southwest. After the meeting, a man in the audience whom she had never seen before asked whether she knew that death squads were forming in Detroit. She was a target, he told her, and should stop her work.

The following month, while visiting family members in Chicago, Murray stopped at an office of the American Friends Service Committee in downtown Chicago. When she left the building around 3:30 that afternoon, she tried to hail a cab on the other side of the street. Another cab, which had been waiting a few doors away, pulled up first. As Murray got in the cab, she noticed she had forgotten her briefcase upstairs and apologized to the driver, saying she'd get another cab in a few minutes. But when she returned, the cab was still waiting for her. As the driver pulled away, he asked her whether the American Friends Service Committee was still located in the building. Alerted by the coincidence of the question, she asked the man how he knew about the committee. He said he was Puerto Rican, and asked Murray what she did for a living. When she told him she worked with Central American refugees, he told her that members of death squads were very aware of the Sanctuary movement. "Don't you understand," he told Murray, "that your family can be kidnapped? If you're on multiple mailing lists, your name will come up as a 'target' in government files," he warned her. "You can be assassinated. You could be killed in your apartment and they could torch the building to make it look like an accident. You better stop your Central America work before you're considered a traitor."[6]

Arson in Arizona

In late July 1985, the Glendale, Arizona, home of Francisca Cavazos, a political activist and an organizer for a local farmworkers' group, was entered by unknown persons while she was on a trip to Nicaragua. Cavazos had recently been interviewed by a local journalist about her upcoming trip. Her landlord found her apartment door unlocked and open and called the police. They determined that nothing had been stolen. The landlord secured the apartment and the episode was forgotten. When Cavazos returned the following month, she found that a second entry had taken place. This time, a fire had been set in the apartment, according to Glendale police. The fire, which had been set

in the bathroom, had apparently burned itself out. But the Glendale Fire
Marshall told a local reporter it was clear the intruder had attempted to
burn down the townhouse where Cavazos lived. "You're always aware
that when you do organizing you'll be a visible target. I certainly
interpreted the incidents as political. Someone breaks into my home and
takes nothing? No TV, stereo? Nothing of value was touched. It looked
like everything was in order. Then, after the article appeared, someone
tries to burn the whole place down. These incidents only confirmed my
political convictions," she said. "But it also makes you become more
aware and be a bit more fearful. I'm not so afraid for my personal safety.
I'm an adult. I know what I'm doing. But I'm more fearful about my two
sons. That preoccupies me more than anything else. One way they get
to people in Central America is through their loved ones."[7]

Targeting Churches

January 3, 1987: The Arlington Street Church in Boston was broken
into Saturday night, the night before the Rev. Victor Carpenter was to
deliver a sermon on why the church had recently voted to join the
Sanctuary movement and provide shelter to political refugees from El
Salvador and Guatemala. To enter the church and reach its inner offices,
thieves opened two sophisticated police locks. The church's sanctuary
file in an administrator's cabinet had been rifled. "They had special tools
to get through the locks. Every locked door was opened and every
drawer gone through. They knew exactly what they were doing,"
Carpenter said. "The government took a real [public relations] beating at
the Tucson trial (at which 11 Sanctuary leaders were convicted of
violating immigration laws). This was meant as a signal to all churches
to discourage them from joining the movement."[8]

January 7, 1987: The office of Rev. Timothy Limburg, pastor of the
Christian Reformed Church of Washington, D.C., was burgled for the
second time within a month. "In December, I went to my office on
Sunday morning to find the door had been jimmied. The office was a
mess. A bottle of ink had been thrown against the wall. I called the police,
who told me fingerprint people would be by later. They never showed
up. When I began to clean up the office, I realized this was not simple
vandalism. I found they had rifled a box of old records in my closet. They
went through old canceled checks and old income tax returns. One thing
they found—and obviously examined—were two old passports of mine.
One was issued in 1976 when I visited my brother in Managua. He's been
active in Central America work for a long time. The second passport I

used to go to Guatemala in 1981. I had no idea the passports were still around. But they found them and looked them over. Then on January 7, the office was broken into again. This time, they went through all the files in the outer office. They took the office copy of the church directory, our only updated copy with the names of new members. That was an act of intimidation. They're telling me, 'We can get in whenever we want.' At this point, I'm far more angry than I am intimidated. I think it's outrageous that this happens in this country. It can't go on."[9]

Car Breaks in Los Angeles

April 4, 1987: Catherine Suitor, a staff member of the Los Angeles CISPES office, found her car had been broken into overnight. "When I went out that morning, I found everything in the glove compartment had been thrown on the front seat. The car contained about $700 in new clothes. They had all been searched and left alone. The only thing missing was one used man's overcoat belonging to a CISPES colleague. He had just returned from Europe, and his coat contained names and addresses of solidarity organizers in Switzerland. That was the only thing stolen." The burglary of Suitor's car was one of four break-ins of cars belonging to CISPES members at different locations around Los Angeles within a month. Glynnis Golden, coordinator of the American Friends Service Committee Central America Program in Pasadena was broken into on the night of March 23. Golden estimated that thieves took between 60 and 70 pounds of files on sanctuary and refugee assistance groups. She left the files in her car for an hour while she stopped into the office of another organization. She added that an expensive stereo, as well as jewelry and a watch, were left untouched by the burglars.[10] In the next two months, cars and offices of nearly a dozen other Central America activists were broken into.

The Bureau Goes Public

At the beginning of April, 1987, FBI agents in six cities visited the employers of volunteers belonging to a group called TecNica, an organization of engineers and computer professionals which provides technical development assistance to Nicaragua. Special Agents in Chicago, Washington, New York, San Francisco, San Diego and Seattle went to the personnel offices of firms employing TecNica members—including firms like AT&T and IBM—and requested employers to summon the volunteers. Some agents proceeded to tell the volunteers that they were acting in the interests of the Soviets and Cubans, and warned that they could get into serious trouble—despite the absence of any law against traveling to Nicaragua. Marilyn McMahon, a technical writer in San Francisco, said an FBI agent contacted her software company after she had given a computer course in Managua on TecNica's behalf. "The agent said she wanted to chat with me about my beliefs about Nicaragua," McMahon said, adding the agent told her, 'If you won't talk to me, I'll call your boss and get to you that way.' It doesn't look like information-gathering so much as trying to cause trouble for me," she concluded. Another TecNica volunteer in Chicago, Ellen Finkelstein, who was interviewed by an FBI agent with her personnel director present, said, "It was quite frightening to be subjected to this kind of pressure. I feel it was a clear attempt to jeopardize my job and reputation." She added that two FBI agents "told me I was a dupe of the Russians and was being given a chance to stop doing something I might regret later."Added Rep. Don Edwards, chairman of the House Judiciary Subcommittee on Civil and Constitutional Rights: "These visits have the odor of harassment. They have the odor of politics. The FBI is supposed to stay out of politics."

Perhaps by coincidence—perhaps not—TecNica was the group with whom a young engineer named Benjamin Linder had been associated. Linder was murdered by contra forces in the spring of 1987, while helping to construct a small hydroelectric generating station in Nicaragua.[11]

On May 17, 1987, a staff member of the New Institute of Central America, at the Old Cambridge Baptist Church, entered the office to find a map of Nicaragua torn off the wall and left, in two pieces, on the floor. Muriatic acid had been poured over 40 computer discs containing information on programs run by the Central America solidarity group. It was the eighth of nine political break-ins at that church since 1984.[12]

Death Squads: A Transcontinental Reach?

Perhaps the most horrifying tale of assault and intimidation followed the string of break-ins at offices and cars of West Coast political activists in the spring of 1987. In June of that year, Yanira Corea, a 24-year-old Salvadoran woman who worked as a volunteer at the Los Angeles CISPES office was driving to the Los Angeles airport with her three and a half year old son when a car driven by two Hispanic men forced her off the road. While one of the men kept pounding and kicking her car, the other tried to pull her out of the door. Although she managed to escape, the man did get a book of hers containing a photo of her son Ernesto. The boy was so traumatized by the event that he did not speak for three days after the incident. Two weeks later, she received a letter with her son's photo. The letter, containing petals of dried flowers, bore the notation: "Flowers in the desert die," a traditional warning of Salvadoran death squads. The following Tuesday, as she approached her car outside the Los Angeles CISPES office, a man came up behind Yanira and put a knife against her back. The man and two others (she later identified them as two Salvadorans and one Nicaraguan by their accents) drove her around the city in a van for six hours. They cut the initials EM (for the Spanish words for death squad) into the palms of her hands. One man punctured her neck with a knife blade. Another raped her with a stick. All the while, they kept interrogating her about CISPES, about her brother who is a union activist in El Salvador, and about individuals involved in CISPES. Her wounds were confirmed by both an investigating officer of the Los Angeles Police Department and a doctor in a Los Angeles hospital who examined Corea.[13]

On July 10, three days after Yanira Corea's abduction, Marta Alicia Rivera, a member of the Salvadoran teacher's union, received a threatening letter which had been left at her apartment. The note read: "For Marta Alicia and her terrorist companions, for being a traitor to the country, you will die together with your companions. You saved yourself in El Salvador. Here you will not." The note included the names of 17 other CISPES members. It concluded with the line: "Flowers in the desert die."[14]

Five days later, Fr. Luis Olivares of Our Lady Queen of Angels Church in Los Angeles, received a similar letter. Olivares had been marked for death by an Escuadron de la Muerte.[15]

Two days after that, Ana Maria Lopez, a Guatemalan refugee who worked with the Guatemalan Cultural Center, was abducted outside the First Unitarian Church in Los Angeles. Two men with guns and plastic masks and Salvadoran accents forced her into a Toyota. During the drive, they told her they knew she supported Salvadoran organizations and warned her to stop. They interrogated her about her work with Guatemalan and Salvadoran groups and questioned her intensely about several Americans she had worked with. She was released after two hours.[16]

Yanira Corea's nightmare did not end after her abduction, rape and torture. Shortly after the incident, Yanira, with her mother, a brother and her son, moved into a new home with an unlisted phone. Within two days, she began receiving more threatening calls—most of which involved the safety of her son.

In October, when Corea had recovered enough to go public with her experience, she agreed to a short speaking tour in New York, Philadelphia and Washington. While arrangements were being made, her father, who lives in El Salvador, received a letter from within the country telling him to make his daughter cancel her appearances. Yanira refused to back out. Just prior to her first appearance, on November 5, she went to the office of Madre in a building on West 27th street in New York to meet some members of the press. (Madre itself had been burgled the previous month, when thieves took computer disks from the organization which provides nutritional and literacy aid to women and children in Central America. Shortly thereafter, Magic Fingers, a commercial computerized mailing list firm which Madre used, was also broken into. The only thing stolen was one hard-disk computer containing Madre's mailing and subscription lists.)[17] That Wednesday in November, Corea sat with a reporter and photographer from the *Boston Globe* for a two hour interview. At the end of the conversation, the photographer left the office and went down the hall to use the bathroom. When she returned, she spotted a torn piece of paper stuck under the office door. The paper was the top half of a flier advertising a speaking appearance by Corea the following Friday evening. Next to her photograph was written in a crude hand: "Sabes donde y como esta tu hijo?" which translates to: "Do you know where and how your son is?" Next to the scrawled, handwritten line was a drawing of a decapitated torso. Next to it lay a crudely drawn child's head.[18]

$$\underline{3}$$

The FBI's Sister City Program: From Dallas to San Salvador

In 1977, three years before the birth of CISPES, Dr. Franklin Agustin Martinez Varela, an evangelical Protestant minister, mounted a major religious crusade in his native El Salvador. The open air services in the towns of Santa Ana and San Miguel, as well as a three-night crusade in the Cuscatlan soccer stadium in the capitol of San Salvador, attracted more than 100,000 people, many perhaps drawn by the distribution of thousands of posters, bumper stickers and free bibles.[1]

But the spiritual message of the born-again minister had strong political roots. For as much as Varela believed in the goodness of God and eternal hope of redemption through Christ, he also believed that the anti-Christ struggling to dominate the soul of the world was personified by communists—from Moscow to Havana to San Salvador. The crusade, which was actively supported by then-President Carlos Romero, was designed to counter the spreading doctrine of "liberation theology"—a philosophy which purported to reconcile Christianity and Marxism and which was seen by Romero and his ferociously anti-communist colleagues as a new ideological tool for the communist exploitation of the predominantly Roman Catholic nations of Latin America.

It was not until four years later that Varela discovered a more secular arena in which to fight the advance of world communism in Central America. Instead of using the pulpit of the Baptist church, he found himself at the threshold of the inner sanctum of the Federal Bureau of Investigation.

Varela's decision to bring his lifelong struggle against communism to the United States was not entirely voluntary. On April 2, 1980, during a visit to his parents' home in San Salvador, he found himself on the porch of the house in a shootout with members of the FMLN guerrillas

35

who had ambushed and attempted to assassinate his father—Col. Agustin Martinez Varela, former director of the Salvadoran Military Training Academy, former director of that country's National Police, former Minister of the Interior and, in 1980, the Salvadoran Ambassador to Guatemala.

Franklin's diminutive mother, Aida, who was getting dressed in the bedroom when the shootout erupted, ran onto the porch clad only in a brassiere and skirt, passing shotgun shells along to Franklin and his father. When the fierce battle subsided some twenty minutes later, five FMLN members lay dead on the street outside the Varela household. A bodyguard assigned to Col. Varela's home lay dead on the lawn. Three weeks later, the Varela family, escorted to the airport by a bodyguard provided by Eugenio Vides Casanova, the director general of the Salvadoran National Guard, flew to Los Angeles where they hoped to find a refuge from the threat of assassination that hung over the family.[2]

Following the family's arrival in Los Angeles, Franklin Varela, who would soon adopt the more American sounding surname of Varelli, was approached by Special Agent John Esparza of the FBI's Los Angeles Office.[3] Esparza told Varelli that the FBI was gearing up for a major investigation of Salvadoran terrorism. Did Varelli think he might be interested in working for the Bureau? the agent asked. When Varelli indicated he was, indeed, very interested, he learned that the investigation would be coordinated by the Dallas FBI office which, in FBI parlance, would be the "office of origin" of the probe. In December, Varelli, his parents, and his younger brother Fernando, moved to Dallas. Shortly thereafter, Varelli received a call from Special Agent Daniel Flanagan, a tall, handsome dark-haired physical culture buff with a penchant for gold jewelry. Flanagan had recently been reassigned to the Dallas office where he would be working in the FBI's elite counter-terrorism squad. In his previous assignment, Flanagan had worked in New York where he posed as a wealthy Wall Street broker who was underwriting a think tank devoted to U.S.-Soviet cooperation. Flanagan's role brought him into regular contact with Soviet delegates to the United Nations where he worked as an FBI counter-intelligence specialist. Flanagan talked to Frank at length and, finally, recommended that Varelli visit the Dallas FBI office on North Lamar to sign on as an FBI analyst.

In short order, Varelli impressed Flanagan, Jim Evans, Parks Stearns and others in the Dallas FBI office with his extensive knowledge of Central American terrorism. He concurred with the concerns of the Bureau that the beginnings of a massive influx of Salvadoran refugees coming north over the Mexican border—either on their own or with the help of members of the newly emerging Sanctuary movement—could, indeed, be a channel by which Salvadoran left-wing terrorists could be infiltrating the United States to plan a campaign of covert violence. And he let the FBI know that while they were, by training, unprepared to deal with the convoluted and splintered realities of Salvadoran politics, that he, Varelli, had access to intelligence sources in El Salvador who were quite frustrated with the inaction of the State Department and the CIA and who might be very happy indeed to establish a direct relationship with the FBI. At one point, Flanagan visited the Varela household, where he met Frank's parents. Flanagan told Varelli's father that he knew a great deal about the colonel's background—apparently from CIA sources in Mexico—and that everything he had learned about the senior Varela's career as director of the National Police and Minister of the Interior indicated he was an extremely effective member of the Salvadoran security establishment.[4] Flanagan concluded that the FBI was indeed fortunate to have Frank Varelli assist the Bureau in their fight against the looming threat of left-wing Central American terrorism.

It was in those early meetings in Dallas that the seeds were sown for Varelli's first major mission for the FBI: a clandestine return to San Salvador to set up a secret channel between the Bureau and the National Guard of El Salvador.

The mission was one of the Bureau's first international initiatives that would become legitimized later that year under a new Presidential order giving the Bureau international reach in its mandate to protect the United States against global terrorism. From the perspective of liberal U.S. citizens or left-wing Salvadorans, however, it would become yet another instance of foreign exploitation of a country whose history was shaped by international power struggles and stamped with a tradition of repression, conflict and violence.

A History of Desperation

When explorer Pedro de Alvarado left the company of Hernando Cortes in Mexico in 1525 to explore a small area to the south on the Pacific Coast, he was lulled by the lush abundance of the Valley of Hammocks, with its rich, volcanic soil, luxuriant foliage and spectacular coastal sunsets. But Alvarado's enchantment was short-lived. Unlike the Aztecs, who had greeted the company's arrival in Mexico with great gifts and a reverential deference to the white-skinned visitors, the Pipil inhabitants of the area that would three centuries later become El Salvador were a ferociously independent people. Over the next 25 years, the native population mounted a succession of rebellions against its Spanish conquerors until, by the end of the 16th century, nearly 80 percent of the indigenous population had been decimated by war and disease.

From its beginnings, the history of El Salvador has been a history of unrelenting power struggles, of periodic uprisings followed by periods of brutal repression by a series of military and civilian rulers. By the end of the 19th Century, a group of wealthy land-owning families had virtually abolished El Salvador's traditional export crops of balsam and indigo to establish large, lucrative coffee plantations. They were helped by President Rafael Zaldivar's order in 1880 to expropriate communal lands inhabited by the native population for the coffee growers, a decision that was backed by the creation of an armed rural police force.

The succeeding years of peasant revolts, economic depressions and the proliferation of security and police forces led, in 1931, to the election of a socialist president, Arturo Araujo, who was promptly overthrown by the Minister of War General Maximiliano Hernandez Martinez. The following year, the Salvadoran Communist Party, led by Agustin Farabundo Marti, led an attempted overthrow of the military government. That revolt resulted in "la matanza," a massacre of between 10,000 and 30,000 Salvadoran peasants, leftists and trade unionists at the hands of Maximiliano Hernandez Martinez who, almost 50 years later, would be honored when a newly-formed Salvadoran death squad was named after him.

By 1970, according to United Nations data, the top 10 percent of the country's landowners owned about 80 percent of El Salvador's agriculturally productive land. At the same time, crushing poverty contributed to the deaths by age 5 of 38 out of every 100 children. By 1976, a U.N. report cited El Salvador's unemployment rate as the highest in the Western Hemisphere. Nearly 50 percent of adult Salvadorans were unemployed or underemployed. Around this period, elements of the Salvadoran leftist community split over whether to pursue reforms through armed struggle or electoral strategies. While some radicalized students and workers formed guerrilla bands under the umbrella of the People's Revolutionary Army, a coalition of Christian Democrats, Social Democrats and Communist Party supporters mounted a slate headed by presidential candidate Jose Napoleon Duarte and his vice-presidential running mate, Guillermo Ungo.

Their apparent electoral victory in 1972, however, fell apart when Col. Arturo Molina, the candidate of the Salvadoran military, seized power. His troops occupied the National Univerity and arrested 800 student protestors. At the same time, Duarte was captured and put on trial for subversion. The military judge who rendered the guilty verdict that resulted in Duarte's exile was the director of the Salvadoran Military Academy, Agustin Martinez Varela, father of Frank Varelli. In 1977, President Molina was succeeded by his Defense Minister, Gen. Carlos Romero. Shortly after his installation, Romero's security forces killed more than 100 demonstrators opposing what they claimed was his fraudulent election.

While the United States had generally turned a blind eye to the repression perpetrated by El Salvador's military dictators, State Department and CIA officials traditionally used U.S. aid to leverage favorable treatment of U.S. economic interests in El Salvador. Behind-the-scenes manipulations usually succeeded in maintaining pro-U.S. leadership in San Salvador. Whle the Carter Administration slightly modified that pattern, it did nothing to fundamentally alter it. Reacting to the continuing human rights abuses and escalating polarization, officials in the Carter Administration pressured the Romero government to curtail abuses and ensure electoral reforms. The succession of Salvadoran military leaders was interrupted by a coup in October, 1979, led by a Carter-supported junta which included members of the country's left wing as well as of reform-minded military officers. In the spring of 1980, following the resignations of several members of the junta, Jose Napoleon Duarte was appointed to the ruling body. Nine months later, he assumed the presidency with Washington's blessings.

U.S. officials described Duarte as moderate—able to communicate with both sides, to help the country attain political security and economic justice, in short, a grand mediator who might help El Salvador find a middle road to democracy and stability. The choice could hardly have been worse. Rather than emerging as a force for stability and reconciliation, Duarte became a lightning rod for all sides of the conflict—each of whom saw him as a representative of the other side's agenda.

To the anti-communist elements in El Salvador's business and military leadership, Duarte seemed the front man running interference for a long-term Soviet-Cuban plan for the communist take-over of El Salvador and, ultimately, all of Central America. They saw Duarte as a mere puppet of Jimmy Carter, U.S. Ambassador Robert White, and the Carter State Department in their deceitful sell-out of El Salvador. And they saw their salvation in the incoming administration of President-elect Ronald Reagan.

But if Duarte personified the political nightmare of the Salvadoran right wing, his failure to implement meaningful land reform and to bring the security forces and death squads under control left him with virtually no support among the FMLN rebels in El Salvador or the left-wing and liberal activists to the North.

At the same time that Reagan's transition chief, and soon-to-be Director of Central Intelligence, William Casey, was advising the new President to make a dramatic show of U.S. political and military resolve in Central America, thousands of U.S. citizens found themselves sickened by the increasing brutality in El Salvador.

The previous March, Roman Catholic Archbishop Oscar Arnulfo Romero preached a sermon at the Metropolitan Cathedral in San Salvador in which he called for an end to the violence. Addressing the members of the military, the National Guard and the National Police, Msgr. Romero told them: "Each one of you is one of us. The peasants you kill are your brothers and sisters…In the name of God, I beg you: stop the repression." The next day, March 24, 1980, as he was celebrating mass in a hospital chapel, Archbishop Romero was assassinated by a sniper. The death of the compassionate Archbishop, who had become increasingly known for his advocacy on behalf of the poor and oppressed in El Salvador, propelled him into international martyrdom.

The revulsion of U.S. citizens was heightened in November of 1980, following the kidnapping of 20 leaders of the leftist FDR party. The mutilated bodies of six of the leaders were discovered outside San Salvador the next day.

The brutality hit North Americans hardest on December 4, 1980, when the bodies of four recently murdered U.S. churchwomen, Maura Clarke, Jean Donovan, Ita Ford and Dorothy Kazel, were discovered in an unmarked grave near the airport.

Near-daily reports in the news media of the institutionalized terrorism of the Salvadoran security forces and the increasing atrocities perpetrated by the country's death squads—which, in turn, provoked sabotage, assassinations and bombings by the leftist FMLN—led U.S. citizens to form a number of new organizations, as well as to reinvigorate existing groups, around the issue of U.S. policies in El Salvador and Guatemala.

To liberal and leftist activists, Duarte appeared as the handmaiden of the Reagan State Department, holding power by the grace of U.S. military force. To them, Duarte appeared as the Reagan Administration's adopted surrogate, sanctioning the increasing U.S. military presence in the country while turning a blind eye to the rampant abuses of the Salvadoran security forces and death squads which propelled the flight of an endless stream of exploited, impoverished and terrified refugees.

In fact, their assessment of Duarte was not entirely wrong. Duarte was listed in the CIA's files as an asset, a source of intelligence from whom the Agency benefitted, even if it did not control his activities.[5]

It was this perception of El Salvador, Duarte and the Reagan agenda that gave rise to the Committee in Solidarity with the People of El Salvador (CISPES)—a small group, born in 1980, that would grow in the next few years to over 300 chapters in virtually every major city in the United States. Formed initially as a vehicle to protest U.S. policies in El Salvador, CISPES' membership grew to include people concerned about conditions in Guatemala and Honduras as well. And when the Reagan Administration turned all its guns on the tiny country of Nicaragua—mining that country's harbors, blockading its ports and fielding a small CIA-created army of Nicaraguan contras—the U.S. liberal community gave birth to a profusion of CISPES-type groups which rallied citizens around the Nicaraguan cause and against U.S. military intervention in the region.

CISPES remained the first and largest of the Central America-oriented political groups of the 1980s. And depending on one's point of view, the group either arose spontaneously to protest what its members saw as offensive and unjust U.S. policies or covertly as a diabolically clever creation of Moscow and Havana which insinuated itself into the mainstream of U.S. political life in order to undermine the forces of democracy and render the U.S. vulnerable to an onslaught of international communist terrorism.

CISPES: Two Versions

Even before it sent Varelli on a secret mission to El Salvador, the FBI had acquired material from the Salvadoran authorities which was to provide the basis for its first investigation of CISPES. That material, which the Salvadoran National Guard claimed to have seized in raids on rebel safehouses, was passed to the CIA which, in turn, provided it, via the State Department, to the FBI.

It was that material which, eight years later, would be found by the Senate Intelligence Committee to be bogus and which, in retrospect, appears to have been the first links in a chain of disinformation which was used to discredit left-leaning political groups in both the U.S. and El Salvador. The initial body of disinformation was generated either by the Salvadoran security forces or by the CIA using the Salvadoran imprimatur, and passed to the FBI in order to provide official justification for its two investigations of CISPES—first for suspected violations of the Foreign Agents Registration Act (FARA), and, later, when that first probe proved groundless, for the less well-defined crime of international terrorism.

Two bodies of material in particular were critical to the FBI's "predicate"—the FBI's term for a body of evidence sufficient to launch an investigation. One package of material consisted of documents said to have been compiled by Shafik Handal, head of the small Salvadoran Communist Party. The documents allegedly included a report titled "The Moscow Plan for Latin America," a long-term strategy inspired by Moscow to work through Havana for the spread of communism throughout Central America. Shafik Handal's diaries also reflected contacts with officials in Soviet bloc countries, including Vietnam, Cuba and the Soviet Union, in which he solicited guns, ammunition, uniforms and other materiel, as well as arrangements for training the Salvadoran rebels.

A second raid reportedly yielded several documents, including travel diaries, from Shafik's brother, Farid Handal, detailing his visit to the United States in early 1980 in which he met with officials of a number of leftist groups, including the U.S. Communist Party, the U.S. Peace Council, the Institute for Policy Studies, the Washington Office on Latin America, and Amnesty International, as well as with Cuban intelligence agents assigned to the Cuban mission to the United Nations.

The purpose of Farid Handal's trip, according to the diaries, was to promote the establishment of a network of "solidarity" groups in the U.S. to support the Salvadoran rebels and oppose U.S. military aid and intervention on behalf of the ruling junta which had been installed the previous year by the Carter Administration.

According to the documents, Handal met with leaders of the U.S. Communist Party and members of the Cuban mission to the United Nations, who directed him to certain left-leaning members of Congress, including Rep. Ronald Dellums of California, whom they said would be responsive to his pleas for support for the Salvadoran guerrillas. Handal, himself, according to intelligence reports, formally severed his official ties with the Salvadoran Communist Party before the visit so he could truthfully tell North Americans that he was not a communist.[6]

Farid Handal also met with Sandy Pollack, a former member of the pro-Cuban Venceremos Brigade and an official of the U.S. Peace Council, which is alleged by intelligence experts to be a Soviet front organization. According to information held by the State Department, FBI and other agencies, Pollack, after meeting with Handal, proposed setting up a conference involving a number of liberal and left-wing groups to establish a nationwide network of committees in solidarity with the

Salvadoran guerrillas. Out of two 1980 conferences—one in Los Angeles and one in Washington—there emerged the initial structure for the Committee in Solidarity with the People of El Salvador.

The formation of CISPES—and its potential for developing a U.S. constituency on behalf of the Salvadoran guerrillas—was especially alarming to Administration officials who claimed that the Nicaraguan Sandinistas were supplying arms to the Salvadoran rebels.

It was the uncorroborated information from the Handal papers, among other data from the intelligence community, which persuaded the FBI—with its newly strengthened mandate as the lead domestic agency in the battle against terrorism—to plan an investigation of the newly-born CISPES.

But as the Senate oversight committee found in 1989: "The FBI [took] the position that it [would] investigate regardless of whether the information on which the investigation is based was verified. The document that provided the basis for the FARA investigation of CISPES—the so-called Farid Handal trip report—was never verified by the FBI. Moreover, the document did not, on its face, show foreign direction or control of CISPES...FBI files do not explain why the Justice Department requested an FBI investigation on the basis of an unverified document received from the State Department that did not on its face show direction and control by a foreign power."[7]

In fact, participants at the two founding meetings of CISPES in 1980 paint a very different picture of the beginnings of the organization than the documents reported to have been provided to the CIA by the Salvadoran security forces. According to CISPES founders, the 1980 gatherings of religious and political activists were marked by confusion, conflicting agendas and very different sets of long-term goals. Rather than a united conspiracy of the left directed by a hidden Soviet or Cuban hand, the delegates found agreement on only two points: that the violence in El Salvador was escalating dramatically and that increasing amounts of United States aid to the Salvadoran government seemed only to fuel the escalation of atrocities.

Many people at those early meetings knew little about El Salvador. What they did know came from the stunning revelations of the murder of four U.S. churchwomen at the hands of the death squads and the assassination of Archbishop Romero.

Contrary to the FBI's belief that CISPES was the creation of the Cuban and Salvadoran communists, officials of the group maintain that their movement was strictly a grassroots North American reaction to the escalating violence. And while several representatives of the FDR—the political wing of the Salvadoran rebels—were invited to address one of the founding conferences, the purported plans of Farid Handal played no part in the formation of the group. "We're not directed by anyone from El Salvador. The diaries are irrelevant to us," said Beth Perry, a founding member of CISPES. "The Reagan Administration used the diaries to totally misrepresent CISPES and to support the position of the FBI that we were controlled by a foreign hostile power and that we were aiding and abetting terrorists." If, in fact, CISPES was conceived as an organization devoted to the support of left-wing Salvadoran terrorism, it would never have attracted the wide public support it did, according to CISPES members. Such a group, they add, could only have operated as a tiny, underground organization, with little support and less visibility. "What Farid Handal may have wanted to do and what we decided to do is as different as day and night," Perry said.[8]

Michael Lent, another founding member of CISPES, makes a different point about the Handal material. "There is absolutely no reason to believe that the so-called Handal diaries are authentic. I have seen nothing to indicate they are not forgeries or fabrications."[9] Lent's observation was apparently supported by the final report of the Intelligence Committee.

Other intelligence experts offered a third interpretation of the Handal material. "The most probable explanaton for Handal's visit is that he came to enlist political and financial support for the cause of the FMLN. That interpretation makes his visit no different from, say, similar public relations activities by countries like Taiwan, South Africa or, to take another example, Nicaragua—overt lobbying efforts to enlist public support in a legitimate and legal way," said one Washington expert who asked not to be identified.[10]

The Hidden Hand of the Private Network

In 1981, however, officials in the FBI's counter-terrorism unit saw CISPES as a direct organ of the Salvadoran communist rebels. To the Bureau, CISPES presented a two-pronged threat. On one hand, CISPES could function as a legitimate public group that secretly concealed terrorists, provided weapons and money to the FMLN and, if undisturbed, might provide the support network for a cadre of terrorists within the United States. Even under a completely legal scenario, CISPES, with its nest of experienced organizers and its propaganda expertise, was generating political support for the Salvadoran rebels, undermining the policies of the President and the Director of Central Intelligence and, ultimately, contributing to prolonging the war in El Salvador.

In early 1981, the Bureau requested authorization from the Justice Department to initiate an investigation of CISPES for violating the Foreign Agents' Registration Act. The FBI's submittal to the Justice Department included, among other material, a magazine article on Salvadoran terrorism which cited verbatim the secret intelligence material contained in the alleged Handal diaries. The article concluded: "What is incredible is that to date the Justice Department has taken no action against CISPES as an unregistered foreign agent. In El Salvador, the Reagan Administration appears to be trying to encourage unity between Salvadoran moderates and Conservatives to stop armed terrorist aggression by Moscow's proxies. But it will take sustained American support to defeat this threat to the security of our Hemisphere. A move against the unregistered foreign agents of the U.S. Committee in Solidarity with the People of El Salvador would show the Communists we mean business."[11]

What would shock members of Congress who demanded an accounting of the CISPES investigation from the FBI seven years later was the revelation that the article, which the FBI used in its official submission to the Justice Department, appeared in *The Review of the News,* a publication of the John Birch Society. Its author was John Rees, the long-time police informant and watchdog of the left. At the time, Rees was working with John Birch Society's Larry McDonald to establish Western Goals. That foundation would, in ensuing years, become one of the most influential players in a network of private right-wing groups that aided the Reagan Administration, both through its cooperation with the FBI, and, later, through its role in the "private network" as a money-laundering operation used by Lt. Col. Oliver North to conceal the sources of covert aid to the Nicaraguan contras. An initial goal of the new foundation was to compile "the country's largest private computerized database of subversives" in order to help construct a file of political activists to replace the FBI's database which had been ordered dismantled by Congress four years earlier, following revelations about the FBI's highly intrusive COINTELPRO investigations.[12]

Eight years after the Handal diaries were used by the FBI to launch the largest investigation of political dissenters since the 1960s, a Senate investigating committee concluded that Rees' article: "cited documents allegedy captured from the files of the Salvadoran Communist Party...The article asserted without documentation that CISPES was composed of groups 'initiated by the Communist Party U.S.A....and Farid Handal.' " Calling the diaries "alleged," and "unauthenticated," the investigators concluded: "The FBI's CISPES file does not reflect any Justice or State Department characterization of the nature or reliability of the alleged captured document or any effort to evaluate its bona fides. The [FBI's] Inspection Department was unable to find any information directly corroborating the statements in the purported Handal document."[13]

In retrospect, it is apparent that the Salvadoran National Guard provided to the CIA a set of documents which were either falsified to implicate CISPES in an international terrorist network, or deliberately misinterpreted to create the impression that the group was doing the bidding of a foreign hostile power. What is most ironic is that this disinformation, generated by the Salvadoran security forces in collaboration with the CIA, was later used to prove that CISPES was, itself, a group set up to generate disinformation, manipulate the media, convey propaganda—a set of activities that would make it the target of a fullblown, nationwide FBI terrorism investigation.

In the spring of 1981, the FBI's counter-terrorism officials wanted to develop their own sources of direct intelligence in their fight against international terrorism. The CIA frequently used the FBI according to its own agenda. It withheld information, often passed along incomplete or outdated material, and frequently ignored the needs of the Bureau altogether. If the Bureau's effort against CISPES and the FMLN were to succeed, the FBI needed an ally whose intelligence was as good—or better than—the CIA. The solution lay in a collaboration between the Federal Bureau of Investigation and the National Guard of El Salvador. And the person to arrange that collaboration was the hitherto untapped treasure chest of Salvadoran contacts and information—Frank Varelli.

Oddly enough, supervisors in the Dallas FBI office—as well as in Headquarters, managed to ignore a teletype which was written after Varelli had come into contact with the FBI but before he actually signed on to work for the Bureau. Much of the airtel, which was sent on February 11, 1981, is blacked out. But the unredacted portion is as prophetic as it is futile: "FM Director TO Dallas: Receiving offices are reminded that it is natural for recently arriving exiles in this country to direct whatever forces they can against their present or former enemies, thereby in effect using the FBI as a political weapon in their struggle."[14]

The teletype suggests that, had its warning been heeded, the history of the FBI in the 1980s might have been very different. But, in all probability, the FBI would likely have found another Franklin Agustin Martinez Varela to use in the Bureau's secret war.

Back Channel Partners: The FBI and the National Guard

With the approval of his superiors in the Dallas FBI office, Varelli made arrangements to return to El Salvador in the spring of 1981 to establish a channel of communications that, for the next five years, would help guide the Bureau in its fight against Salvadoran immigrants and U.S. political activists opposing the Reagan Administration's policies in Central America.

Varelli's arrival in San Salvador on April 10, 1981 was an emotional homecoming. He was met by his lifelong friend, Antonio Villacorta. The former Jesuit priest had been selected by Col. Eugenio Vides Casanova, director of the National Guard, to conduct ideological counter-insurgency training for the Guard and to handle the Guard's public information and press relations.[1] Unknown to all but a very few people in the Salvadoran government, Villacorta was also Vides Casanova's hand-picked secret intelligence operative who reported directly to him rather than to the official head of the G-2 Unit of the National Guard.

But there was another, deeper connection between Varelli and the National Guard. As a young man in training at the Salvadoran Military Academy, Vides Casanova had been a top student of Varelli's father, Col. Agustin Martinez Varela, who, at the time, was commander of the cadet company of the Military Academy of El Salvador. As the senior Varela's career progressed through his assignment to the General Staff Command, his appointment as director of the National Police and, later, as the Salvadoran Minister of the Interior, Vides Casanova served under him on several occasions. In fact, Vides Casanova had met young Franklin when the boy was only three days old when his father brought his infant son to the Academy on a fine spring day in 1950 to show him off. Seventeen years later, when Varelli enrolled in the Academy as a cadet,

Vides Casanova was his captain—just as his father had been Vides Casanova's captain nearly two decades earlier.

Varelli's father held Vides Casanova in enormous admiration, as much for his character as for his military prowess. To Col. Agustin Martinez Varela, Vides Casanova epitomized integrity, honor and patriotism. He was a devoted family man and a very hard-working soldier. He was also a very good friend.[2] After five FMLN gunmen ambushed Varela and tried to kill his wife and sons, it was Vides Casanova who ordered a 24-hour protective watch by National Guardsmen at the Varela home.

The young Varelli had always been struck by the gentle, almost courteous manner of the handsome director of the National Guard. "His eyes do not have the ferocious kind of look that many commanders have. He had a non-aggressive, almost passive, manner—even when he ordered us to perform the most torturous kinds of exercises at the academy. I remembered him as a gentleman in all respects," he recalled.

But to human rights groups and critics of the Salvadoran military, the tall, courtly Vides Casanova personified a cruel and repressive type of terrorism. During his tenure as Director General of the National Guard—from his appointment in 1980 until his elevation to Minister of Defense several years later—Vides Casanova was said to have presided over a campaign of detentions, tortures, disappearances and political assassinations by government security forces and private right-wing death squads that involved tens of thousands of victims.

By the end of 1983, the reign of political violence had become such a political liability that then Vice President George Bush, along with Lt. Col. Oliver North, traveled to El Salvador to warn the Salvadoran military that unless they drastically cut back on human rights abuses, they would alienate Congress and jeopardize the entire program of U.S. aid to their country.[3]

The day after his arrival in San Salvador, when Varelli arrived at the Salvadoran Officer's Club for his appointment with Vides Casanova, the moment was electric. Vides Casanova greeted Varelli like a lost son. When Varelli produced a personal letter from his father to Vides Casanova, the soft-spoken colonel glanced at the signature at the bottom of the letter. His green eyes began to water as he looked away from Varelli. After a long moment, Vides Casanova indicated a doorway into his private office. The two men moved into the room and closed the door. Vides Casanova sat down and slowly read the letter from beginning to end.[4]

As he read, Varelli sat across from Vides Casanova's desk scanning the elegant wood paneling which concealed the steel reinforcement and soundproofing material in the walls. On one wall was mounted a battle map of El Salvador, with marking pins and small flashing lights. Vides

Casanova wore three gold stars on his uniform indicating his rank as colonel. On his lapel he wore the gold seal of El Salvador. His automatic weapon lay on a bookcase behind his chair, next to a bank of radio communications gear which punctuated the silence with the crackling of intermittent messages. When he was done, he put the letter on the desk, smiled at Varelli, and asked: "What is it we can do for you?"

Varelli told Vides Casanova that he had, by pure coincidence, come across an old acquaintance, a man named Daniel Flanagan, who was now an FBI agent. Flanagan, Varelli told Vides Casanova, had not only persuaded Varelli to work with the Bureau but had confided in him the FBI's need to establish a direct channel of communication between the Bureau and the National Guard. The FBI wanted the help of the Guard to work more effectively in stopping the flow of communists from El Salvador into the United States and also to prevent or intercept communications between communist support forces in the U.S. and the FDR-FMLN in El Salvador. Only recently, Varelli added, the President had commissioned the FBI to take the lead in the battle against terrorism; the White House was concerned that the U.S. was losing control of its own borders.

Vides Casanova was puzzled. He didn't see how the FBI could help the National Guard. The Guard already had direct access to the American Embassy—and they communicated daily with the CIA. Vides Casanova added that he was not happy with the response of the U.S. authorities. He was especially disturbed by the rampant propaganda emanating from the United States which, he said, was constantly undermining the efforts of the Salvadoran government by distorting facts and deceiving the public about what was happening. "Even if every one of our operations were conducted with complete adherence to human rights and regulations and due process, we would still be made to look bad because of the communist propaganda. And the U.S. government does nothing at all about that." It was the propaganda, especially in the international press, that was hampering the government's efforts to win the war, Vides Casanova complained.

"That is exactly how we can help you," Varelli told Vides Casanova. He explained, as Flanagan had told him, that the special counter-terrorism unit of the FBI for which he was working had the direct sanction of the White House. "This FBI unit wants to be sure it gets the most accurate information which it will disseminate to the White House. The White House, in turn, would see to it that the true story of El Salvador would be properly conveyed both to the public and to Congress."

Beyond that, Varelli added, the FBI wanted a secret channel so that it could work with the National Guard to squeeze the communists both in El Salvador and in the United States. That kind of operation required instantaneous knowledge of meetings and plans of members of the FDR-FMLN and other Salvadoran guerrilla groups. At the same time, the FBI would furnish the National Guard with the plans and operations of "terrorist support" groups in the U.S., as well as with the latest propaganda that was being generated in North America.[5]

The more the passionate Varelli talked, the more enthusiastic Vides Casanova became. To Vides Casanova, the prospect of helping the FBI in its fight against terrorism while, at the same time, reaping the benefit of the Bureau's intelligence on North American agitators, was tremendously encouraging. The director of the Guard saw the initiative as the beginning of a new El Salvador policy on the part of the Reagan Administration, the first step in a diplomatic coup against the Junta and a reversal of the demonic and destructive policies of Jimmy Carter's CIA and State Department. He was also impressed by the FBI's special treatment of Varelli which Vides Casanova took as a sign of the high priority of this operation. Varelli related to Vides Casanova that Flanagan frequently told him to take special care with his reports as they were going to the White House. As a result, Vides Casanova finally agreed to a direct, clandestine channel of communication with the Dallas FBI office.

He was especially excited by Varelli's explanation that both the FBI and the members of the Salvadoran right wing shared a common rival: the CIA. It had long been the conviction of Vides Casanova and other members of the security forces—as well as of the elite businessmen who controlled much of El Salvador's industry—that the Carter Administration had virtually delivered their country into the hands of the communists by installing a ruling junta which contained several avowed socialists. In permitting the junta's imposition of "instant socialism" on their country, Vides Casanova believed the Carter Administration had played directly into the hands of the leftists. By this time, moreover, it was clear that the emerging head of the junta was Duarte, a lifelong socialist whose agenda included a rapprochement with the communists and a gutting of El Salvador's security forces. In the entire transformation of the country, the chief agents of President Jimmy Carter were his hated State Department, personified by former Ambassador Robert White, and the duplicitous and dangerous CIA, which had provided clandestine support to Duarte.

At one point, Varelli produced a stack of newspaper clippings from his briefcase and laid them on Vides Casanova's desk. The articles condemned the murderous right wing in El Salvador while lionizing the poor, oppressed supporters of the FMLN who wanted only peace and justice. If the escalating violence of the rebel guerillas was ever mentioned, it was parenthetically and far down in the article. Vides Casanova was dismayed by the false and biased picture of El Salvador that they represented. "How can the government of the United States permit these kind of lies?" he asked Varelli. Vides Casanova made it clear that any joint operation involving the FBI and National Guard must be geared toward influencing Congress and the media. And it must prevent the work of North American leftists spewing out all their propaganda on behalf of the FMLN.

Varelli told Vides Casanova that since he would be working at the center of the FBI's CISPES investigation, he could personally guarantee the thrust of the Bureau's efforts. One such task, he said, was the rebuilding of files on U.S. leftists that had been ordered destroyed during the Carter Administration. Another was to clamp down on destructive propaganda. All the FBI needed in exchange, Varelli said, was speedy, accurate, expeditious information on the movement of Salvadoran communists and their contacts inside the United States.

Vides Casanova was clearly excited by this time. No one had ever presented a proposal like this before—especially no one like Franklin Varela, whom he personally knew to be a dedicated and devoted anti-communist. Vides Casanova knew the CIA had its own man in the intelligence unit of the National Guard. He knew the man communicated to the State Department and the Pentagon. But, for all that, nothing ever seemed to happen. He didn't know how to distinguish between all the mixed signals emanating from Washington. Here, at last, was an answer. With the chain of command stretching from the Dallas FBI office to the White House, the FBI could tell the National Guard where U.S. policy was really going, how it was to be implemented, and how President Reagan viewed developments in El Salvador. It was, he concluded, an offer he could not refuse. It represented his country's best, and perhaps, last hope for the future. At the end of the meeting, Vides Casanova hugged Varelli by the shoulders for a long moment. It was a hug that contained the aspirations of a generation of Salvadoran patriots—people who felt themselves under siege from the communists and betrayed by the U.S. State Department and CIA, and who believed with their hearts they were El Salvador's only remaining guardians of freedom, defenders of capitalism and protectors of western civilization.

A Secret History of Repression

To implement the new collaboration, Vides Casanova approved an arrangement whereby Varelli would work directly with Villacorta, the

National Guard's chief of public information and disinformation. Varelli revered Villacorta for his extensive knowledge of history, as well as his range of skills and talents in a number of disciplines. Villacorta dazzled Varelli with his knowledge of philosophy, theology, Marxism, capitalism, virtually all the social sciences and humanities. The two men had spent countless evenings in El Salvador discussing the best ways to counter the advance of communism. They dissected the effects of what they saw as the Carter Administration's efforts to destabilize the country. In the year since Varelli had moved to the U.S., Villacorta and two colleagues were already making plans to defect to the U.S.—and to use their treasure of intelligence materials as bait to secure the approval of U.S. authorities to grant them political asylum. But the deal never materialized.

Nevertheless, the inventory of Salvadoran intelligence represented an enormously valuable prize to an agency like the FBI, charged with combatting Central American terrorism.[6]

The data included documents purportedly seized in raids on FMLN safe houses or confiscated from captured rebels. One report included a war plan of the Salvadoran Communist Party. Material seized from an armed group with the acronym GAR (Grupos de Accion Revolucionaria) detailed when and how they had been trained, the names of their Cuban instructors and maps of Cuban training installations. Another confiscated document contained methods of guerilla operations, names of members and the organization of urban terrorist cells. One document indicated that the Christian Ecumenical Movement had been infiltrated by communists—especially Protestant and Catholic church workers in El Salvador and the United States. Many of those churches would later become active participants in the Sanctuary movement.

From another source, Varelli obtained a copy of a super-secret political and military history of El Salvador compiled and updated by the General Staff Command of the Salvadoran military to help the FBI understand the nature of the communist threat in El Salvador and Central America and the recommendations for controlling its spread. The extraordinary report[7] elaborates a history of Soviet designs on El Salvador dating back to 1932 when the revolt led by Agustin Farabundo Marti threatened to restore a socialist president who had recently been overthrown by the military. The intelligence specialists who compiled the assessment saw virtually every reform movement in the last 50 years as part of a long-range Soviet plan for eventual communist domination of the world. But the remarkably candid secret report also acknowledged that recurring surges of popular discontent were prompted by indiscriminate repression and generalized economic exploitation at various periods in El Salvador's history. "Although the communists have tried to force the government to take repressive measures, care must be taken not to do it in a general and indiscriminate way. The armed forces must always try to isolate the subversive cells from the rest of the population to maintain constitutional and civil liberties." This was a lesson which was apparently lost on the report's readers within the FBI's counter-terrorism unit.

The report also acknowledged the institutionalization of a network of private paramilitary squads as well as the maintenance of a secret database of subversives. "In the face of urban terrorism," the report noted, "anonymous harassment of the communist leaders has been increased. Those leaders know they will be individually responsible for all terrorist acts that may take place. Harassment is used as a tool of discouragement...Anonymous propaganda and massive campaigns of pamphlets and fliers in which death threats and threats of kidnapping against communists is part of the permanent plan of harassment to which they will be subjected."

In recounting the government's brutal response to the 1932 uprising, in which 10,000 to 30,000 campesinos are said to have been murdered, the report noted that: "The government abruptly suspended the process of voting—but not without having obtained lists of all the people affiliated with the Communist Party all across the country." Those lists were to form the core of the database of terrorists, communists and sympathizers that had been perpetually updated by each new generation of Salvadoran military and police forces.

But those databases, which were so central to Varelli's mission on behalf of the FBI, also proved to be an overwhelming source of anxiety and danger to the members of the Salvadoran security forces.

The Secret of the Database

Varelli and Villacorta knew that, in order to successfully identify the movement of known and suspected terrorists and to track lines of communication between communists in El Salvador and activists in the United States, the FBI needed at least a partial database of known Salvadoran communists with which to compare names of Salvadoran refugees who were apprehended at the border or inside the U.S. But the database itself had become a source of dense intrigue among political and military leaders in El Salvador. In October, 1979, after the junta was installed, it issued a proclamation calling for the dissolution of the country's numerous police and intelligence units and their consolidation under the control of the General Staff Command. One such agency, Ansesal, a presidential police and intelligence force, was ordered disbanded.

Shortly after the installation of the junta, Maj. Roberto D'Aubuisson, an Ansesal official who would later be widely accused of being a mastermind of the Salvadoran death squads, asked a superior what he should do with the store of Ansesal files in the presidential palace. Were they to fall into the hands of the communists, it would be a disaster for the country and its security forces. D'Aubuisson was told to take care of the files any way he wanted to—destroy them, give them away—just get them out of the palace. D'Aubuisson secretly took them to his home.[8]

In January of 1981, three months before Varelli's arrival in San Salvador, the junta ordered all databases and files to be turned over to the General Staff Command of the Salvadoran military. The order, designed to bring the various security forces under the junta's control, covered the National Guard, the National Police, the Treasury Police, Customs Police, and municipal police departments.

While members of the junta justified the order as a way to streamline an unmanageable array of bureaucratic fiefdoms and to bring to heel the human rights abuses of the security forces, men like D'Aubuisson, Villacorta, and Nicolas Carranza of the Treasury Police, saw the order as part of a scheme by Duarte and his socialist cronies to emasculate the country's security forces in order to pave the way for the establishment of a Marxist-Leninist regime. (Their fears, coincidentally enough, echoed complaints by members of the intelligence community and the FBI several years earlier when a committee of the U.S. Senate ordered the Bureau to deactivate its files on suspected communists and radical activists in the United States.)

The order generated a frantic flurry of activity among the various police and security forces. While all the other police agencies complied with the command, the National Guard did not. Inside the Guard, which held the country's largest collection of political files, Villacorta evaded the order by turning copies of some files to the General Staff Command, while, at the same time, copying the entire archive to be hidden around the country. Several months later, D'Aubuisson, who had secreted the contraband Ansesal files, secretly fed them back to Villacorta who, along with Constantino Rampone and two aides, began to copy them and secretly disperse them to a network of allies throughout the country.

In April of 1981, when Varelli arrived in San Salvador, he found Villacorta and his associates furiously copying the files they were secretly receiving from D'Aubuisson. The men were operating out of a ware-house-type room, about 50 by 20 feet, stacked to the ceilings with cartons of documents, lists, materials seized in raids on FMLN safe houses which included diaries, communiques and materials on the secret organizations of terrorist and political cells. Frantically they processed the documents on an overworked photocopier which kept breaking down. The room was a blizzard of papers and boxes. The men worked furiously 18 hours a day. At any moment, they could be discovered by agents of Duarte who would cashier them and destroy their vital but illegal secret operation. Varelli spent hours of his visit during Holy Week in 1981 driving around the streets of San Salvador looking for available photocopiers to help process the overwhelming mass of documents.[9]

The material they copied included three lists which Varelli delivered to the FBI office in Dallas on his return. One list, compiled by Salvadoran security forces, included the names of 300 Salvadorans who had studied in the Soviet Union or other Eastern bloc nations. "We knew they were engaged in academic studies, but, at that time, we could not prove they were engaged in military training. Later, we learned that various communist universities specialized in different aspects of political and military warfare," Varelli explained.

The second list, compiled by the ministry of defense, contained the names of 103 "Traitors to El Salvador." The list contained a mixture of known combatant guerrillas as well as leftist and Marxist political leaders and ideologues.

The third list, which was actually a compilation of names from seven death squads, including more than 1,000 names of people who had been sentenced to death by the private assassination teams. While it included the names of known terrorists, it also included liberals, socialists and homosexuals, some of whom were known to have been communists or communist sympathizers. But some of those names were put on the lists because of personal rivalries or family feuds, Varelli explained later.

Those were the lists Varelli brought back to the FBI at the end of April in 1981.[10]

Beginnings of the Miami Network

He brought back two other key pieces of information as well. During the visit, Varelli was invited to a very private meeting of representatives of a council of elite, ruling families in San Salvador. At an elegant house in San Bonito, a wealthy area just outside of San Salvador,

Varelli was greeted by the 80-year-old "Professor" Alfredo Peccorini. Peccorini had already involved other members of the Salvadoran establishment in the war against the communists through his establishment of a conservative Salvadoran think tank called the Center for Socio-Political Studies of El Salvador (CESPDES). Much of the material developed by CESPDES dealt with the identities of emerging leaders of the FMLN-FDR, as well as descriptions of their terminology, their methods of operation, their recruiting and indoctrination techniques, and their links with various sectors of Salvadoran and U.S. society.[11]

In addition to its function as a private intelligence group, CESPDES also published material which was designed to counteract what its members saw as an enormous blitz of propaganda and disinformation by members of the Salvadoran left. In the next four years, CESPDES material would prove a useful source of intelligence for the FBI.

As other members of the group arrived—lawyers, doctors, architects, a few military people—the meeting focused on a plan to set up a propaganda operation inside the United States to counter the message of North American liberals. If the Salvadoran rightists organized a public relations outlet, then the press would cover them just as it covered the activists of the left. (Later, the operation fizzled for lack of interest from the North American press.) The members of the council saw the battle as much as a war of information as a war of guns and bombs. Their main goal was to neutralize the success of CISPES and counteract the message of the leftists in order to win the support of Congress and the U.S. public.

The new operation, Varelli learned, was to be based in Miami, where several Salvadoran businessmen were in the process of setting up an organization partly to disseminate propaganda and partly to gather intelligence on U.S. and Salvadoran activists. The operation, which would come to involve Salvadorans in Los Angeles, San Francisco, Houston (where the operation utilized a Wang computer to record its collected intelligence), New Orleans, Miami and other cities, was aimed at discouraging U.S. leftists from supporting the FMLN rebels and their political wing, the FDR. It was an operation that would work for several years in a loose partnership with the FBI. "The council decided that the North American leftists were obvious targets for the operation. They provide the platform for FMLN ideas. They are able to exert political pressure on Congress. The families wanted to create a situation here where some of the groups could be intimidated into silence," Varelli said.

During the meeting, the participants questioned Varelli intensively about the propaganda efforts of the communists. Did he feel they were effective? Why were the U.S. intelligence agencies falling down? What were the FBI's needs? How could they help? "The best way they could help," Varelli told them, "was to channel everything they learned to the FBI."

Six years later, Varelli would explain that one of the reasons he decided to go public "was to make sure the FBI will never do this again to anyone. They will not misuse people like this. They blew it. They were not dealing with dogs. They were dealing with human beings—with ambitions, desires, goals, dreams and feelings."

Reflecting on the way in which the Salvadoran right wing has been characterized in the U.S. media, he added: "Please. In this area, you're dealing with human beings. The liberals will swear we drink blood, but my friends of the right were not criminals. They were not sadists or people who followed the Hitler mentality. The people I dealt with were people that had dreams and aspirations and hopes. They had families and children. They went to mass on Sundays and took communion. They participated in Red Cross activities and in Little League. The only difference was they had the determination to take a stand against communism. They were trying through their work to improve the country and themselves in an honest way. But one day a bunch of communists—Soviet- and Nicaraguan-backed terrorists—came in and started to bomb their houses, rape their wives and kill their brothers and sisters. The next day a socialist government was imposed by the U.S. which put into effect reforms that not even the Cuban revolution could impose on the Cuban people 20 years after Castro took power. These were people who were doing nothing more than defending themselves and their way of life."

But others see Varelli's defense of the private right-wing Salvadoran establishment, with its close links to the death squads, as gratuitous at best. A number of students of Salvadoran history point out that the Salvadoran military, aided by secret paramilitary forces, has controlled the country through an unending rule of terror and repression since at least 1932—long before Fidel Castro and the Sandinista regime in Nicaragua came on the scene.

A Network of FBI Sources

By the time Varelli left El Salvador 19 days after he arrived, he had mobilized a very impressive intelligence network for the FBI, one that included figures in the country's private and public sector and that was not totally dissimilar to a larger, more activist, more far-flung network that would come to operate several years later under the coordination of a Marine lieutenant-colonel assigned to the National Security Council.

In an extensive report to the FBI compiled in late May after his return from El Salvador, Varelli assured the Bureau it would receive timely, complete and reliable information on every relevant development within the FMLN. The material was to provide current and detailed information on churches—especially those religious groups which were attracted to the ideology called Liberation Theology; on labor unions; on the nation's health care sector; and on developments within El Salvador's two main universities.

In all, Varelli reported to the FBI that he had recruited 14 principal intelligence sources to assist the Bureau in its fight against terrorism. In addition to the National Guard, for instance, he recruited an official in the passport section of the Salvadoran immigration department. This person would come to pass information to the FBI on virtually every politically significant Salvadoran or American who applied to travel to or from the United States. He enlisted the cooperation of an official of the Ministry of the Interior—an arrangement which guaranteed the FBI access to information about developments in every city in the country. He recruited an employee in the Ministry of Culture who passed along reports on foreign visitors and cultural exchange programs involving delegations from socialist countries. He recruited several physicians to provide information about doctors who were involved in labor organizing as well as about medical workers who were aiding the guerrilla forces. The physicians would, Varelli hoped, be able to track the flow of medical aid raised by CISPES and other groups directly to the communist forces. He developed a channel of communication with a member of the National Association of Private Enterprise (ANEP), a politically-active business group with ties to private death squads. And he developed a channel with a military official who was known to be involved with several Salvadoran death squads, as well as with similar paramilitary groups in Guatemala.

It was from the National Guard that Varelli acquired a final piece of information—at the end of his trip to El Salvador—that would serve as the springboard for his next four years with the FBI.

Three months earlier, in January, 1981, the FMLN had mounted a nationwide general offensive which was designed to lead to a general uprising which it hoped would paralyze the ruling regime. But the offensive was a failure. The army, which had learned about some of the FMLN plans in advance, squelched a number of guerrilla operations. And the mass uprising, with the exception of a few pockets of activity, never materialized.

In the wake of its military failure, the FMLN decided it was time for a major tactical shift. The thrust of the new offensive would be, not armed insurrection, but propaganda aimed at securing international support.

About the time Varelli was leaving El Salvador at the end of April, the National Guard acquired the text of a recent presentation by Roman Mayorga Quiroz, a leading strategist for the FDR, the political arm of the FMLN communist rebels. In his presentation at UNAM University in Mexico, which was titled "A Political Solution for El Salvador," Mayorga Quiroz laid out the strategy of the FDR-FMLN for the coming years of the Reagan Administration.

"The U.S. does not want a Marxist regime," he noted. "Even though they are sending weapons, they will not dare send in troops. In order to hamstring the Reagan administration, three measures are proposed:

"1) The FDR-FMLN will increase to the maximum its political-military actions (in order to demonstrate force).

"2) We are escalating international pressures on the U.S. (through sympathetic leftist governments.)

"3) We will erode the base of the U.S. Republic. (For this purpose, 180 groups of solidarity with the People of El Salvador have been created in the United States.)"

Mayorga Quiroz added that the creation of the solidarity groups was based on the Vietnam precedent.

"These measures are based on the fact that the U.S. is not a fascist government; that debate exists; that public opinion is powerful enough to stop Reagan. But our problem is time.

"Since the defeat of the U.S. in Vietnam was gained through public opinion, let us use public opinion once again to force Reagan to deliver El Salvador."

Opening the Show in Texas

It was this last piece of intelligence—the explicit plan of the FDR to set up 180 groups inside the U.S.—that forever altered Varelli's role with the FBI from the intelligence analyst he was hired to be to an undercover operative, which is what he became.

When Varelli brought the Mayorga Quiroz material to the FBI, he underscored the effectiveness of the tactic by pointing out that just days after Mayorga Quiroz' speech, the FDR-FMLN won official recognition from the governments of France and Mexico.

When he explained the FDR strategy of setting up 180 groups inside the U.S., the response of the Bureau was swift and unequivocal: Find the 180 groups.

Thus began the saga of "Gilberto Antonio Ayala Mendoza"—a poor Salvadoran political asylum applicant whose family had been murdered by the death squads in El Salvador—and whose identity could be verified by his social security card, two driver's licenses, and other identity material provided by the FBI to support Varelli's "legend." Through his Mendoza cover, Varelli began to provide the FBI's Dallas office—which would come to coordinate the entire nationwide investigation—with an unending flow of information from both the right and the left.

From El Salvador came regular communications from Villacorta and Rampone at the National Guard's Intelligence Unit. Some came via telephone, other material by mail (either from El Salvador or from various ports of entry within the U.S.), and some came directly by couriers.

By the happiest of coincidences, on a May morning in Carrollton, Texas, Varelli went into the Alpha-Beta Supermarket where he stumbled onto a roadmap of the movement in opposition to Reagan's Central America policies. In the supermarket's magazine rack, Varelli's eye was caught by the cover of a magazine featuring the white hand of the death squads. The magazine was *Mother Jones,* a small, California-based left-liberal journal which had devoted an entire issue to Central America, the emerging political issue of the 1980s.

Using the *Mother Jones* list of Central America-oriented political groups around the country, many of them just forming, together with address and phone numbers, Gilberto Mendoza began writing to each group for its literature and, in short order, found himself on the mailing lists of group after group, as magazines, fliers, pamphlets and newsletters flooded the Post Office box which had been procured for him by his case agent, Dan Flanagan.

While Flanagan grilled "Mendoza" mercilessly on his legend (the cover-story of an undercover agent), the FBI procured a post office box, a bogus telephone number (which actually rang in the FBI office in Dallas), two different drivers' licenses, a social security card and a secure telephone in his home.

It was over that phone—rigged with an FBI-issue tape recorder—that Gilberto Mendoza put his first moves on the newborn Committee in Solidarity with the People of El Salvador.

"Gilberto" and "The Doctor"

If Frank Varelli had never been born, he would have existed as a figment of Bill Casey's imagination. The short, spectacled, mustachioed Varelli grew up in a crucible of political violence which hardened in him a ruthless and obsessive hatred of communism. From mentors in the Salvadoran military he learned the street ways and strategies of the FMLN guerillas and how they fit into the right-wing version of a larger terror network driven by Moscow, Havana and the PLO. But Varelli's study of human nature was no less rigorous than his study of history. An evangelist by training, he developed a deep understanding of what motivates people—an understanding that served him well as one of the FBI's most effective undercover agents.

As "Gilberto Mendoza" he appeared to his fellow CISPES members as humble, deferential, ingratiating and a valuable source of information about developments in El Salvador. In tape recordings of his phone calls to CISPES members, Mendoza's Colombo-like manner is disarming and, when one understands his real purpose, chilling:

(Call No. 1)[1]

Mendoza: Hello, is this the number of CISPES?

Woman: Yes, it is.

M: Well, I'm trying to get this material that came out in the *Mother Jones* magazine. And I wanted to know how I will go about getting that.

W: Ok. What materials were you interested in?

M: Well, I got it here. This one is "El Salvador on the Threshhold of a Democratic Revolutionary Victory." The other one is called "El Salvador: A Brief Overview." One is four dollars and the other is seventy five cents.

W: Listen, I need to look through my materials. I think I have the brief overview. If I can have your address, I'll send you what I do have that might be interesting.

M: Well, I think that would be fine.

W: Another thing is, I'll write on the material the date of our next meeting in Dallas. You might like to come to that.

M: I'm very interested in finding out more.

W: Well, we're having a dinner a week from tonight—a fundraiser—for us to keep working on the issue. And there'll be a speaker there. I'll send you all this material plus the dates of the dinner and of our next meeting. Could I have your name and address?

M: Let me get it because I just moved here. Just a second please. OK. Let me give you this one. My name is Gilberto Antonio Ayala Mendoza. Do you speak Spanish?

W: Just a little bit. Can you spell it?

M: (Spells it) And my address is PO Box 57294. And at the bottom you put 1505 Slocum, Dallas, Texas 75207.

W: Listen, would you mind if you gave me your phone number so if something comes up I could call you?

M: Ok. Just a second please…I'm calling here from a friend's house. I'm at 624-1939.

W: Thanks very much.

In fact, the phone number Varelli gave to activists was a direct line to the terrorism unit in the Dallas FBI office. Whenever anyone called for Frank, his "roommates" would take the message and call him at home. Shortly thereafter, Varelli would return the call from his home telephone which had been outfitted with an FBI-issue recording device. If the call dealt with plans for an upcoming meeting or demonstration, Varelli would call other members, or drop by the CISPES office, to get estimates of how big and how important the event was. Depending on the timing, he would either call Flanagan or drop by the FBI office, or else send in a written report on the upcoming rally and the need for law enforcement coverage. In the case of a local event, Flanagan would notify the Dallas police. For a statewide or nationwide demonstration, the state police or, additionally, all the FBI field offices would be notified of CISPES' plans.

CISPES' Salvadoran Pipeline

(Call No.2—a woman named Uli, with a noticeable German accent, answers)

M: Hello, good morning. Could I please speak with Linda?

U: Well, Linda's not here. Sorry.

M: Well my name is Gilberto Mendoza and I just wanted to find out if you're having a meeting this week of CISPES.

U: Well, I don't think so but you could call someone else of the CISPES people. Joe Crews' office. If you want the number, I can get it for you.

M: Please, because I would like to find out because usually we have them on Thursdays.

U: Well, wait a moment please.

M: OK

U: Here I've got Joe Crews' number It's 767-0032...You want another number of somebody else?

M: Yes, please, in case I don't get to talk to him.

U: There's Hilda's number. You know Hilda?

M: Yes, yes.

U: Hers is 843-4943.

M: OK. I'll call either one of them and I'll find out if they're gonna be having a meeting...

(A few minutes later the phone rings again)

M: Hello. Is this Uli?

U: Yes.

M: This is Gilberto again. How ya doin?

U: Fine.

M: I'm calling back because I called those two numbers you gave me and Joe's not gonna be in today. And the other number has been disconnected.

U: Oh gosh.

M: Do you have somebody's else's number?

By the end of the conversation, Varelli had acquired six more home phone numbers of CISPES activists.

As time went on, Mendoza proved to be a valuable source of both inspiration and information for CISPES. As a refugee, he was the kind of articulate and moving victim that personified CISPES' concerns. He was, in fact, well served by the oratorical skills he had developed as a ministry student and which had proved so successful during his crusade several years earlier in El Salvador.

Posing as a member of the underground community of undocumented Salvadorans, Mendoza provided a constant flow of information about what was going on in El Salvador. But while his CISPES colleagues thought he was conveying the latest information from the refugee network, Mendoza drew on other sources for the information he passed along at CISPES meetings.

"Before attending a CISPES meeting or demonstration, I'd call down to the National Guard office—or to other sources in El Salvador—

to get some general information about developments down there—new government initiatives, developments in the labor unions, word about political changes which were in the wind," Varelli said. At the meetings, he'd tell the CISPES activists that he had called friends who told him the latest plans of the government. "I tried to sound knowledgable. That's why CISPES treasured everything I had to say. I don't know why they never figured it out. I always had fresh information and I always seemed to be able to contact somebody in a position of knowledge."

The information flow, moreover, went both ways. During those same calls to the G2 unit of the National Guard, Varelli would tell Villacorta about CISPES' latest plans for demonstrations, lobbying efforts or letter writing campaigns. The National Guard, in turn, would publicize CISPES' plans in advance, hoping to keep organizers of the group distracted and confused.

"CISPES thought the information was obtained independently by the Guard, when, in fact, we were collecting it and passing it on to the National Guard so that they looked like source of origin. The Guard would have a press conference and announce that a demonstration protesting the Reagan Administration policies in El Salvador would be taking place in Washington or New York and that communist elements were involved in the preparations and that confiscated documents from intelligence operations revealed there was a link between CISPES and Cuba or Nicaragua or the Soviet Union. At the same time, we could use information from the National Guard to show to FBI Headquarters to impress on them the importance of our connection with the National Guard and how necessary it was to keep this channel of information open."

(Call No. 3)

Sister Linda Hajek: Hello.

M: Linda? This is Gilberto. How ya doin?

H: Fine. How are you?

M: Oh, just fine. Listen, I was sorry I wasn't able to make it this last Saturday. I have a friend who owns a truck and I've been helping him take materials different places. You know, going to Denton, going to Austin and different places. I just been staying a little busy trying to make a little money. I just wanted to call you today to let you know I haven't forgot you and I still want to continue coming and I also have the things I promised you.

H: That's great. Also, Gilberto, we met a very interesting young man from El Salvador.

M: Oh really?

H: Who came out in December. He is interested in working with the refugees down in Harlingen in South Texas. So Ron, in our group, drove on down there and went to the detention center and talked to lawyers who are working with them and what we want to do now is to have a tour for this young man, Roberto, who will be coming to Dallas probably in a couple of weeks.

M: Oh, fantastic, fantastic!

H: So we might be calling on you. First of all, I'd like for you to meet him and have a chance to really talk to him.

M: Yes, yes.

H: Secondly, you might be able to help if we need some translating.

M: Yes, I'd be more than delighted to.

H: Good. Well, listen, we're having a meeting on Thursday night at the Intercultural Center at SMU.

M: Fantastic. And you're doing fine?

H: Yes, I'm doing real fine.

M: Well, I'm glad to hear that. You know, sometimes I don't have the words to express how I feel inside. But the last time I was there, I felt such a warm atmosphere that I felt like I was at home, you know. Because there are moments that I do miss my country so much. But all the people make me feel at home and didn't make me feel like a stranger. And I really appreciate that and God's gonna bless you for that.

H: Good, good. Well, we look forward—we are really glad you are with us. Thanks for calling, Gilberto. Bye-bye.

Varelli subsequently decided to avoid meeting the man Linda Hajek mentioned since he was afraid he might be recognized. But he later told the Bureau the man might be a terrorist, since, Varelli added, he was interested in the locations of police and fire stations and power plants in the Dallas area.

Night Calls of "The Doctor"

Those were the daytime calls of Gilberto Mendoza.

The nighttime calls of the "Doctor" were very different. The "Doctor" was an invaluable secret link from the FBI to the elite intelligence unit of the Salvadoran National Guard.

Late at night, flanked by piles of notes and documents, Varelli cradled the phone between his shoulder and ear listening to the voice at the other end. The waves of conversation arced high over the moonlit Caribbean, overheard only by the silent satellites of the National Security Agency which had been requested by the FBI, at Varelli's suggestion, to monitor the calls in case there were ever a question of which master was being served.[2]

V: This is the doctor. We are monitoring the activities of these people. There is one organization called Coalition for a New Foreign and Military Policy. At this moment, I have in my hand a legislative update, number 13, for the Coalition. Their central offices are at 120 Maryland Avenue, Northeast, Washington, D.C. 20002. The phone number is: 202-546-8400. The letter is dated 4th October 1981. Aid to El Salvador: Reagan rejected.

NG: Got it. Now write this down. Salvadoran Ecumenical Aid Committee. Tell this to our good friend [amigo was the codeword for the FBI] that this organization is a front. A lot of respectable people could be part of the executive board. But the secretariat is manipulated by the LP-28 [an armed guerilla force in El Salvador]. Write down Jose M.A. from Cuernavaca. This gentleman is the one that is the link to those in this country we are talking about. This must be publicized: that this man is a link to all the aid that is being collected and that indeed, all the dinero is going to the guerrillas down here. That is a fact. In San Salvador, the church is La Iglesia Bautista Emmanuel. Pastor Sanches Pallacias belongs to FAPU [one of the five Salvadoran armed forces comprising the FMLN].

V: That fits with the document that was seized and confiscated titled Ecumenical Cells in 80 and 81.

NG: This is intimately related to the liaison commission of the DRU [the highest revolutionary directorate of the Salvadoran rebels.] Through the information I just gave you, you'll be able to complement information you have and finish the documentation you are working on for our friend [the FBI]. Be sure to say the information—in case it is used publicly—was not obtained here. Absolutely. It can not be used to compromise our channel.

V: Understood. Next I have in my hand a proposal for the creation of ecumenical cells. [The document was confiscated from a woman at the Texas border by Customs officials acting on a request from the Dallas FBI office.] See Annex 1, page 17. Under Roman numeral V number 6 dash 1. El Salvador and Mexico. A—local people responsible. In El Salvador, Iglesia Bautista Emmanuel.

NG: Bingo. It checks with my information.

V: Senora Christina de Amaya. Also Reverendo Carlos Sanchez.

NG: That's the name I gave you earlier. That's FAPU.

V: The little girl was carrying the papers in her clothing when Customs nabbed her.

NG: Perfect! Good work!

The "little girl" to whom Varelli referred was at the time being held at the El Paso office of the FBI, captured by INS border patrol agents in Las Nueces county on the Texas-Mexican border. In June, 1981, Varelli got a call from Flanagan telling him that the woman, who gave her name as Ana Estela Guevara Flores, had been arrested by agents along with twelve other people. The woman was found to be carrying a number of documents in her clothing, including a booklet of sermons by Archbishop Oscar Romero and letters of introduction to church activists in Puerto Rico. Varelli told Flanagan to call down to Las Nueces and have the group held for interrogation. By the time he called down, the twelve people traveling with the woman had already been deported, but she was still in custody.

"When I learned that the other twelve had been deported, I called the National Guard to meet them at the airport. We wanted to know if we could learn their names and destinations in the U.S.. But it was too late. By the time the National Guard contacted the San Salvador airport, they had already arrived and left the airport," Varelli said.

On orders from Flanagan, agents from the FBI's El Paso office took the woman from Las Nueces to a more secure jail. They sent her documents to the Dallas office. The next morning, Varelli received the documents which, to his eyes, looked very compromising. In addition to the Romero sermons, there was a proposal for a Latin American Ecumenical Movement as well as a diary which described a recent trip by the woman to Managua.

"I started to read material and it was clear. She had been to Managua. She had been affiliated with members of the Communist Party in El Salvador. She was quoting a lot of passages of Msgr. Romero about 'Liberation Theology.' She had booklets that were strictly Marxist." In a small book of phone numbers, one entry caught Varelli's eye. It was a phone listing for a building in San Salvador which sat opposite the American Embassy. Next to the number, someone had written the word "surveillance." The phone number belonged to the fourth floor of that building, CIA personnel confirmed to the FBI. That meant that anyone with access to that office could look directly into the offices of the U.S. Embassy.

When Varelli studied the woman's photograph, he determined that she had recently cut her hair, altered her make-up and, in subtle ways, changed her appearance. On closer scrutiny, she reminded Varelli of Norma Guevara, a "commandante" of the FMLN guerrillas who had recently been released from prison under an amnesty program. Varelli asked the National Guard to forward a photo of Norma Guevara.

Meanwhile Flanagan was on the phone to the El Paso FBI office making arrangements for the woman to undergo a polygraph examination. When preparations were complete, Varelli got on the phone and began dictating specific questions for the agents to ask the woman.

"I told the agents to be very careful what words they used. If, for instance, they were to ask her whether she has participated in any armed robberies, she'll say no and the needle won't move. That's because she has a different concept. What we would consider a criminal act would be to her simply an action to further the liberation of the oppressed people. So she wouldn't respond to general questions about crimes on a polygraph. For it to work, you have to ask whether she has 'expropriated' or 'liberated' something. The idea is to use the same terminology the revolutionaries use."

If the FBI had any doubt about Varelli's suspicion, they soon evaporated. As Varelli continued to dictate questions, the polygraphing agent told him: "She's failing all the questions."

In particular, she failed two questions which were key to the issue of her true identity. First, she was asked if she knew the name Norma Guevara. She said no, but the needle on the lie detector showed she was lying. Next, she was asked if she knew Mario Aguinada Carranza, a member of the FMLN who had worked in the past with Norma Guevara. Again, she answered in the negative. Again, Varelli recalled, she was contradicted by the movement of the polygraph.

When she was confronted with the polygrapher's findings, she said she did know Norma's name—but only from reading about her in the Salvadoran press. She continued to deny any knowledge of Carranza. When she was confronted with the fact that she had obtained a false passport in Guatemala and a fraudulent birth certificate in Mexico, she explained she obtained them from people who helped her enter the U.S.

As the woman elaborated her story, the agents became more and more agitated. The phone lines between Dallas and the National Guard were burning up. Flanagan contacted headquarters who notified the FBI's Legal Attache in Panama. In short order, the CIA station in El Salvador was involved in checking aspects of her story. Still the woman insisted she was not "Commandante Norma" of the FMLN but Ana Estela Guevara Flores, a poor Salvadoran maid who was seeking refuge in the United States.[3]

As FBI agents in Texas worked to sort through the inconsistencies in her story, CIA personnel in San Salvador were checking on names of people in notebooks the woman carried. Simultaneously, the San Juan field office began checking on Puerto Rican names in her papers—a number of whom turned out to be sympathetic to the Puerto Rican FALN.

Varelli's Media Event

"Things were looking very good for us at the time," Varelli recalled. "The leads were checking out. The FBI was preparing to take credit for a major interruption of a terrorist channel of communication." Varelli knew that the real Norma Guevara had been arrested in El Salvador almost a year earlier and that her fingerprints were on file with the security forces. To confirm the Bureau's suspicion about the woman, the Dallas FBI office asked the National Guard to forward the woman's fingerprint cards. As it turned out, her prints were on file with the National Police—an agency that was much more closely tied to the U.S. Embassy and the CIA than the National Guard. When the fingerprint cards arrived, they showed that the woman was not the well-known "Commandante Norma." When Varelli and Flanagan shared this information with Villacorta at the National Guard, he told the FBI the cards were phony. "Don't trust what the National Police is sending you. It appears she's being protected by people in the Junta and the National Police," Villacorta told the bureau. By this point, the contest over the identity of the woman had blossomed into a full-blown inter-agency rivalry, pitting the CIA and Salvadoran National Police against the FBI and the National Guard.

Villacorta also forwarded a photograph of Norma Guevara to Dallas. To Varelli, the facial structure of the woman in detention matched exactly the structure of the face on the National Guard's photograph of "Commandante" Norma.

"Flanagan was confused and very uncertain about how to handle the situation. I explained to him that the FBI was being set up, that the woman is Norma Guevara, but that we we're being sent phony prints by the National Police acting on the direction of the CIA," Varelli said.

At that point, Varelli and Villacorta began to plot an ingenious scam using a local Texas television reporter as their unwitting agent. The reporter, who at the time worked for a CBS affiliate in Dallas, had been trying to arrange an interview with the Varela family, who were rumored to have been very important people in El Salvador. Varelli called the reporter and told him to meet him at a hotel restaurant at two o'clock that afternoon. At the meeting, Varelli confided that he worked for the FBI. "I'll share some information with you if you promise never to reveal the source—and I will give you a second source to use to confirm the material. If you abide by those rules, I'll give you the story," he told the reporter, who called his editor to clear the arrangement.

Varelli told the reporter that later that day, the National Guard in El Salvador would be holding a press conference to announce the capture in Texas of a confirmed terrorist named Norma Guevara. After Varelli filled him in on the details of the arrest and the background of Norma Guevara, he told the reporter he had to cite the Salvadoran National Guard public information division as the source of the story.

After the men parted, Varelli called Villacorta and told him to schedule a 6 p.m. press conference to announce the capture of Commandante Norma in south Texas. Varelli told Villacorta that the Guard should mention that the source of the information was CBS news.

At 6 o'clock sharp, the reporter led the local news program with a story that a well known Salvadoran female terrorist had been arrested by U.S. authorities in Las Nueces county. Two minutes later, the phone rang in the National Guard office where Villacorta stood, surrounded by reporters. As he hung up the phone, he announced to the assembled press that CBS had just announced the arrest of a FMLN terrorist in Texas.

At that point, Varelli poured himself a half glass of scotch. As he sipped it, the phone rang. It was Flanagan asking whether Frank had seen the news on TV. Both men chuckled softly. The coup was a quiet secret within the counter-terrorism unit. And Varelli got a special airtel from Headquarters congratulating him for his work.

Nevertheless, the fingerprint cards and the information from the National Police indicated the woman was not the guerrilla leader the National Guard claimed she was. In retrospect, Varelli explained, it didn't really matter. "Suppose she's not Norma Guevara. Then we've made a mistake. Suppose she's really Ana Estela Guevara Flores. She still deserves to be in a terrorism file. She was carrying subversive literature. Beside, if we had really arrested the wrong person, the real 'Commandante Norma' would have come forward and humiliated the FBI in front of the whole world. More important than the disposition of this particular case is that we proved to the National Guard that the Bureau was willing to go beyond normal channels to see the operation through to its conclusion. Remember, this was one of our first joint operations and it gave the FBI tremendous credibility in their eyes." To Varelli, as well as the National Guard and the FBI, the success of the operation far outweighed the fact that they were indicting an innocent woman whose possession of "subversive" sermons had marked her for surveillance, disappearance or death should she ever return to El Salvador.

The Guevara Flores case, moreover, yielded the first tangible clue regarding the FBI's assistance to the National Guard in helping the Guard monitor and apprehend leftists who, in fact, were known to be innocent of terrorist activities. A teletype, which incorporated information developed in Dallas, was sent from the FBI's Legal Attache in Panama to FBI Headquarters. According to the teletype:

"Subject [Guevara Flores] is not a known guerrilla/subversive." But, acknowledging the interest of the Salvadoran security forces in the woman because of her possession of "subversive" literature, the teletype noted: "If subject is deported back to El Salvador, they [Salvadoran security forces] would desire to be notified of the date and flight number...and perhaps copies of documents found on the subject could be furnished the captain of Taca [the Salvadoran airline] for passage to El Salvador National Guard, to the attention of Col. Eugenio Vides Casanova, Director General." But whatever credibility the FBI gained with the National Guard, it subsequently lost with the federal judiciary. In 1986, a federal circuit court decided that, not only was Guevara Flores not the well-known rebel leader, Norma Guevara, but that she had demonstrated a "well-founded fear of persecution" that had to be taken into account by immigration authorities.

Connections Found or Fabricated

The following month, the FBI forwarded to the Defense Intelligence Agency a communique from the National Guard which illustrates the subtlety with which the new operation combined information of genuine counter-terrorist value with other material which was designed to discredit innocent opponents of Administration policies.

On July 17, the Guard sent the FBI a bulletin concerning an armed revolutionary group, GAR, several of whose members had recently been arrested by Salvadoran security forces. The Guard bulletin noted that members of GAR had been involved in numerous assassinations of police and military personnel, as well as armed robberies, sabotage of public facilities and extortion of civilians.

In a subsequent section of the Bulletin, the National Guard indicated that, at the direction of the Salvadoran Communist Party, "members of the most radical elements of the GAR were to promote in North America a strong and violent campaign of agitation and propaganda on behalf of FMLN-FDR, *having obtained immediate support from different sectors of North American society. Among the groups providing support were labor unions, Gay Power groups, Pro-Abortion groups, groups involved in the women's liberation movement, and organizations that are opposed to the strengthening of the military forces of the US.*"[4]

While the GAR had, in fact, compiled a record of armed guerrilla attacks in El Salvador, there was absolutely no indication that the group received any support from activists in the gay, abortion rights, women's liberation or Nuclear Freeze movements. In fact those groups had been included in the communique by Villacorta at the direct request of the FBI.

"In planning my meeting with Villacorta," Varelli recalled, "Flanagan told me specifically to get some of these groups included in communiques from the Guard. If we could find a real connection among the various political groups, that was fine. If not, we were under orders to create those connections." While some of the women's rights, and gay and Nuclear Freeze groups did lend secondary support to CISPES, there was absolutely no indication that they were aiding terrorist elements in Central America.

The communique—and others that followed—served two purposes. On the one hand, it conveyed accurate intelligence on developments within the FMLN guerilla groups. On the other hand, it provided deliberate disinformation to be used to discredit and neutralize legal and non-violent political organizations. "Can you imagine if gay rights groups, abortion rights groups, the Equal Rights Amendment groups were known to support a group which had killed more than 20 police and soldiers in one year?" Varelli asked. "Once the FBI had this data in their files, they could proceed to investigate all those other groups. What is even worse," he added, "the FBI knew that this material from the National Guard was strictly disinformation. But they passed the same material along to the Secret Service, the Defense Intelligence Agency and other agencies in the intelligence community without alerting them to the fact that it was completely fabricated."[5]

Allies in the Shadows: The FBI's Private Network

While Frank Varelli was the first FBI employee to infiltrate and report on developments within CISPES, a network of private, right-wing organizations was also at work spying on emerging liberal and left-wing Central America groups, disrupting their activities and providing material for the FBI's files. Many of the same groups that gathered intelligence on religious and political groups, including CISPES—and disseminated a blitz of distorted, scurrilous material tying them to purported international communist-inspired terror networks—would later be shown to have formed the propaganda and funding core of the Reagan Administration's private contra-support network.

In the context of domestic intelligence gathering, their affiliation with the FBI had been authorized by a little-noticed provision of a presidential order signed by Ronald Reagan in 1981 which permitted the FBI to "contract with…private companies or institutions…and need not reveal the sponsorship of such contracts or arrangements for authorized intelligence purposes."[1]

A number of the domestic conservative groups who aided the Administration's secret campaign to support the contras and to neutralize opponents of its Central America policies worked with other foreign governments and organizations under the umbrella of an international organization known as the World Anti-Communist League. The League's membership includes some of the most ultra-conservative and reactionary elements in the non-communist world. Founded in 1967, WACL has included in its membership a number of former Nazis and Nazi collaborators and counts among its various regional affiliates Guatemalan and Salvadoran death squad leaders, including Mario Sandoval Alarcon, a former vice president of Guatemala known as the "Godfather of the

Death Squads." League members were invited to Taiwan's Political Warfare Academy for training in counter-insurgency and police techniques, as well as to Argentina, where they were trained in brutal interrogation techniques by members of the Argentine military.[2]

During the 1980s, WACL's chief spokesman in the United States was Retired Major General John K. Singlaub, a former Army chief who resigned his commission after openly criticizing President Jimmy Carter's proposal to reduce US troop strength in South Korea. In 1980, Singlaub founded a US branch of WACL and, four years later, became chairman of the League. In that capacity, he helped facilitate covert military support from League members to anti-communist resistance movements in a number of countries, including Mozambique, Angola, Ethiopia, Vietnam, Laos, Cambodia, Afganistan and Nicaragua, whose former dictator, Anastasio Debayle Somoza, was an influential member of the League before his ouster by the Sandinistas in 1979.

As League chairman, Singlaub told a WACL conference in 1984: "Our struggle with Communism is not a spectator sport...We have opted for a course of action which calls for the provision of support and assistance to those who are actively resisting the Soviet-supported intrusion into Africa, Asia and North America."

At the time, Singlaub was assuming the role of the leading publicly visible figure involved in securing weapons and money for the Nicaraguan contras under a private-sector initiative apparently conceived by the late CIA director William Casey and coordinated by Lt. Col. Oliver North from the National Security Council.

Back in the winter of 1980, following Ronald Reagan's election, Singlaub traveled to Central America, along with another WACL official, former Defense Intelligence Agency chief Daniel O. Graham, to tell officials in El Salvador and Guatemala that the emphasis of the Carter administration on human rights was being downgraded and that counter-terrorism and hemispheric security would be the dominant policies of the new Administration. One Guatemalan official quoted Singlaub and Graham as telling military leaders in that country that "Mr. Reagan recognizes that a good deal of dirty work has to be done." Within weeks of the Singlaub-Graham visit, the level of death squad activities in Guatemala increased dramatically.[3]

From the Moon Files

One of the more prominent United States-based offshoots of a member group of the World Anti-Communist League was the Rev. Sun

Myung Moon's organization. While most publicity about the Moon organization has centered on stories of the psychological "captivity" and "deprogramming" of young members of the cult, as well as the federal tax evasion conviction of the Rev. Moon in the late 1970s, the organization, with its large accumulation of capital, has been a major player in international right-wing circles for 20 years.

The international spread of the Moon organization has been paralleled by the proliferation of Moon-funded organizations within the US to promote the profoundly anti-communist and anti-democratic ideology of the Moon church, which itself has been alleged by a number of researchers in and out of Congress to be directed by the Korean Central Intelligence Agency.

One of the more active Moon groups in the early 1980s was a campus organization created under the acronym CARP, the Collegiate Association for the Research of Principles. In early 1981, CARP strategists determined that Central America was becoming a critical arena in the fight against the advance of Marxism-Leninism. As a result, they mounted a campaign on more than 100 campuses around the country to counteract the activities of groups like CISPES by presenting support for the Salvadoran junta and its emerging leader, Jose Napoleon Duarte.

CARP members began to make their intentions known to the FBI as early as April 1981, when Moon activists wrote a barrage of letters to the FBI informing the Bureau of their activities. In short order, the entries in the FBI files, some of which are headed "Miscellaneous - Non-Subversive," grew into a more active partnership between the Bureau and CARP. And by the spring of 1981, CARP members were infiltrating CISPES meetings and sending reports into various FBI offices.

One entry, headed "ATTN: FBI" noted an exchange between a CARP activist and the public affairs director of a student-run radio station at the University of California at Santa Barbara. According to the CARP activist: "Cory [the station director] is well-educated in Marxism and is a supporter of the [Salvadoran] FDR. He tried to convince me that the Soviet Union is not involved in El Salvador, yet he freely admits the role of Cuba. Just before we made our arrangement, he was in a conversation with a local CISPES. It was about some program from Havana."[4]

Another submission from CARP reads: "Enclosed are many articles and clippings culled mostly from communist-inspired front groups. CARP at California State University at Long Beach has gathered these materials in the hope that they will be of assistance in determining the message and strategy of the left on campuses."[5]

The 48 pages released by the FBI, which constitute only a small portion of the Bureau's files on CARP, includes submissions from Moon groups on campuses as diverse as Columbia University, Boston University, the University of Wisconsin, and the University of Chicago. While the FBI released CISPES-related references to CARP, it declined to release any of the entries in the Bureau's main file on the Moon organization.

The activities of CARP allegedly went beyond intelligence gathering into more active forms of political harassment and disruption. A number of FBI documents note the outbreak of fights and rock throwing incidents at CISPES demonstrations that involved members of CARP. To a casual reader, the FBI notations seem to be neutral accounts by observing agents. In fact, CARP's relationship to the FBI—at least in Texas—was much more active. At the SMU campus in Dallas, for instance, where CARP had a contingent of about 75 members, Special Agent Dan Flanagan would go the campus once a month to pay the Moonies for their support services to the FBI. In addition to supplying intelligence to the Bureau, the Moonies started fights among the audience whenever CISPES held a rally or demonstration on campus. After a series of such incidents, CISPES moved off the SMU campus to the Martin Luther King Center, much to the relief of authorities at the university who were concerned about the violence that seemed to follow CISPES campus events.[6]

"The Moonies were a major support group," Varelli recalled, adding that in 1982, agents in the FBI's Washington Field Office prepared a Moon contingent to hold a demonstration in support of a visit by Duarte which had generated a number of oppositional demonstrations by CISPES and other groups.

In Dallas, Varelli said, they reported to Flanagan at least once a month on the various groups they were collecting intelligence on. "In several of their reports, they mentioned 'Gilberto Mendoza,' this poor Salvadoran who was talking a lot of crap and who nobody knew where he came from. Flanagan paid them a minimal amount, but it was enough to secure them as a source. It's standard procedure to hook a source with money, even if it's very little. The money formalizes the relationship. And the existence of signed receipts can be used in the future to force continued cooperation," Varelli said. The collaboration of the Moonies with the Bureau, Varelli added, was an open secret in the Dallas counterterrorism unit.

A second private group which flourished during the Reagan era was the Washington-based Council for Inter-American Security. The group disseminated reams of material during the 1980s purporting to prove linkages between a Soviet-inspired global terror network and liberal and left-wing American groups opposed to US foreign policies. CIS also expended considerable effort to improve the public image of the reputed Salvadoran death squad leader Roberto D'Aubuisson. When the FBI's CISPES files were pried open in 1988 by a lawsuit brought by the Center for Constitutional Rights, they were found to contain several reports written by J. Michael Waller, a researcher whose work has been sponsored by the nongovernmental Council for Inter-American Security.[7] But Waller's work to connect American political dissenters to an international communist-terrorist plot was part of a public-private partnership. According to several contracts on record, Waller's research—which helped swell the FBI's files on Central America groups—was also financed by no less a source than the Reagan Administration's Department of State.[8]

Western Goals:
The Strange Case of John Rees

Of all the emerging private conservative organizations working to support the policies of the new Administration, none was more effective than Western Goals. Housed in a townhouse in Alexandria, Virginia, this foundation turned out a series of publications designed to expose the "communist-terrorist" menace inside the country.

One of the purposes of the foundation was described in a statement of purpose by founder Larry McDonald: "In the field of Marxists, terrorism and subversion, Western Goals has the most experienced advisors and staff in the United States…The Foundation has begun the computerization of thousands of documents relating to the internal security of our country and the protection of government and institutions from Communist-controlled penetration and subversion."[9]

A long-time colleague of McDonald and a key figure in the work of the new foundation was John Rees—the same right-wing journalist whose article was used by the FBI to launch the first CISPES investigation and whose writings were cited by the Denton Committee to brand nuclear peace groups as Soviet "active measures" front groups.

In assembling a board of directors, McDonald wasted no time in soliciting a man who was already prominent in international right-wing circles—John Singlaub.

Beginning in 1982, the foundation—under the guiding hand of Rees, himself a long-time confidant of Singlaub—began publishing a series of books targeting liberal and progressive activists involved in a range of causes and organizations. *The War Called Peace* dealt with the array of US peace groups supporting nuclear arms reduction and the nuclear freeze movement. *Broken Seals* attacked the National Lawyers Guild, the Center for National Security Studies, the American Civil Liberties Union and other groups which had, in the previous decade, been in the forefront of the effort to demand stronger Congressional oversight over the CIA and the FBI. *Ally Betrayed...Nicaragua* catalogued the role of the Carter Administration in "selling out" the Somoza regime in that country and permitting the establishment of the Sandinista regime in its place. *Soviet Active Measures Against The United States* laid out an elaborate theory of contacts and linkages which purported to explain how domestic political and religious groups, such as the Washington Office on Latin America and the National Council of Churches, were being used by the KGB as fronts for Moscow's political operations.

In defense of his activities, Rees has pointed out that he has never been successfully sued for libel, a fact he attributed to his knowledge of libel law, his meticulous research and his dependence on open source information for most of the material he has compiled on left and liberal activists.[10] But another reason Rees may have avoided such litigation lies in the limited nature of the circulation of Western Goals materials. At least in the early days of the foundation's operations, very few of the group's publications made their way into left-liberal circles. According to former employees of the foundation, the publications were circulated, almost exclusively, to John Birch Society chapters, other groups on the far right, local police departments, the Bureau of Alcohol, Tobacco and Firearms (BATF), the Central Intelligence Agency and the FBI.[11]

In a suit against the Bureau and the Washington, D.C. police department, the Institute for Policy Studies introduced a deposition by Rees in which he testified that he had supplied information about the group to the FBI both by phoning FBI agents and providing the Bureau with copies of his publications. In the deposition, Rees listed a number of law enforcement agencies as recipients of his newsletter, including the Internal Revenue Service, BATF, the Secret Service, Customs, the Drug Enforcement Agency, the FBI, and the Maryland, New York and Michigan State Police.[12]

People familiar with Rees' operations over the last twenty years— he began his own newsletter, *Information Digest,* in 1967, around the same time he began working as an informant for the Newark Police Department—are amazed at his resilient ability to stay in business despite a series of discrediting events.

Rees, who was born in Great Britain and came to the United States in 1963, worked for a spell for the *London Daily Mirror*. His career as a mainstream journalist was aborted, however, when superiors at the paper discovered he had been trading on his professional standing by receiving free meals and hotel reservations. When officials at the paper discovered Rees' unethical activities, they fired him from the paper and paid off his bills.[13]

He first came to the attention of the FBI when he began dating a woman who was secretary to the FBI's Legal Attaché at the U.S. Embassy in London. The woman was reportedly prepared to marry Rees when she learned he was already married, according to an FBI document.[14]

Rees gained a measure of notoriety in 1964, shortly after his arrival in the United States, when he moved to Boston and gained the confidence of Grace Metalious, the author of *Peyton Place*, who was terminally ill. Hours before Metalious died, Rees brought a new will to her room at Beth Israel Hospital. He persuaded her to sign the document, which left her entire estate, then valued at nearly $150,000, to Rees, cutting off her husband and three children. Metalious' lawyer at the time said that the author fully understood her actions in leaving her estate to Rees. The attorney quoted her as saying, "I have complete trust in Mr. Rees with regard to my children." It was only later, when Rees learned that the liabilities and outstanding claims against Metalious' estate were greater than her assets, that he renounced his claim to her legacy.[15]

Rees subsequently married a black woman and moved to Newark where, in 1967, he launched "New Careers," a program designed to provide jobs for poor black residents of that city. At the same time, capitalizing on his wife's contacts in Newark's black community, he began secretly reporting to the Newark police on activities of black activist groups in the city.[16] But his Newark career was cut short when the U.S. Labor Department, which partially funded his "New Careers" program, determined that Rees overcharged the city some $7,500. The department also blocked payment of another $12,000 to a job training firm for which Rees was a consultant.[17]

The following year, Rees moved to Chicago where he began to work as an undercover informant for the Chicago Police Department, infiltrating groups opposing the U.S. involvement in the Vietnam War. Rees offered to testify on his findings before the House Un-American Activities Committee and to share his material with the FBI as well. But, at that time at least, officials at FBI headquarters determined that Rees was next to useless as a source of reliable information.

In a 1968 internal memo, Special Agent Alex Rosen wrote to several top deputies of J. Edgar Hoover about Rees' offer, noting that, during his stay in Newark, "he attempted to sell himself and his services to the FBI. The interviewing agents believed his interests were self-serving and that he came to the FBI thinking this would enhance his credentials in contacting other clients." The memo added that Rees "talked in generalities regarding persons and events connected with racial and criminal problems in Newark and furnished no information of value."

The FBI memo concluded that: "Rees is an unscrupulous, unethical individual and an opportunist who operates with a self-serving interest. Information he has provided has been exaggerated and in generalities. Information from him cannot be considered reliable. We should not initiate any interview with this unscrupulous, unethical individual concerning his knowledge of the disturbance in Chicago as to do so would be a waste of time."[18]

Despite his rebuff by the FBI, however, Rees stepped up his political spying activities, drawing on local police contacts he had cultivated in Newark, Chicago, New York and elsewhere. During the early 1970s, Rees gathered extensive material on political activists from various police officials, informants and private political spies with whom he exchanged information. That material was recycled in his *Information Digest*, which, in turn, went to a number of law enforcement agencies who, in turn, used it to compile files on political activists.[19]

The bizarre and damaging secret flow of unsubstantiated and scurrilous reports surfaced in 1976 when an investigative arm of the New York State Assembly conducted an investigation into the compilation of hundreds of thousands of files by the New York State Police on political groups and activists. They discovered that information reported in *Information Digest* "was casually used to create dossiers on a wide spectrum of Americans whose only crime was to dissent on what the *Digest* authors considered the left of the political spectrum. This information was, in turn, kept in state police files throughout the nation and widely disseminated. For police officials to have participated in this procedure is a shocking commentary on the decline of democratic safeguards."

"It is important to note," the investigators added, "that this was a national police procedure. *Information Digest* was the string that held together a network of hidden informants whose information was recorded by police departments throughout the nation without the individual involved knowing of the process and without independent checking by the police as to validity and source of this derogatory information."[20]

Noting that material was compiled by both John and Sheila Louise Rees, his third wife, who, at the time worked as a Congressional staffer for Rep. Larry McDonald, the investigators asked McDonald to elaborate on his relationship with Rees and his wife. McDonald, however, declined to comply.[21] Even without McDonald's testimony the investigators unraveled a longstanding covert, deeply concealed network of information-sharing on liberal activists which assumed greater proportions the further the investigators dug into it.

To avoid having to identify Rees and his newsletter as the source of many of their political files, officials in the New York State Police classified *Information Digest* as a "confidential informant" thereby investing it with the same aura of authority as an undercover asset who had actually infiltrated groups which were the subject of its reports.[22]

The material's authoritativeness was further enhanced when it was forwarded from the files of the New York State Police to other law enforcement agencies around the country in response to inquiries about political activists. When other agencies received the Rees-generated information, they assumed it was reliable since it bore the imprimatur of the New York State Police. "Few liberal organizations escaped being targets of derogatory reports or of infiltration by the agents of *Information Digest* who hid behind a maze of false names and Post Office boxes taken out under mysterious circumstances," the report added. "Opponents of the Vietnam war, including journalists, union leaders, campus dissenters, state and national politicians and liberal organizations were frequent targets. At times, personal remarks about the lifestyles of targets were included."

Elaborating on Rees' mode of operations, the report quotes "a highly-placed source" as explaining that Rees would go to one police department with information. While collecting payment as an informant, Rees would gather new material and pass it along to other police departments, either in exchange for pay or for yet new material.

The report detailed Rees' work with the Washington, D.C. police between 1971 and 1973. The relationship began prior to a major anti-war demonstration in May 1971, which resulted in the jailing of more than 12,000 protestors. Before the rally, Rees suggested to D.C. police officials that they rent an office for him and install listening devices to monitor leftists he would invite to the office. Using the alias John Seeley, Rees opened the Red House Book Store, which was conveniently located one floor below the headquarters of the Vietnam Veterans Against the War. The store, which provided an easy listening post for Rees, was rented and paid for by the intelligence division of the Washington D.C. police department.

Investigators for the New York State Assembly concluded that: "*Information Digest's* raw, unevaluated, editorialized and frequently derogatory information was used to develop dossiers on thousands of patriotic and decent Americans who had committed no crime and were not suspected of committing a crime...It should be noted that the extraordinary cost of maintaining a million-card file on innocent civilians could be put to use to curtail real criminal activities."

The New York investigation succeeded in eliminating one subscriber—the New York State Police—from Rees' list of clients. But the resourceful Rees, aided perhaps by his association with McDonald, lost little time in cultivating a new client, the FBI—which had, just ten years earlier, determined him to be "unscrupulous, unethical and unreliable."

It was also during the late 1970s as well that Rees worked with a partner in the private spy business who had personal connections to two men who would become among the most powerful people in the country: Ronald Reagan and his Attorney General, Edwin Meese.

For several years, Rees worked with Patricia Atthowe, a security consultant who compiled files on political activists, especially those opposed to nuclear power, which she used in her security work with large West Coast utilities such as Pacific Gas & Electric. According to the notes of two Los Angeles detectives who interviewed Richard Miller, then a vice-president of PG&E: "Atthowe and [her organization] provided good information. Ronald Reagan could verify Atthowe's reliability. Atthowe's husband was a deputy with the Alameda County Sheriff's Department and Edwin Meese was a District Attorney in Alameda County at about the same time."[23]

It is unclear how, and at what date, Rees managed to establish a new relationship with the FBI, but the climate in 1980 was clearly conducive to the Bureau's cultivation of private-sector resources like Rees. The first document on file which speaks to a formal relationship between Rees and the FBI surfaced in December 1981, when an assistant United States Attorney in New York testified, in a case involving the National Lawyers Guild, that: "Some federal agencies received information about the National Lawyers Guild from John Rees or S. Louise Rees or both, sometimes in the form of *Information Digest,* and from time to time they were compensated by the FBI for furnishing information."[24]

During the 1980s, Rees attained greater public visibility when he began to write a column for the Moon-owned *Washington Times.* But toward the end of the Reagan Administration, he again managed to become an embarrassment to the FBI.

In 1987, Jonathan Dann produced for KRON-TV in San Francisco a three-part series on private political spies. Dann reported in the final segment of the series that in 1982 the State Department published a list of groups which it declared were "Communist fronts" controlled by the KGB and the Kremlin. One group on the list was the Women's International League for Peace and Freedom, a long-standing peace organization. When members of the group learned they had been branded as agents of Moscow by the State Department, they filed a Freedom of Information request to ascertain the origin of the charge. They learned that the State Department's report quoted, word for word, from a Western Goals publication, *The War Called Peace,* written by John Rees. Initially, Rees denied writing the passages quoted by the State Department but, when confronted by Dann with a draft of his own booklet, stating that WILPF "supports revolutionary national liberation movements utilizing terrorism and armed struggle" and that WILPF "is thoroughly penetrated by the Moscow-line Communist party," he conceded it was his work. [25]

Angered by the FBI's red-baiting of the group, and especially troubled by the government's use of scurrilous, unverified information from a private right-wing activist, Congressman Don Edwards demanded an explanation of the FBI's conduct from William Webster, then director of the Bureau. The responses from the FBI's Office of Congressional Affairs were characteristically unenlightening. They are worth noting less for the information they contain than for the glimpse they provide of the impotence of Congress in effectively overseeing the Bureau.

Edwards had asked the FBI how Rees' book came to be retained in the FBI's files and how the portion dealing with WILPF was retrieved and disseminated to the State Department. The Bureau's response was: "A search of our indices does indicate a copy of the Rees booklet was retained in FBI files. It does show that two copies were provided to the U.S. Department of State. The FBI may acquire pertinent public information material and appropriately disseminate that material to other agencies if that information is of possible interest or use to them." [26]

Edwards further asked the FBI whether it had advised the State Department that the document in question was "an unverified report from an outside source whom the Bureau had previously discredited."

In characteristic FBI jargon, the Bureau responded: "The transmittal communication only advised the State Department that the booklet was edited by John Rees and published by the Western Goals Foundation and contained no opinions as to the credibility of the editor, publisher or authors...The decision on the credibility of such a public document in most circumstances is left to the reader. It is noted that the publisher of the booklet, Western Goals Foundation, had as its chairman the late Congressman Lawrence P. McDonald, killed when the Soviets shot down the KAL airliner..."[27]

At the time, McDonald had been en route to a meeting of the World Anti-Communist League.

While the FBI may not have explicitly endorsed the reliability of the material, that subtlety was obviously lost on the State Department. Shortly before Dann's report aired in late 1987, the State Department removed the name of WILPF from its group of Moscow "front" organizations. A spokesman for the State Department indicated that the Department, itself, had no way of knowing whether the allegations about WILPF were true. The reason the group was included on the list was that the State Department received the information from the FBI. It was the FBI's imprimatur on the material that led the Department to believe in its authenticity and accuracy.

The "Active Measures" Equation: Advocacy + Propaganda = Terrorism

Toward the end of 1981, Flanagan called Varelli and asked him to come to the FBI office on North Lamarr. When Frank arrived, Flanagan was clearly upset. The normally taciturn Flanagan waited for "Franco" to sit down at his desk. Then, with a flourish, he pulled an airtel from under a sheath of papers, flipped it over and thrust it in front of Varelli.

"Do you believe this?" Flanagan asked angrily. "Some asshole in the Justice Department is telling us we have to close the CISPES investigation. Do you believe that?"[1]

Varelli read the teletype slowly, word by word. In the teletype, an assistant attorney general had determined that since the FBI had found no evidence that CISPES had violated the Foreign Agents Registration Act—that is, no evidence that it was working directly on behalf of a hostile foreign force—that the FBI must therefore close the investigation and prepare a final memorandum on the probe.

Varelli was devastated. All the FBI's good work, he felt, was going down the tube. Just when they were establishing a surveillance system in a dozen FBI offices, just when Varelli was making real headway in CISPES, getting close to the leaders and gaining their trust, just when the National Guard had come to fully trust its relationship with the FBI, the Justice Department was closing it all down. Did this mean the end of Varelli's FBI career? Did it mean the end of the Bureau's pledge to "squeeze the communists" both in El Salvador and in the United States? He looked at Flanagan in a long moment of silence.

Flanagan looked stonily ahead for a moment and then the small creases of a smile appeared at the corners of his mouth. "Of course, this doesn't mean a fucking thing," he told Varelli. "Of course, you understand that the investigation will continue—just under a deeper cover."[2]

Jim Evans, another member of the counter-terrorism squad, walked into Flanagan's office. Evans, who always reminded Varelli of an aging hippie, looked nothing like an FBI agent. With his balding head and long hair, his thin build and bent posture, he looked like a shopworn refugee from the 1960s. But Varelli knew Evans was a very savvy agent.

"You're going to have to work full time at home," Evans explained to him. "Now, even more than before, do not discuss your work with anyone—especially not with other FBI agents who are not in the counter-terrorism unit. Keep attending CISPES meetings. Send in your expense receipts. We'll use your post office box for most communications. The investigation may be closed for now, but it is not over."

Flanagan noted that while the FBI's official CISPES investigation was being suspended, it would continue under a separate investigation of Salvadoran Leftist Activities being run out of the Houston Office. "We'll be back in it before the year is over," Flanagan added. "Mark my word. The CISPES investigation hasn't really begun. Meanwhile, keep developing information. Keep track of everything you learn. It will not be wasted, I promise you. Just be careful. Nobody is supposed to know about this."

Flanagan's prediction that the FBI's CISPES investigation would be resurrected was to come true with a vengeance the following year. In the summer of 1982 the FBI dramatically upped the stakes in its campaign against political activists. In its initial investigation of CISPES for violations of the Foreign Agents Registration Act, the FBI sought tangible evidence that the group was directly linked to the FMLN. But CISPES was not being paid by the FDR, was not helping provide weapons to the FMLN and was not taking its political direction from any "foreign principal," according to a memo from FBI headquarters to the Justice Department in early 1982.

The following year, however, the Bureau determined that it no longer needed such specific evidence of tangible links between a U.S. group and an international adversary in order to investigate the group. Henceforth, the FBI declared, it would be enough for dissenters inside the United States to publicly espouse positions which conformed to those of, say, the Soviet Union, the Sandinista government of Nicaragua or the Salvadoran FMLN rebels. That, alone, would provide the necessary evidence that the group was, in intelligence parlance, an "active measures front"—and, as such, a legitimate target for an FBI terrorism investigation.

William Casey's Active Measures

While the concept surfaced formally in the summer of 1982 during Congressional discussions about the preparation of new FBI guidelines, it had actually emerged as an informal element of intelligence policy the previous year under the sponsorship of William Casey.

Shortly after he assumed the directorship of the Central Intelligence Agency in 1981, Casey ordered two internal studies done for him by agency personnel. The first was to develop mechanisms for improving coordination between the CIA, on one hand, and the FBI and other elements of the intelligence community, on the other.

The second internal study involved a CIA report on "Soviet Active Measures"—a broad term that included "soft" covert activities designed to influence the political process in other countries. These so-called "active measures" included activities such as propaganda, disinformation, manipulation of news media, the cultivation of foreign opinion leaders and the use of "front" groups by the Soviets or their political clients to promote Moscow's line on particular issues. Significantly, the early CIA study identified CISPES as one such "active measures front," even while the group was barely becoming an organized political entity.[3] Domestically, the political meaning of the "active measures" concept— minus the mystifying jargon of intelligence specialists—was enunciated in a hearing of the Denton committee just a month before a presentation in the summer of 1982 by FBI and CIA officials to the House Intelligence Panel.[4]

In a statement which opened the subcommittee's hearings on the FBI's guidelines, Denton noted that: "...In the reordering of priorities and the restructuring of the entities within the Bureau which deal with substantive foreign counter-intelligence and domestic security, an important aspect of the Bureau's work may have fallen through the cracks...*What seems to be missing...is attention to organizations and individuals that cannot be shown to be controlled by a foreign power and which have not yet committed a terrorist or subversive act, but which, nevertheless, may represent a substantial threat to the safety of Americans and, ultimately, to the security of the country.*"[5]

Despite the FBI's own pronouncements that domestic terrorist events had been declining for the previous three years, Denton continued: "At this time of ever increasing terrorist activity, I believe the American people need an organization that has the ability, the desire, and the understanding of the threat to see through propaganda and false colors so that American people can be informed of the threat represented by organizations committed to the destruction of our freedoms. When I speak of a threat, I do not just mean that an organization is, or is about to be, engaged in violent criminal activity. *I believe many share the view that the support groups that produce propaganda, disinformation or legal assistance may be even more dangerous than those who actually throw the bombs.*"[6]

The following month, the House Select Committee on Intelligence heard presentations by both the deputy director of the CIA and the FBI's director of intelligence that prefaced a dramatic relaxation of the restrictions on domestic surveillance—and that would come to justify hostile government action against virtually any group or movement that expressed opinions which wandered too far beyond the accepted guidelines of mainstream political dialogue.

At a two-day session of the House Intelligence Committee in July 1982, CIA deputy director John McMahon and FBI intelligence expert Edward J. O'Malley laid out for Congress the dangers of "Soviet Active Measures."[7]

Although it was O'Malley who laid out the FBI's concerns about Soviet manipulation of domestic political groups through the use of "active measures," his presentation was actually a follow-up on the earlier study by the CIA's Operations Directorate. McMahon explained to the Intelligence Committee the use of "political front groups" as an element of "active measures" campaigns that, in retrospect, would take on enormous significance in the context of domestic surveillance. "With Soviet and Cuban encouragement and participation, Salvadoran leftists in the spring of 1980 established the FDR, the political front that represents the [Salvadoran] insurgency abroad," McMahon testified. "The [governing body of the FDR-FMLN] called for the establishment of solidarity committees...to serve as propaganda outlets, conduits for aid, and organizers of solidarity meetings and demonstrations. These committees are sometimes organized as part of a broader 'Nicaragua-El Salvador Solidarity Committee,' or 'Guatemala-El Salvador Committees,' or sometimes simply as 'El Salvador Solidarity Committees,'" he concluded.[8]

The presentation to the Intelligence Committee contained an indication of how central the concept of "active measures" had become in the Reagan Administration. To respond to the "active measures" threat, the government convened a permanent inter-agency task force on countering "active measures" initiatives. The group, which is chaired by the State Department and includes representatives of the CIA, the FBI, the National Security Council and the Defense Department, was still active as of the spring of 1990.

The emergence of an inter-agency effort to counter "Soviet active measures" raises the key question of operational links between the FBI and CIA. It is one of the first indications that the FBI's assault on domestic political groups was part of a larger inter-agency effort that involved numerous other elements of the federal intelligence community. And it explains why the FBI felt justified in employing the same investigative techniques against political dissenters that they used against suspected terrorists.

An Early Target:
The Nuclear Freeze Movement

While a range of groups which mobilized around Central America issues became the targets of the most extensive terrorism investigations conducted under the "active measures" designation, it was the overnight mushrooming of the Nuclear Freeze movement that first prompted the Administration's most public denunciation of a political movement as an "active measures" threat. In October 1982, President Reagan himself voiced concern that the Freeze movement was being manipulated by Soviet forces. The rapid growth of the movement—and the sensitivity of the issue of arms control—magnified the Administration's concern about a hidden Soviet hand manipulating the groundswell of opposition to U.S. arms control policies.

By mid-1982, the list of groups and communities endorsing the Nuclear Freeze was formidable. It included 17 state legislatures, 276 city councils, 450 town meetings and 56 county councils. Nearly three million citizens signed Freeze petitions. And, in addition to a large number of mainstream religious groups, including 140 Roman Catholic bishops, labor and civic organizations, the Freeze's supporters included the former Director of the CIA William Colby, former Defense Secretary Clark Clifford and Gen. James Gavin.[9] Nevertheless, the Freeze movement—which was one of the largest and fastest spreading grassroots movement of the 1980s—acted as a lightning rod for the most conservative elements in the government.

Just a few days before Reagan's remarks, for instance, Sen. Jeremiah Denton, head of the Security and Terrorism Subcommittee of the Senate Judiciary Committee, charged that the wife of Sen. Dale Bumpers (D-Wyo.) chaired a group called Peace Links which was subversive in nature and which "lends itself to exploitation by the Soviet

Union." Denton charged that at least four groups represented on the Peace Links board "are either Soviet-controlled or openly sympathetic with, and advocates for, communist foreign policy objectives." To support his allegations, Denton put into the record nearly 50 pages of right-wing extremist literature which purported to show direct links between the Soviet KGB and the Nuclear Freeze movement.[10] Similar material, virtually all of it lacking any credible substantiation, flooded out from *Readers Digest, Human Events* magazine, the *National Review* and other politically conservative organs. One such group charged that at least 13 Freeze sponsors—from SANE, to the American Friends Service Committee to Friends of the Earth and Physicians for Social Responsibility—"have all been identified as communist front organizations." The source of that information was a group called the Young Americas Foundation—whose material on CISPES would subsequently turn up in the files of the FBI.[11]

That climate of red-baiting, provoked by the sudden mass popularity of the Freeze movement, provided an encouraging environment for the FBI. The Freeze movement peaked in 1982 when ABC-TV broadcast a terrifyingly realistic fictional account of the outbreak of a nuclear war between the two superpowers. The week the film was to be aired, a group of the nation's most prominent scientists took out a full page ad in the *New York Times* urging the public to support the Freeze movement. The ad bore an address with a post office box for members of the public to send donations and letters of support. At the direction of headquarters, FBI agents put a mail cover on the post office box and entered the names of everyone who responded to the ad in the Bureau's terrorism files.[12]

An Allegation of Forgery

The only illegal act among the eight categories of activity included under CIA-FBI definition of "active measures" involves the dissemination of forged documents which are designed to mobilize opinion against the U.S. and in favor of either the Soviet Union or, at least, of Soviet positions on various issues.

One operation which is alleged to have involved political forgery was the dissemination by CISPES in late 1980 of a document which purported to be a "dissent paper" by a group of State Department employees who, in apparent disagreement with the Administration's El Salvador policies, warned that the President and his Secretary of State were leading the U.S. into an inevitable military intervention in that country by pursuing counter-productive policies. The authenticity—or lack thereof—of the document has never been proved. Nor has its authorship. Nevertheless, the allegedly bogus "dissent paper" was the subject of a brief flurry of press coverage, climaxing with a March 6, 1981, column by Flora Lewis of the *New York Times,* in which she relied on the "dissent paper" to support a column critical of U.S. policies in El Salvador. Three days later, however, Lewis denounced the dissent paper as "spurious" and apologized to her readers for treating it as a legitimate document.[13]

Aside from forgeries, the other activities covered by the term "active measures" include such time-honored components of political advocacy as manipulation of the media, the use of sympathetic indigenous organizations (labeled as "front groups") to disseminate propaganda, the use of disinformation and the cultivation of opinion leaders sympathetic to a particular point of view. According to the FBI report on "active measures," "Soviet political influence operations in the United States are designed to cultivate contacts with political, business, academic, and journalistic leaders and secure their collaboration. This does not necessarily require the actual recruitment of the individual, only his cooperation. Typically, the Soviets will play upon themes such as peace and disarmament, detente and peaceful coexistence to secure the cooperation of their target...The major objective of these exercises is to inject the Soviet voice into foreign government, political, business, labor and academic dialogue in a nonattributable or at least unofficial manner."

Commenting on the development of "active measures" strategies in the late 1970s and early 1980s, the FBI's O'Malley declared that "...the Soviets now make greater use of ad hoc front groups. These groups, which do not have an overt tradition of close association with communist and Soviet causes, try to attract members from a broad cross-section of the political spectrum. Nevertheless, they are dominated by pro-Soviet individuals and are, as a rule, covertly financed by the Soviet Union...Examples of such organizations include the Salvadoran solidarity committees."

Referring to several case studies of "Soviet active measures," the report again stressed that groups concerned with the situation in El Salvador must be regarded as either witting or unwitting agents of the Soviet Union. Noting the Soviet Union's ideological support for the rebels in El Salvador, the report cited the emergence in 1980 and 1981 of a network of El Salvador-oriented "solidarity" groups as part of a "classic Soviet active measures campaign that included front groups, covert press placement, disinformation and manipulation of mass organizations."

To William Casey and his colleague William Webster, it was apparently inconceivable that growing numbers of American voters felt so troubled by their government's involvement with a "death squad" regime and its indirect role in forcing the exodus of thousands of terrorized or displaced Salvadoran and Guatemalan refugees that they might be moved by their own consciences to support an opposition movement. In fact, a large majority of U.S. activists who rallied around the cause of Central America had little history of political activism, let alone ties to the Soviet Union.

The earliest core of the Central America movement comprised a number of veteran left-wing activists, some of whom had traveled to Cuba in earlier years to cut sugar cane and provide assistance to Castro's revolutionary Cuba. Other political veterans had been radicalized by their knowledge of United States policies in Puerto Rico and, in particular, the use of the FBI and other military and intelligence agencies to undermine the Puerto Rican independence movement. Others had become politically active in the 1960s and 1970s in response to the injustices which were highlighted by the Civil Rights, anti-war, black liberation, feminist and gay liberation movements. To them, Central America in the 1980s was the new battleground of a war for social justice which had been running like a skein through the history of the United States in the 1900s.

The consciousness of veteran Central America activists was marked by such events as the CIA's 1954 coup against Jacobo Arbenz, the popularly-elected president of Guatemala. It was solidified by what the left perceived as the isolation of Cuba by the United States following the revolutionary victory of Fidel Castro and Che Guevara over the exploitative and repressive regime of Fulgencio Battista, the Cuban dictator who turned the island into a Mafia-dominated casino park for wealthy North Americans. And it was cast in stone following the CIA's bankrolling of a nationwide transportation strike in Chile in 1973 which led to the overthrow and subsequent assassination of Salvador Allende, one of the few popularly elected socialist presidents in the Western Hemisphere.

To many of these veteran activists, who defined their politics as variously as anti-imperialist, pacifist, socialist, feminist, anarchist or communist, the history of the United States' relations with its Central and South American neighbors has been a history of domination, exploitation and imperialism. Whether or not that perception conforms to mainstream views of U.S. policy in the region is irrelevant in considering the federal invasion of their personal and political privacy as suspected terrorists under the FBI's heading of "active measures." Absent any

evidence that they have broken the law, their victimization by the federal
police is most simply illegal, if not under the FBI guidelines, then under
the First Amendment to the U.S. Constitution.

A much larger component of the Central America movement
involved citizens with little history of political activism but with humanitarian impulses which revolted at the ongoing slaughter of civilians in
the cities and villages of El Salvador and Guatemala. Large numbers of
mainstream church members became appalled by the intransigent poverty of Central America, the endless atrocities of right-wing death squads
and reprisals by the FMLN leftist rebels, and the burgeoning U.S. population of illegal refugees fleeing the intolerable violence of Central
America. It was these citizens, flowing from the Friends Meetings and
the Jewish synagogues, as well as the Baptist and Lutheran and Methodist
and Roman Catholic churches, who came to comprise the backbone of
the Central America political movement of the 1980s, and its religious
counterpart, the Sanctuary movement. Their numbers were supple-
mented by groups of students for whom the political activism of the
1960s was a phenomenon of an earlier period of American history.

But the various impulses behind the largest political movement of
the 1980s mattered little to William Webster's FBI. Carrying on in the
tradition of Hoover, the Bureau targeted not only CISPES but hundreds
of other Central America groups in the firm belief that they were "active
measures" fronts taking their orders directly from the Soviet Union, Fidel
Castro, the Nicaraguan Sandinistas or the FMLN.

Even O'Malley, when pressed to identify areas of American decision-making that had been affected by Soviet propaganda and disinformation efforts, was unable to cite any U.S. policy that had been
skewed by Soviet attempts to influence the political process. In his
Congressional testimony, O'Malley conceded: "It is often difficult to
determine the significance or impact of Soviet active measures. In
addition, it is difficult to judge the effectiveness of Soviet active measures
operations, although the fact that the Soviet leadership continues to use
and fund such operations...suggests a positive assessment of their
value."[14]

What is most troubling is that under the doctrine of "active measures" anyone who promotes a position on any issue—whether it
involves Third World development, arms control or foreign policy—that
might happen to conform to or support an official Soviet position is a
candidate for investigation by the FBI as an agent of Moscow or, at least,
a tool of "Soviet active measures."

In the U.S. system of government, conflicting opinions—as well as the introduction of overstated or even falsified material to justify those opinions—are to be resolved through their free airing in open political debate. Under that tradition, virtually every technique covered under the umbrella of "active measures" has become an accepted and acceptable part of mainstream political activities in this age of mass media and mass marketing.

As Rep. Romano Mazzoli, a member of the House panel, noted during the hearings: "[The types of Soviet active measures cited by the CIA] sounds very much like a political campaign to me. Those are the things that we use in American political campaigns, if you just drop the 'communist' part of it...This is really an effort to control public opinion or to influence public opinion, which is really what we do as a kind of part and parcel of our political activity in this country."[15]

Nevertheless, the concept of "Soviet active measures" became a key element in the FBI's second—and far more dramatic—probe of domestic political groups in the 1980s. As O'Malley told Congress in 1982: "FBI investigation of Soviet active measures falls under the authority and guidelines of Executive Order 12333, the Attorney General's Foreign Counter-intelligence Guidelines, and related statutes. Under these guidelines, the FBI has the responsibility to detect and prevent espionage and other clandestine intelligence activities conducted by or pursuant to the direction of a foreign power. Active measures fall in the category of other clandestine intelligence activities."[16]

A Private Use of Active Measures

The zeal with which the "active measures" theme was picked up by private right-wing activists was reflected the following spring in a speech by John Rees to the Conservative Caucus.[17]

In his presentation, Rees first made the audience aware of his very close relationship to the Bureau's counter-intelligence division. "The title of the talk I prepared for this morning was Soviet Activities in the U.S....In the case of classical espionage, which the FBI is supposed to monitor, I noted that one of the KGB spies deported from France this week has the same name as the third counselor at the Soviet Embassy on 16th street [in Washington]. When I called the FBI to see if there was a relationship—whether they were brothers or came from the same family—experts in counterespionage at the FBI had not yet made that connection..."

Rees then laid out the nature of "active measures." Getting down to specific cases, he cited the campaign in Congress against the

Administration's policies in El Salvador. "When the [human rights] certi-
fication program of the President is put into effect in Congress, first of
all, and absolutely by coincidence and with no coordination, the terrorists in El Salvador step up their campaign—and take measures like
blowing up generating stations, etcetera, that achieve national publicity
in the United States thanks to the *New York Times,* the *Washington Post*
and the *Los Angeles Times.* This is all designed to show that the legitimate
needs of the Salvadoran people are better met by the communist terrorists than by anyone else."

"Then various congressmen—usually in the case of El Salvador led
by Tom Harkin and Ed Markey—will unleash a series of lies based on
forgeries provided to them by the Cuban DGI [the Cuban intelligence
service]. These will then become issues and there will be street protests,
attempts to blockade the State Department... The overall effect is to
discredit whatever intelligent policies we try to develop in Central
America. And at no time do you see this program being initiated unless
you see as an initiator a member or former member of CPUSA [U.S.
Communist Party] or one of the front groups, like the National Lawyers
Guild, that is organizing, funding and taking care of logistical activities.
That is a prime indicator that it is an 'active measures' campaign."

For Rees—as for the FBI and for Bill Casey—the involvement of a
left-wing group in a protest against Administration policies provides
sufficient proof that the protest is a Soviet-manipulated effort designed
to injure or embarrass the United States government.

It was the kind of thinking which would find a bizarre and vivid
form of fruition in the creation of the FBI's Terrorist Photo Album.

$$8$$

An Album of Terrorists, An
Underground of Spies

The summer of 1982 saw the beginning of another FBI operation—
one which gave full expression to the concept of "active measures" and
which, five years later, would provide the Bureau with the occasion for
blatant dissembling to members of Congress.

During the official hiatus in the CISPES investigation—after the
closing of the Foreign Agents Registration Act probe and before the
opening of the terrorism investigation which would begin in March
1983—Evans and Flanagan instructed Varelli to compile entries for the
FBI's "Terrorist Photo Album." The operation was to be named "Pipil"
after an Indian group that originally inhabited the area that is now El
Salvador.

The idea was to compile a book of entries on known and suspected
terrorists—or people who were providing support to known terrorists—
that would provide basic identification data, photographs and a summary of the Bureau's investigative interest in the individual.[1]

To compile the album, Evans put Varelli in touch with an employee
in the FBI's photo lab who gave Varelli a crash course in the use of
photographic equipment. The Bureau provided film, lenses and filters,
and paid for the rental of a tripod and the purchase of hundreds of sheets
of photographic paper. When Varelli completed a roll of photos—many
of which were shot from books, newspapers or magazines—he would
drop the film off at the FBI office in Dallas where the photo lab would
develop and print them according the specifications of the photo album
format.

When Varelli submitted the completed album forms, he would
include only a number in the box on the upper right hand corner of the
page reserved for the photo. He would submit the photographs under

97

separate cover with the corresponding numbers on the backs of the pictures.

The material in the entries came from a variety of sources. Most of the material about left-wing Salvadorans and FMLN members came from the National Guard or the private, right-wing CESPDES institute, in San Salvador. Some of the material came from *Replica,* a right-wing Spanish-language publication put out by members of a secret ultra-conservative society called the Tecos in Guadalajara, Mexico. Much of the material on grassroots U.S. activists came from other FBI field offices responding to queries from the Dallas office. Varelli relied on material from Western Goals and John Rees' publications, whose acquisition was approved by the FBI, for much of the material on U.S. political figures. When it was finally submitted to Headquarters for routing and filing, the album contained about 700 entries.[2] But, as Varelli was to testify to Congress in 1987, "in reality, the album frequently contained the names of people who simply opposed the Central America policies of President Reagan." The subjects of the album ranged from individuals with documented involvement in political violence to such prominent, and non-violent, Hispanic politicians as Lopez Portillo, then president of Mexico. In addition to entries on a number of U.S. political and religious activists, it listed Senators Christopher Dodd and Claiborne Pell, Representatives Michael Barnes and Patricia Schroeder and former U.S. Ambassador to El Salvador Robert White as having "terrorist tendencies."

Some of the entries are revealing in the light they cast on the FBI's definition of terrorism which, according to the entries, ranges from activists with known ties with Soviet bloc agents to members of the United States Congress.

An entry on Sergio Mendez Arceo, a Catholic bishop of Cuernavaca, Mexico, reads: "He runs from his diocese a network of nuns and priests and lay people that are friendly to the FDR-FMLN of El Salvador and the FSLN of Nicaragua. They collect intelligence, buy and sell guns and serve as couriers for the communist guerrillas of El Salvador. Mendez Arceo has participated in [several conferences] in which the Catholic bishops proposed the Liberation Theology option for the poor. This new theology proposes a merging of Christianity and Marxism-Leninism. CIA Mexico reports contacts between Arceo and KGB-DGI agents. A member of the Green Party of West Germany presently active in CISPES in Dallas reports that money collected at meetings is sent to Mendez Arceo for guns for the FDR-FMLN. Teletype to all FBI offices. SECRET. Urgent."[3]

Another entry in the album portrays Sister Peggy Healy, one of the major activists in the Sanctuary movement, who was convicted in 1986 of violating immigration laws by helping shelter illegal Salvadoran aliens in this country. The "Terrorist Album" entry notes that she is a staff member of the Washington Office on Latin America and is pro-Sandinista and pro-Castro. Under the heading "Narrative of Activities," Varelli wrote: "She is a nun with the Maryknoll Order. Maryknoll is the popular title for 'The Catholic Foreign Mission Society of America.' It is a community of priests, brothers, sisters and lay people that are supposed to be spreading the gospel all over the world. Instead they are front runners in preaching the Marxist-Leninist 'Liberation Theology'. In El Salvador as well as Nicaragua, the Maryknoll priests and nuns are guilty of aiding, protecting and supporting the communist terrorists of the FDR-FMLN and FSLN. WOLA, the Washington Office on Latin America, is a powerful pro-Castro lobbying organization with staff members drawn from the National Lawyers Guild which seeks to influence the U.S. Congress and public on behalf of numerous leftist terrorist and communist groups from Latin America. Operating under the banner of 'human rights violations' they are operating against the U.S. government."[4]

A less specific but equally vituperative entry accompanied a photo of Robert White, the U.S. Ambassador to El Salvador during the Carter presidency. Of White, Varelli wrote: "Fired by the Reagan Administration in Feb. 1981 because of White's open support for the Marxist-Leninist fronts of El Salvador, the FDR-FMLN. Because of his left wing positions, White is hated by the right wing groups of El Salvador and has been sentenced to death by the Maximiliano Hernandez Martinez Death Squad. He was very instrumental in the formation of CISPES in the U.S. and works very close to Sandy Pollack (CPUSA). Teletype to all FBI field offices. SECRET. Attention Boston, Ma. and Washington, D.C. Robert White is actively pushing to stop present administration policy in El Salvador via CISPES, Solidarity World Front, Communist Party of the United States of America. Urgent to all Bureau offices."[5]

Fingering Congressional Terrorists

In one segment of the album, the FBI managed to squeeze the names of seven terrorist "supporters" into one entry—that of Rep. Patricia Schroeder who for a short time considered mounting a run for the presidency in the 1988 election. According to the FBI album: "She is openly working on behalf of the Sandinista Government in the U.S. through the Nicaraguan Network (NNSNP) and CISPES. Schroeder is actively raising money for the Sandinistas. Schroeder is involved in operation HAND (Humanitarian Aid for Nicaraguan Democracy). She has ties with other pro-Sandinista members of Congress: Tip O'Neill, Christopher Dodd, Michael Barnes, Ed Boland, Edward Kennedy, Ron Dellums. WARNING. She could be the target of right wing groups. Strong resentment in right wing circles in the U.S. and El Salvador against her. Advise if she travels abroad."[6]

In the Bureau's defense, the entry on Schroeder and the other members of Congress were not included in the final edition of the album which was subsequently retained in FBI Headquarters. That version contained far less than the 700 entries prepared by Varelli at the request of Davenport, Evans and Flanagan.

Nevertheless, when FBI Director William Webster responded to a query about the album from Schroeder in the spring of 1987, the response was less than candid. Webster told Schroeder: "This document purports to be a completed form sheet containing your photograph and information about you for inclusion in the FBI Terrorist Photograph Album. This document, which...was brought to your attention by the attorney for Frank Varelli, is spurious. While the form itself appears to be a form used by the FBI in the preparation of its Terrorist Photograph Album, I have been assured following a careful hand search of the entire album that you do not appear in our album nor have you ever appeared in our album, nor would we have the slightest basis for including you in our album."[7]

While Webster's response apparently laid the issue of the Terrorist Photo Album to rest for Rep. Schroeder, as well as for much of the press, which accepted the FBI's denials at face value, an FBI document dated September, 1983, confirms the extent of the operation.

"TO: DIRECTOR, FBI

"FROM: SAC, DALLAS

"SUBJECT: EL SALVADORAN LEFTIST ACTIVITIES

"Routed to FBI Offices in: Chicago, Houston, Los Angeles, Miami, New Orleans, New York, Norfolk, San Antonio, San Francisco, San Juan, Washington Field Office, Dallas:

"For information of receiving offices (DELETED) has compiled over 1,000 photos of individuals known to have participated in leftist activities in El Salvador and the United States.

"Dallas will periodically supply pertinent photos and background to the Bureau and receiving offices with FD-432 for inclusion into Terrorist Photograph Album."[8]

The Dodd Memo

A second document, initialled by both Webster and Revell, indicates, moreover, that, with Webster's approval, the FBI lied to members of Congress concerning both the album and the Bureau's investigations of legislators who opposed Reagan Administration policies in Central America. In the spring of 1987, alarmed by Varelli's allegation that he was included in the FBI's terrorism files, Sen. Christopher Dodd, a leading opponent of the Administration's policies of support for the Nicaraguan contras and for its practice of increasing military aid to the government of El Salvador, wrote Webster to formally request that "I be provided at the earliest possible opportunity all material in the FBI files in reference to myself which resulted from Mr. Varelli's activities."[9]

In his response to Dodd, Webster assured the senator of his "sensitivity" to Dodd's concerns and promised that, on finishing an internal inquiry, "I will be pleased to see that you are furnished information on the material developed regarding the Varelli allegations as it relates to you."[10] What Dodd was not told was that Webster's letter to him constituted a successful, and fairly routine, type of legalistic obfuscation by which FBI officials have traditionally concealed the truth about their operations from members of Congress and others charged with overseeing the agency.

Within the Bureau, Webster's letter to Dodd was circulated, along with an internal memo, that left no doubt as to the FBI's intention of withholding the truth from Dodd.

The internal memo, which was initialled by both Webster and his second-in-command, Oliver Revell, reads:

"NOTE: This letter is in response to a letter from Senator Dodd of 2/23/87 wherein he requests that he be provided, at the earliest opportunity, all material in the FBI files in reference to himself which resulted from Mr. Varelli's activities. Congressional Affairs Legislative Counsel Larry Rissler spoke to Senator Dodd's Administrative Assistant and agreed to furnish him the material on Dodd regarding the Varelli allegations that would be furnished to any Congressional Committee. *There was no agreement to provide all material in the FBI files in reference to Dodd which resulted from Varelli's activities...*"[11]

In other words, at the same time that Webster was signing a letter to the senator which seemed to promise him a complete explanation of his place in the album, he was also initialling an internal memo which, in effect, authorized his FBI representative to lie and withhold the requested material from the senator.[12]

In fact, the material indicates that Dodd was regarded by the Bureau as a significant "agent of influence" of an "active measures" campaign of the Nicaraguan Sandinista regime. To Varelli and like-minded agents in the Bureau's counter-terrorism unit, people like Dodd were as deserving of the label "terrorist" as were people like the infamous Abu Nidal. The only difference to the "true believers" within the FBI was that the latter committed acts of "physical terrorism" while the former was dedicated to a "terrorism of the mind," to use Varelli's description.

It was also during the summer of 1982, according to Varelli, that the FBI opened an investigation of members of the Jesuit order in the U.S. because of its association with the "Army of the Poor" in Guatemala and its work on behalf of Salvadoran refugees. The FBI subsequently expanded its investigation of religious groups to cover the Capuchin order in Milwaukee, the Tucson Ecumenical Council, the Unitarian Universalist Committee in Boston, the Dominican order in Chicago and the Sisters of Mercy in New York. Members of those orders, horrified by the plight of Salvadoran and Guatemalan refugees, had bought stock in Western Airlines which, at the time, had a contract with the Immigration and Naturalization Service to ferry Central American deportees back to El Salvador and Guatemala. As a result, some of the religious activists, including the Rev. John Fife, a prominent figure in the Sanctuary movement, used their shares in the airline to mount a stockholder vote which forced Western Airlines to terminate its contract with INS.[13] One result of their victory was that the INS turned to Taca, the Salvadoran airline, to transport deported refugees. Another result was the creation of new FBI counter-intelligence files on the religious activists.

The Miami Network

At the time Varelli was compiling Terrorist Photo Album entries for the FBI, he was also facilitating the Bureau's exchange of information with a group of private operatives established by a handful of Salvadoran expatriate businessmen in Miami. The initiative, about which Varelli had been briefed during his visit to the home of Professor Peccorini in San Salvador in 1981, involved the establishment of a propaganda and intelligence-gathering operation in the United States. It followed the formation, in the late 1970s, of several new death squads in El Salvador.

The squads in El Salvador presented themselves initially as neighborhood defense patrol groups whose mission was to protect the population from attacks by rebel guerrillas. They were composed of from 15 to 20 people, including off-duty military and police personnel working in conjunction with private anti-communist activists. Many of the private death squad patrons provided equipment or logistical support—trucks, jeeps, nightscopes, for example—as well as physical support. One squad might include four military officers plus bodyguards and another ten to twelve civilians. They worked in small groups of five to ten people, intimidating, threatening or assassinating people they saw as a threat to the stability of the country.

Frustrated by the reluctance of the junta to turn the country's full military power against the guerrillas, the death squads soon escalated their activities from community defense to a full-blown battle against known and suspected leftists. In the couple of years after the 1979 installation of the junta, the death squads were, by many accounts, fairly tightly focused on known political enemies and their supporters. But as time passed, the squads began to widen their sights, attacking households and villages throughout the country and killing not only confirmed political and paramilitary operatives but their relatives, neighbors and children—as well as personal enemies of death squad members.

The most highly visible Salvadoran identified with the death squads has been Roberto D'Aubuisson—an official in El Salvador's executive security force, Ansesal, until it was disbanded in 1979. D'Aubuisson also coordinated the operations of Orden—a vigilante organization of rural farmers designed to promote Salvadoran-style democracy and to set up system of surveillance to monitor the activities of the Salvadoran left. In late 1980, both Ansesal and Orden were disbanded, casualties of the newly-installed junta's attempts to bring the most virulent of the nation's security forces under the control of the government. The shift, however, served to stimulate the growth of a more privatized network of death squads, many of which were said to be under the direction of D'Aubuisson and Col. Nicolas Carranza, head of the Treasury Police.

The public-private death squads saw their mission as protecting the country from the communist guerrillas as well as El Salvador's more moderate leftist elements, including the Christian Democrat Party. Between 1979 and 1982, for instance, right-wing death squads are said to have assassinated more than 260 members of that party, including 35 mayors.[14]

It was around the end of 1981 that the private Salvadoran intelligence-gathering apparatus was established in the United States. Based in Miami and operating through a network of Salvadoran activists—including a number of former National Guard and death squad members—the operation utilized a Wang computer in Houston to store and collate information gathered in cities where CISPES was active and where there was a significant Salvadoran population.[15]

To their Miami-based Salvadoran organizers, the new North American operation seemed the most natural way to combat what they viewed as the move of the Salvadoran communists to bring the war in El Salvador into the United States under cover of CISPES and other sympathetic organizations.

When former members of the Salvadoran military or security forces turned up in cities like Los Angeles, San Francisco, Houston, Dallas, New Orleans, Miami or Washington, D.C., they would be put in touch with the organizers in Miami who would welcome them into the network.

As the bands of Salvadoran activists grew to between 50 and 100 people in those southern and western cities which harbored large Salvadoran populations, they began to gather as much information as they could on CISPES and other groups sympathetic to the Salvadoran rebels. Working in small cell-like groups of three or four members, members of the secret network would spy on liberal groups, monitor rallies, speeches and other political events and, according to some reports, terrorize members of CISPES in an effort to stop their propagandizing on behalf of the FMLN rebels.

The operation funneled material to the FBI—at first to the Dallas office, but, according to Varelli, the Miami-based Salvadorans subsequently dealt directly with the FBI's Miami office.[16] The operation was so extensive and so successful, that Varelli was amazed to learn, when he traveled to Miami in 1985, that the Salvadorans knew as much, if not more, about domestic Central America groups as did the Federal Bureau of Investigation.[17]

The Decoy or the Duck

Michael Ratner, Margaret Ratner, Chip Berlet and Dr. Ann Mari Buitrago saw it coming from the beginning. The only problem was that for the longest time they couldn't tell which direction it was coming from.

The Ratners worked at the Center for Constitutional Rights, a public interest group of liberal and left-wing lawyers based in lower Manhattan. For them, as well as for Berlet, a political researcher who had been involved in cases involving the FBI and the Chicago Red Squad, and Buitrago, one of the country's foremost experts in the use of the Freedom of Information Act, the election of Ronald Reagan began to raise alarms as early as the winter of 1980. They were concerned not only about the candidate's rhetoric but about the composition of his transition team and the Heritage Foundation recommendations for strengthening the nation's domestic intelligence apparatus.

In general, however, those early signs were dismissed, if not ignored, as left-wing paranoia. The leadership of the Washington office of the American Civil Liberties Union, for instance, declared that civil liberties and government surveillance would not be significant issues in the 1980s. Instead, it argued, the emphasis of the Reagan Administration would be almost exclusively economic—and the battles of the coming years would involve issues of economic justice and the rights of the poor rather than issues of free speech and civil liberties. In fact, Morton Halperin, of the ACLU, accused attorneys at the Center for Constitutional Rights of raising a specter of alarmism without giving the administration an opportunity to prove that it was not bent on subverting the intelligence and law enforcement communities to do its political bidding.

But while the Ratners, Berlet and Buitrago were concerned about what they saw as the coming crackdown on political freedom, it was not the FBI that first caught their attention, but a new Senate committee—the Subcommittee on Security and Terrorism (SST)—which was created by the incoming Republican majority in Congress to focus public attention on the threat of international terrorism and the peril of domestic subversion.

Created as a subcommittee of the Senate Judiciary Committee, the SST was staffed by Senators Orrin Hatch of Utah and John East of North Carolina, and headed by Alabama Senator Jeremiah Denton, a member of the Moral Majority who spent seven years as a prisoner of war in a Vietnamese prison camp. Along with Senator Jesse Helms, East, Hatch and Denton believed that the greatest threat to the United States was the danger of "creeping communism." And, to that end, the committee set out to expose the danger of internal subversion.

The Terrorism Cover

In his opening address at the first meeting of the subcommittee in 1981, Denton declared: "The subcommittee plans to investigate certain organizations which, within the United States, engage in, or have engaged in acts of terrorism, including bombings, acts of sabotage, aircraft hijacking, armed assaults and homicides."[1]

But the political implications of Denton's proclamation came clear in short order when staffers in Hatch's office leaked the fact that the SST planned to investigate, among others, three left-liberal institutions that had never been associated with terrorism or violence of any sort. According to those early leaks, the SST would take on the Institute for Policy Studies (IPS), a left-liberal think tank in Washington which provided substantial input to Congressional deliberations on a range of domestic and foreign policies; the North American Congress on Latin America (NACLA), a left-wing research institute in New York which conducted a number of studies critical of U.S. economic and diplomatic policies in Latin America; and *Mother Jones,* a left-liberal magazine which featured investigative reports on corporate excesses, environmental abuse and social injustices.[2]

In the spring of 1981, concerned by the emergence of SST, Margaret Ratner drafted a letter of opposition to the subcommittee which read:

"In the 1950s, the country was convulsed by a series of political acts which made a mockery of the concept of democracy. Hundreds and thousands of people saw their lives and livelihoods destroyed as the House Un-American Activities Committee and the Senate Internal Security Subcommittee engaged in their nightmarish witchhunts for dissidents...These committees were determined to ruin all who opposed their interpretation of 'Americanism'... History has since repudiated that tragic period…[Today, however] we are alarmed by the establishment of the new Subcommittee on Security and Terrorism. This new subcommittee has wrapped itself in a thoroughly vague mandate: it will investigate 'terrorist activities' and matters relating to 'national security.' Yet, who is to define those terms? Is opposition to the committee itself a 'threat to national security?' Will those who maintain their constitutional rights of free speech and assembly be deprived of their human rights as they were at other times in this nation's history? Committee member John East has remarked that 'the biggest threat to civil liberties today is terrorism.' But we assert that the committee, itself, poses the biggest threat to our civil liberties."[3]

Noting that such committees have traditionally operated more by holding public hearings and generating publicity for their causes than through actual legislative initiatives, Ratner accused the Administration of planning to use the SST to "rally support for the concept of a terrorist threat and to act as a propaganda machine to generate fear." The public success of the committee would subsequently be used, she wrote: "to allow us to support regimes such as the one in El Salvador; to grant the FBI and the CIA the extra support required if they are to carry out more illegal and repressive operations… to control dissent…and, finally, to curtail civil liberties."

At the same time that the attorneys at the Center for Constitutional Rights were warning activists about the new Denton committee, Berlet, who had worked with the National Lawyers Guild and who had written extensively on the FBI abuses of the 1960s, was becoming increasingly concerned at what he saw as a new climate of red-baiting not only of political groups but also of left-wing and liberal journalists.

In an article in *Alternative Media,* Berlet noted that the SST and other elements close to the Reagan White House were taking aim at such outlets as Pacifica Radio, *Covert Action Information Bulletin* and *Mother Jones.* "Charges that the media is part of the Soviet plan for world conquest have escaped the confines of conservative living rooms and are now ringing in the halls of Congress…Publications on the Right are calling for investigations into how alternative media groups are part of a KGB disinformation campaign," Berlet wrote, noting that the Heritage report identified even mainstream journalists "who may engage in subversive activities without being fully aware of the extent, purposes or control of their activities."[4]

No More Witch Hunts

In June 1981, Berlet, the Ratners and other activists organized simultaneous conferences around the theme of "No More Witch Hunts" in 19 cities, including Chicago, Detroit, Houston, Los Angeles, New York, St. Louis and Washington. In New York, "No More Witch Hunts" took the form of a street fair on West 8th Street, in which participants were exposed to a frightening array of surveillance technology—high-tech bugging devices, infra-red night-vision telescopes, and wigs, fake mustaches and make-up kits used by undercover infiltrators.

In Chicago, the conference attracted more than 1,000 people and featured an address by Mayor Harold Washington. The event was endorsed by nearly 90 organizations—including the Illinois branch of the ACLU, the American Friends Service Committee, the Gray Panthers, the Gay and Lesbian Coalition of Chicago, the Mobilization for Survival, the United Auto Workers and the Women's International League for Peace and Freedom. Whether by coincidence or design, the names of the majority of those sponsoring organizations were discovered, seven years later, to have been entered into the FBI's terrorism files in the course of the Bureau's investigation of CISPES and the octopus-like spread of the Bureau's probe into a vast array of domestic groups dedicated to reducing the risks of nuclear war, to protecting the environment, to advocating for the rights of the poor and disenfranchised, and to criticizing the policies of the Reagan Administration in Latin and Central America.

During the following year, Berlet began to hear about problems encountered by activists returning from Cuba and El Salvador. They included extensive interrogations and delays by Customs officials, threats of prosecution in the face of legal, protected activities, and the specter of lawsuits against several activist groups under the Foreign Agents Registration Act. While a number of complaints came from leftists who had visited Cuba, others were surfacing in the network of newly formed peace groups which were mobilizing around the issue of nuclear weapons reductions.

As a result, Michael Ratner and Berlet, under the auspices of the National Lawyers Guild, conducted a series of secret meetings with representatives of activist groups. The meetings, which were held in Chicago, Los Angeles and New York, focused on civil liberties and on legal strategies to protect those liberties. Focusing on such areas as immigration law, travel rights, visa procedures and FARA issues, the strategy meetings laid the groundwork for combatting what several

Guild members saw as a coming clampdown on basic freedoms of travel and assembly. But, at that point, with activists focusing on the Denton subcommittee and the cascade of red-baiting right-wing literature, very little thought was given to what pursuits might be occupying the energies of the FBI.[5]

Toward the end of 1982, Michael Ratner and Ann Mari Buitrago drafted a lawsuit on behalf of a number of activist organizations that challenged the 1981 Reagan Executive Order which had loosened restrictions on intelligence gathering by the FBI and CIA. But the suit was thrown out of court on the grounds that the plaintiffs, who at that point could not cite any actual instances of harassment or illegal government spying, had no legal standing.[6]

It was not until a year later—toward the end of 1983—that the first reports of break-ins and mysterious surveillance began to surface. At that point, the Center decided to set up a clearinghouse for all such incidents. They created a small operation named the Movement Support Network whose function was to receive, verify and publicize complaints of political harassment. At first, the list of such complaints was tiny. In 1983, for instance, some members of a Wisconsin committee on Central America were interviewed by FBI agents who indicated they were interested in any knowledge of international terrorism on the part of any members of the group. But the Bureau stopped the interviews shortly thereafter, when Sen. Robert Kasten inquired about the FBI's activities.[7]

The following year, the Center began to receive complaints from people traveling to Nicaragua. Some had been interviewed by FBI agents, or had learned that their employers, neighbors or landlords had been interviewed by agents. Others had been detained by Customs officials and had personal papers confiscated on their return. But those harassments were official in nature—and while they offended and, in some cases, intimidated American travelers to Central America, they were far less unnerving than the flow of terrorizing events that would begin to gain nationwide momentum in the coming years.[8]

While the early efforts of the attorneys at the Center, as well as Berlet and Buitrago, were directed at the red-baiting of the Denton Committee, it was not until 1984 that they began to suspect the hand of the FBI in the campaign against political activists. In retrospect, it was a case of mistaking the decoy for the duck.

Priming the Bureau's Files

If 1981 had been the year of Frank Varelli's education in the ways of the FBI, 1982 was the year he reciprocated. Although the Bureau had put a temporary hold on many of his official responsibilities, Varelli worked furiously to fill what he saw as critical gaps in the FBI's knowledge of the operations and connections between various "terrorist" groups. In his discussions with Flanagan, Evans and others, as well as his reviewing of thousands of teletypes from other FBI field offices as well as from the CIA, Varelli found himself appalled at the lack of knowledge of the FBI agents about the operating principles of terrorist groups in general and about the situation in El Salvador specifically. Not only did few agents have any working knowledge of Spanish, their preparation for induction into the counter-terrorism squad appears to have consisted of their reading the collected speeches of J. Edgar Hoover on the evils of Communism and the threat of internal subversion. As a result, agents misspelled Hispanic names, mangled the acronyms of various Central American groups and, in some cases, had no idea of the backgrounds of various groups and individuals who fell under their scrutiny.[9]

Encouraged by Flanagan and Evans, Varelli developed a virtual curriculum on Central American terrorism for members of the counter-terrorism unit. He spent hours constructing elaborate charts showing the structure of various armed revolutionary groups, as well as the linkages between groups in Central America and their connections to political groups inside the United States.[10]

That August, Flanagan forwarded to headquarters a map of the U.S. on which Varelli had indicated the explosion of CISPES chapters and other groups which had sprung up in opposition to Reagan Administration policies in Central America. The map indicated that within the previous year and a half, nearly 60 chapters had sprouted all over the country.[11]

While some of the chapters bore the name CISPES, others went under the name Inter-Religious Task Force on Central America, Religious Task Force on Central America, Casa, Central America Solidarity Committee and Central America Network. To Varelli, the development of these groups presented a chilling parallel to the proliferation of armed guerrilla groups in his native El Salvador. Inside the United States, the network was branching out everywhere. Quietly and away from the glare of publicity, Varelli pointed out, a nationwide network was forming which could readily conceal an inner core of terrorists and saboteurs who would be undetectable to law enforcement and intelligence agents.

Varelli reminded colleagues at the FBI that a traditional strategy of the Salvadoran communists involved the constant creation of new groups, as well as the renaming of old ones, to create a popular impression of strength and diversity far beyond the groups' actual numbers—and to keep the security forces off balance. When agents in other FBI field offices were confused as to whether a new Central America-oriented political group in their jurisdiction should be investigated or not, Varelli—drawing on information from sources in El Salvador as well as from the slew of liberal and left-wing publications to which he subscribed—demonstrated links between new groups and CISPES, apparently to the satisfaction of the agents in other FBI field offices.

Whenever a new group came to Varelli's attention, he would draft an airtel to the appropriate field office requesting them to open a preliminary investigation of the group. Without such investigations, there was no way to know which of the splinters were engaged in disinformation and propaganda, which ones could be serving as conduits for money and weapons to the Salvadoran communists, and which ones might be planning violent actions.[12]

Varelli was alarmed, for instance, at the speed with which events in El Salvador became known to the North American groups. If a bomb went off, a union meeting was dispersed, or a military mission was mounted by the Salvadoran Army, the North American groups would know about it within hours. But it was difficult to predict for the FBI which events in El Salvador would trigger demonstrations, rallies or other reactions in the U.S.. As a result, Varelli arranged for the National Guard to call the Dallas FBI office whenever violence erupted in that country so that other field offices could be alerted to the possibility of civil disturbances erupting in reaction to developments in El Salvador.

He also worried that the quiet proliferation of the groups indicated a possible plan to catch the country's law enforcement apparatus by surprise at some future date when all the groups would emerge in an awesome and unsuspected show of strength. "They can go very slowly. Time is on their side," Varelli explained. "The FBI's manpower is extremely limited, given the proliferation of groups. If tomorrow all the groups in the nation were to publicly join together, people would be shocked and frightened by the sudden show of strength. It's part of a strategy of creating preliminary conditions for revolutionary action."

What seems to have eluded Varelli's mind, with its extreme conspiratorial bent, was the fact that political activists in the United States frequently lend their names to multiple organizations. The community of people concerned about Central America in the mid-1980s was still a relatively small number, with members of one group subscribing to publications of other organizations. What Varelli was seeing was not the formation of an underground terrorism network but, rather, the growth of a belief by liberals around the country that their government's policies in Central America were not working and that poverty and repression were flourishing, especially in El Salvador and Guatemala.

Privatized Intelligence Salvadoran Style

In addition to the material the FBI was receiving from the Salvadoran National Guard, the Bureau, through Varelli, received information from several other sources on Central American terrorism. One such source was the private, right-wing think tank in El Salvador known as CESPDES, the Center for Socio-Political Studies of El Salvador. Originally modeled along the lines of U.S. think tanks, CESPDES was initially formed to counteract the barrage of what they saw as leftist propaganda and disinformation in El Salvador. Over time, through its links to the intelligence units of various arms of Central American military and security forces, CESPDES developed extensive profiles of Central American "communist" groups. In addition to its general publications, the group, which included a number of retired military and intelligence officials, generated secret reports, some of them coded, in which they published the identifications of guerrilla leaders, explanations of their terminology, descriptions of various groups' modes of operations, their recruiting and indoctrination techniques, and the sectors of Salvadoran society—churches, universities, unions—which they had targeted. Some of the material forwarded to Dallas by CESPDES, Varelli claims, had been obtained in raids on rebel safehouses or procured via reports of interrogations of detainees by Salvadoran security forces.[13]

It seems clear that much material which purported to be confiscated from "rebel safe houses" was the product of sophisticated fabrication and disinformation by Salvadoran rightists. While some of the material was, in fact, seized in political raids, it was subject to alteration, addition and reinterpretation to justify CESPDES's view of a long-term, global masterplan of the world communist movement. It also seems clear that some of the CESPDES material was used by Salvadoran death squads to identify enemies and compile hit lists. It was certainly used by the Salvadoran security forces to justify large-scale military and police sweeps of suspected leftists and left-wing organizations in El Salvador.

Every week Varelli would receive a six- or eight-page broadsheet put out by CESPDES. He and Villacorta worked out an ingenious system to determine which of the material was authentic and which was incomplete or misleading. After receiving the printed material, Varelli would call down to El Salvador, telling Villacorta, "I have in my hand one through six" referring to, but not mentioning, the pages of the publication. Villacorta would respond: "Use one but don't pay much attention to two. Proceed to three. But be alert to a more detailed number two next week."[14]

The deception was aimed not only at any communists who might get their hands on the publications. It was aimed as well at preventing the State Department, the CIA, even non-authorized FBI agents from knowing the contents of the communications. Flanagan had drilled into Varelli the need to keep the operation totally secret, even from other FBI personnel. "If someone at FBI headquarters felt later on that they wanted to share the material with other agencies, that was ok with us. We had been told the Bureau was being jerked around by the CIA and by DOD, which often withheld material from us. If headquarters wanted to share the material, fine. But it had to be a headquarters decision," Flanagan had told Varelli.

Another source of intelligence from all over Latin America was *Replica,* an ultra-conservative and vituperatively anti-Semitic magazine which seemed to combine a strange mix of military-type intelligence with ultra-right-wing diatribes against, among others, the Roman Catholic Church, the world communist movement and the Democratic Party of the United States. The magazine, whose English-language editions resemble less polished versions of the publications of Western Goals and which, coincidentally, reprinted a number of reports from Western Goals, is published at the Autonomous University of Guadalajara, Mexico—the home of the Tecos.

A super-secret, paramilitary group, the Tecos, who date their organization from 1910, were revived after World War II by a Mexican Nazi who spent the war in Germany and an Argentine Jesuit priest who was an admirer of Hitler. By the early 1970s, the Tecos, supported by a network of anti-communist activists throughout Central and Latin America, formed the Mexican Anti-Communist Federation, with links to death squads in Guatemala, Argentina and Paraguay. In 1972, the Tecos spearheaded the formation of the Latin American Anti-Communist Federation, the Latin American chapter of the World Anti-Communist League.[15] The group was heavily involved in the formulation of the "Banzer Plan" in 1976. The "Banzer Plan," aimed at identifying and

destroying networks of left-wing clergy who were promulgating 'Liberation Theology' in Latin America, called for a shared database, involving
the security forces of ten Central and Latin American countries, to
"maintain up-to-date information about the ideological orientation of the
main religious institutions, as well as to elaborate a file containing the
names of priests and nuns along with their personal background, to be
annually revised." Within two years after the operation of the database,
at least twenty-eight bishops, priests and lay workers were killed in Latin
America, allegedly by right-wing death squads. The Tecos have also
been rumored, but not proved, to have been involved in several assassinations, including the 1984 shooting of a Mexican investigative journalist who published a series on the group.[16]

A good deal of the material contained in *Replica* consists of virulent
political diatribes. A cover story in the summer of 1984 before the U.S.
presidential election begins: "Walter Mondale, sidekick and accomplice
of the wretched James Earl Carter…has demonstrated that he is the ideal
candidate for President of the United States—but of course from the
Soviet point of view. [He] provides the best option for delivering the
world to Communism." Another edition of *Replica,* published just after
a 1985 Congressional vote against contra aid, reads: "The House of
Representatives, controlled by the Democrats, showed that, more than
serving the interests of the United States and the free world, they have
placed themselves at the service of communist imperialism… Perhaps
they will regret their clumsiness and their anti-Reaganism of today when
the United States falls victim to communist aggression. Although then it
may be too late."[17]

Among other international press services, the magazine draws on
material from the *Bulletin of the World Anti-Communist League*. But the
magazine also contains intelligence material on leftist groups, social
movements and revolutionary activists throughout Central America
which is generated by military, intelligence and diplomatic agents of a
number of right-wing Latin American governments, as well as from
officials in South Korea, Taiwan and other countries with membership
in WACL.

As with the booklets and reports of the Western Goals Foundation,
the FBI's CISPES files are bulging with material from *Replica.*

One report in the FBI's files drawn from *Replica* material is headed:
*U.S. Philanthropists financing Cuban and Salvadoran communist op-
erations.* According to the report: "Under cover of being cultural and
literary organizations, in order to protect their real terrorist mission,
Cuban agents of the DGI [the Cuban intelligence arm] are presently

receiving millions of dollars from American philanthropic foundations." The foundations include the Ford Foundation, the Rockefeller Foundation, the Woodrow Wilson International Center for Scholars and Boston's Permanent Charity Fund, among others. The report documents the foundations' funding of academic conferences attended by the alleged Cuban agents, noting, for instance, that: "The Ford Foundation granted $7,500 for the meeting of the Latin American Studies Association (LASA) held in Houston. Officials and writers of the Cuban regime, such as Mirta Aguirre, Santiago Diaz, Maria Rosa Gentile, etc., participated in this event." Another entry in the same report reads: "The link between Castro and the Rockefeller Foundation is Peter Jennings, who in July 1978, was invited by the Cuban government. He traveled in company of six others from the International Center for Tropical Agriculture of Colombia."[18]

While North American liberals, including members of Congressional staffs, have dismissed the *Replica* material as paranoid and absurdly conspiratorial, the fact remains that the FBI files contain masses of material from the publication and it is clear that, rather than being warned to ignore such information, the FBI strongly and consistently encouraged Varelli's use and transmittal of the material.

Forward from Quantico

By the beginning of 1983, the value of Varelli's work had become clear to many of the top brass in the FBI's counter-terrorism apparatus in headquarters. They had landed an extraordinary asset, far more valuable than they had originally envisioned. In early 1983, Varelli's FBI career reached its high-water mark when Flanagan received a teletype from Washington ordering him and Varelli to attend a top-level conference at the FBI Academy in Quantico, Virginia. The three-day conference would bring together the FBI's top counter-terrorism and counter-intelligence operatives from around the country to pool information and determine strategies on countering the growing "terrorist" threat. The featured speaker at the super-secret meeting was to be Frank Varelli.

According to the headquarters document which authorized the conference, "accumulated information from sources and investigation indicate a surge of El Salvadoran terroristic activities in the United States. Sources have furnished information showing financial support coming from front organizations in the United States and discussions by these terrorists to attack military bases in the United States."[19] The document cited no known instances of El Salvador-related terrorist incidents in the U.S.—and no evidence of financial support from any political group in the United States to any armed guerrilla group in Central America. In fact, while Varelli was clearly the source of some of the information, the FBI cited a number of other sources who had reported, independent of Varelli, that groups like CISPES had ties to the PLO and to the Cuban intelligence service.

What is clear from this Quantico conference—and a second conference the following year—is that, while information forwarded by Varelli might have filled in some of the gaps in the FBI's imagined outline of an international terrorist conspiracy, the driving force for the Bureau's offensive against left and liberal organizations came from headquarters, from men high up in the FBI's chain of command, men who were inspired, if not directed, by Bill Casey, architect of the Reagan Administration's intelligence policies.

According to a second headquarters document, the Quantico conference covered a number of topics, including:[20]

"1) Organization and structure of various groups comprising the known El Salvadoran leftist movement.

"2) Identifying the organizational structure of groups in the United States suspected of furnishing support and assistance to the El Salvadoran leftists.

[The first two topics permitted Varelli an opportunity to display a very far-flung conspiracy of groups which he demonstrated by the use of poster boards and flow charts to indicate linkages in an international and domestic terror network.]

"3) Furnishing of direction, support, and assistance by [foreign] governments to the El Salvadoran leftists, both in the United States and El Salvador.

"4) Targeting of organizations and individuals supporting Central American terrorism in the United States.

[Topic four became the occasion to review the FBI's files on both political and religious activists in the U.S., as well as on about a dozen senators and representatives who had been in the forefront of the legislative struggle against Reagan Administration policies in Central America.]

"5) Development of uniform acronyms for the various organizations.

"6) Manpower and other resource needs."

[This topic was the occasion for a long discussion on the methods of recruiting other Salvadorans and Central Americans into the service of the FBI, where they were subsequently deployed by various field offices as informants and spies on domestic groups.]

As Senate investigators later pointed out, one participant in the Quantico conference—an FBI official with experience in Central American affairs—advised officials in both Headquarters and in Dallas to "use caution in directing [Varelli] relative to his direct contacts with Salvadoran intelligence and law enforcement authorities to avoid…confusion…" In other words, at least one FBI official voiced concerns that Varelli's actions, as a go-between for both the FBI and the National Guard of El Salvador, made his information suspect. But, as the investigators concluded: "those concerns were not reflected in subsequent FBI communications during 1983 and they appear to have been completely ignored by FBI Headquarters and by the Dallas field office."[21]

For Varelli and Flanagan, the Quantico meeting was a tremendous success. Both men received warm congratulations from Ron Davenport, the Headquarters supervisory agent in charge of the Salvadoran Terrorism investigations.

Two weeks later, another airtel from Headquarters confirmed just how important the conference had been. The airtel, signed by Oliver "Buck" Revell, the head of the FBI's counter-terrorism and criminal divisions, announced that after a hiatus of just over a year, the Bureau was opening a second investigation of CISPES.[22]

But while the initial investigation was limited to potential violations of the Foreign Agents Registration Act, the new probe would be conducted under a much broader heading—Foreign Counter-intelligence Counter-terrorism.

And where the initial FARA probe was limited to 12 FBI offices around the country, this new, expanded investigation would, in short order, involve all 59 field offices of the FBI.[23]

Storm Flags

It was around the time of the beginning of the second CISPES investigation in the spring of 1983 that movement activists began to hear of an increasing number of harassments by government agents.

Berlet recalled that he began to hear reports from printers at the Salcedo Press in Chicago. People at the press, which publishes material from various left and liberal political groups, began hearing reports of harassment from people who had traveled to Nicaragua or Cuba. One woman said she noticed someone staking out the press's office. Another mentioned that some files in the office were discovered to be missing. "At the same time, I heard similar reports from a political organizer in Oregon, as well as from others on the East Coast. We began to see some sort of pattern emerging, even though we didn't really know what it was. But it was becoming clear by this time that something was happening," Berlet said.

It was shortly thereafter that Berlet began to organize a series of public conferences on the threat of FBI and governmental harassment.

Asked why he and other movement people did not suspect the FBI earlier than 1984, Berlet explained: "Because you are so acutely aware of the propensity to become paranoid, you bend over backwards to be skeptical and un-paranoid." Berlet, who initially set out to work as a higher education policy analyst, explained he was attracted to movement work because "I get passionately upset when I see that the Constitution and Bill of Rights is not enforced. It's just not a fair fight. For doing this, I have seen countless people hurt, jailed, even killed. What you're up against when you take on the FBI, the CIA, the undercover informants who feed the governmental apparatus, is a self-selected group of people who have a messianic vision of themselves. It keeps rising up over and over again. Trying to protect civil liberties is like Sisyphus. It is an unceasing battle. All governments want more power. It makes them more efficient. But democracy, on the other hand, implies inefficiency. So there's always the need to fight back. The battle over domestic civil liberties will never be won. It just has to keep being fought."

For Dr. Ann Mari Buitrago, a longtime movement activist and one of the country's pre-eminent experts in understanding and deciphering FBI files, the secret of the CISPES investigation was foreshadowed by the Reagan Administration's efforts to gut the Freedom of Information Act.[24] As a graduate student, Buitrago had gotten involved with progressive causes during the Rosenberg trials. In the late 1970s, when the FBI released thousands of pages of Rosenberg files on the case, Buitrago found herself fascinated by the challenge of trying to piece those files into a whole picture. That fascination led her to establish, in 1979, an organization called FOIA, Inc., which was devoted to helping scholars, historians, researchers and plain citizens use the Freedom of Information Act.

"In early Reagan years, the Freedom of Information Act came under sustained attack by the Justice Department, the Office of Management and Budget, and all sorts of executive agencies. As the attacks on the Freedom of Information law mounted, we worked with Congressional committees to keep the law alive. That was our main battle during the early period. That's where FOIA, Inc. was most active."

Buitrago, who in 1988 and 1989 would quarterback the effort to secure release of field office documents and work with Central America groups in various cities to decipher what she could of the FBI's operations against those groups, has long seen the Freedom of Information Act as a barometer of the overall activities of an administration.

"The Freedom of Information Act is a wonderful tell-tale. If you see an administration that sets out to attack it, gut it, get rid of that act, that means it is intending to do something it thinks the public will not approve of. It is setting out with something to hide, and repression will follow. You don't have to know what precisely they're up to. If you just watch what they do to freedom of information, you can figure out where to start looking."

Initially, Buitrago's involvement with Central America activists was almost incidental. At the beginning of the decade, Buitrago had concentrated her efforts on a successful federal lawsuit designed to prevent the FBI from destroying hundred of thousands of its files. A few years later, she began to receive frequests from some of the defendants in the Tucson Sanctuary trial for help with their applications for their FBI files. When word surfaced that the government had planted informants in the Sanctuary movement, Buitrago's work with the Sanctuary groups increased. The increased volume of the work prompted her to join forces with the Center for Constitutional Rights which, by 1986, was receiving a growing cascade of complaints about break-ins, intimidations and harassment by government agents.

Two things conspired that year to put Buitrago on a direct track to the CISPES files. For one thing, she noticed that there were a fairly frequent number of CISPES references in some of the FBI responses to Sanctuary movement requesters. "I was analyzing the few scattered documents that were coming back. The name of CISPES kept turning up. So we contacted groups and got more and more of them to request their files. The handfuls of documents indicated something pretty big was going on."

Then, in the late spring of 1986, Buitrago received a copy of an article in the *Dallas Morning News* which focused on the bizarre and still unexplained loss of classified FBI documents by Dan Flanagan, Varelli's handling agent in the Dallas FBI office.

"The article set off all the bells I needed to hear," Buitrago recalled. "Prior to reading the references to CISPES in the Flanagan piece, we had sent a few requests for various organizations. We had no idea which one would find paydirt. When the Flanagan article surfaced, we began to focus specifically on CISPES documents. We began with requests to

Headquarters and to the Dallas FBI office. When one of the Headquarters documents came back with a distribution list of 24 field offices, we proceeded to file for those 24 offices. Later, we filed for FBI documents with every field office in the country."

All that was left, Buitrago recalled, was to educate the press and the public—and to wait for the evidence to come in. But that task would prove harder that it sounded. After receiving the first CISPES-focused requests, the FBI began dragging its feet. First they gave one date for release and then another, steadily moving the release of the documents further and further into the future. It was only after Buitrago and Michael and Margaret Ratner mounted a protracted lawsuit against the FBI, that they finally won release of the CISPES files in the winter of 1987-1988.

"The reason the project was successful was because of our correct analysis. We understood what was right under our noses—that Reagan meant what he said in his early speeches about unleashing the intelligence agencies. We understood the meaning behind his gesture in pardoning Felt and Miller, who had been convicted of illegal black-bag jobs in the 1970s. We understood that meant more repression was coming. Even before we had the evidence on which to base our FOIA lawsuit, we knew we were right in our analysis of the political situation which we were dealing with."

10

The CIA At Home, the FBI Abroad

Around the same time that the FBI dramatically intensified its crackdown on Central America groups, a separate cluster of government agencies was establishing a clandestine operation aimed at secretly pumping the Administration's own brand of propaganda into the consciousness of the American electorate through a covert campaign aimed at securing newspaper space and television and radio time for advocates of Reagan policies in Nicaragua and El Salvador.

The architect of this second line of information control was none other than William Casey, director of the Central Intelligence Agency. Toward the end of 1982, Casey made it clear that the Administration was not doing what it should to win the battle of public opinion and convince the mass of voters to support the Reagan Administration's military intervention in El Salvador and, more importantly, its increasing isolation of the Sandinista regime in Nicaragua and its concurrent mobilization of the contras.

As a result, Casey established an operation designed to control the flow of information on which the voting public would base its attitudes toward Central America policies. The second front of the assault on the U.S. public involved pumping pro-Administration propaganda into the public consciousness via the press, the television networks, and the nation's libraries, to win the "hearts and minds" of the voters for a set of policies which had hitherto been rejected by a substantial portion of voters and their representatives in Congress.[1]

Although the Administration's viewpoint—including much of the real and fabricated intelligence that it used to justify its Central America policies—was made public through a network of conservative publications as well as through a regular program of White House briefings for conservative supporters, Casey feared that the Administration was basically "preaching to the converted." What was needed, he felt, was a new

121

and separate apparatus which would better explain the rationale for U.S. activities in Central America to the public. To accomplish the mission, Casey tapped Walter Raymond, Jr., a long-time propaganda specialist with the CIA. But there was one problem. The CIA is forbidden by law from conducting operations inside the United States. For Casey or his employees at the Agency to run a covert domestic propaganda campaign would be to invite the harshest kind of Congressional retribution should the operation ever be discovered. The problem was difficult—but not insurmountable.

First, Casey drafted an executive order, numbered NSDD 77, to "strengthen the organization, planning and coordination of the various aspects of public diplomacy...relative to the national security." President Reagan signed the order in January, 1983. The effort was to involve government funds as well as financial and logistical support from selected members of the private sector. In a memo on the subject to National Security Adviser William Clark, Charles Wick, director of the United States Information Agency, suggested an initial meeting to which he would invite, among others, David Rockefeller, newspaper magnate Rupert Murdoch, and Joachim Maitre, soon-to-be dean of the Boston University Journalism School who, at the time, was a representative of Axel Springer, the West German conservative publisher.[2]

In July 1982, at Casey's request, Raymond went to work at the White House and, shortly thereafter, assumed his post at the National Security Council where he met on a weekly basis with Casey through most of 1983. Working in close collaboration with Oliver North, Raymond proceeded to implement the creation of an information apparatus designed to "sell" the Administration's policy positions to the U.S. public. Casey and Raymond decided that the operation would best be centered in the State Department, specifically in an obscure office known as the Office For Latin American Public Diplomacy. Over the objections of Secretary of State George Shultz, Raymond had Otto Reich, a veteran of the U.S. AID office, assume command of the Office of Latin American Public Diplomacy (OPD). According to a series of memos from Raymond to National Security Advisers Clark and John Poindexter, the goal of the OPD operation was to bring to bear the expertise of the CIA and NSC to direct a clandestine domestic propaganda effort to sell the Administration's Central America policies to the U.S. public while, at the same time, concealing the Administration's involvement in the public relations blitz.[3]

In one memo to Clark, Raymond referred to a meeting between a group of public relations specialists and Casey in which the group discussed the need to "sell a new product—Central America" to the American public. In the same note, Raymond wrote: "We need an organizer. I would like to lead with our silver bullet. I recommend that Peter Dailey be asked to put the group together and turn it over to an outside coordinator...." Dailey had previously served as the CIA's counsel to Casey. In a follow-up note, Raymond referred to the need for a "sustained effort to garner support for our overall Centam policy, increase understanding of the issues and, in the specific case of Nica, concentrate on gluing black hats on the Sandinistas and white hats on the [contras]." The following month, in a memo to Poindexter, Raymond noted that "Bill Casey called...and would like to follow up on his idea to have a meeting with five or six key public relations specialists...I philosophized a bit with Bill Casey (in an effort to get him out of the loop)...."

That removal of Casey from the "loop" was critical, since the Central Intelligence Agency is prohibited by law from conducting any operations which affect political life inside the United States. Later, in discussions with Congressional staff members investigating the affair, Raymond tried to downplay the illegality of Casey's involvement by suggesting that Casey undertook these activities "not so much in his CIA hat but in his advisor to the president hat."

The involvement of federal agencies in the secret propaganda operation grew in the following year when Reich requested—and received—help from five Army psychological operations specialists stationed at Ft. Bragg, North Carolina, to "look for exploitable themes and trends, and inform us of possible areas for our exploitation." In short, as one official of the Latin American Public Diplomacy office told Alfonse Chardy of the *Miami Herald:* "If you look at it as a whole, the Office of Public Diplomacy was carrying out a huge psychological operation, the kind the military conducts to influence the population in denied or enemy territory."[4]

By the summer of 1984, after one year of operation, the Office of Public Diplomacy had booked more than 1,500 speaking engagements, including radio, television and editorial board interviews; published three booklets on Nicaragua; and distributed material to 1,600 college libraries, 520 political science faculties, 122 editorial writers and 107 religious organizations, according to the office's own report on its activities to the NSC.[5]

By 1985, the operation had gained enormous momentum. It had succeeded in placing a number of op-ed pieces in some of the nation's largest and most influential newspapers, including the *Wall Street Jour-*

nal, the *New York Times* and the *Washington Post,* which were written by authors whose connections to the government operation were never revealed. In addition, the operation secured extensive television time for contra leaders and other proponents of Administration policies.[6]

A May 13, 1985, classified memo from OPD staffer Jonathan Miller to Patrick Buchanan, the president's director of communications, indicated that the article was one part of an ongoing "white propaganda" operation that was placing anti-Sandinista opinion pieces in leading newspapers. One such article that appeared in the *Wall Street Journal* in March of that year was authored by John Guilmartin, Jr., a history professor at Rice University. According to the memo, Guilmartin "had been a consultant to our office and collaborated with our staff in the writing of the piece...Officially, this office had no role in its preparation...."

In the same memo, Miller notes that: "Two op-ed pieces, one for the *Washington Post* and one for the *New York Times,* are being prepared for the signature of [contra] leaders Alphonso Rubello, Adolpho Calero and Arturo Cruz. These two op-ed pieces are being prepared by one of our consultants...."

"Through a cut-out, we are having the [contra] leader Alphonso Rubello visit the following news organizations while he is in Washington this week: Hearst Newspapers, *Newsweek* magazine, Scripps Howard Newspapers, the *Washington Post* (Editorial Board), and *USA Today.*"[7]

While Miller later defended the "white propaganda" operation as "putting out the truth," a legal opinion by the General Accounting Office concluded that the "white propaganda" articles amounted to "prohibited, covert propaganda activities designed to influence the media and the public to support the Administration's Latin American policies."[8]

The operation also arranged briefings of Congressional staff members by apparently independent, academic experts on Central America who were secretly directed by the Public Diplomacy staffers. One such person, Joachim Maitre, at the time a professor of journalism at Boston University, reportedly briefed members of House Speaker Thomas P. "Tip" O'Neill's staff on Nicaragua, while concealing the fact that he was, at the time, on the payroll of the Gulf and Caribbean Foundation, a major contributor of the private contra aid operation.[9] The OPD operation also targeted a number of congressmen—most notably Rep. Michael Barnes (D-MD.), who was at the time chairman of a House subcommittee on Hemispheric Affairs and a vocal opponent of Administration policies.

During the same period, the OPD contracted with a number of right-wing researchers to produce reports discrediting domestic Central

America organizations. One such grant recipient was conservative researcher J. Michael Waller. Waller produced at least four such reports for OPD—several of which subsequently turned up in the files of the FBI.[10]

A final point about the interrelationship of various elements of government which were involved in supporting the Reagan policies in Central America emerges from a reading of a 1986 memo on the status of the public diplomacy effort from Raymond to Casey. Raymond notes in the memo that the Public Diplomacy group "takes its policy guidance from the Central American RIG [Restricted Inter-Agency Group] and pursues an energetic political and informational agenda."[11] The major actors in that RIG—Oliver North of the NSC, Alan Fiers of the CIA, and Elliot Abrams of the State Department—are the same men who oversaw the secret contra supply operation which became exposed when an American cargo plane crashed in Nicaragua in October of that year.[12]

By late 1983, the outlines of an inter-agency effort to promote the Reagan Central America policies had emerged. Following Casey's lead, the FBI adopted the CIA's concern about Soviet "active measures" and incorporated it as a justification for the Bureau to move against political groups whose advocacy on behalf of the Salvadoran leftists and the Nicaraguan Sandinistas qualified them as suspected terrorists. Simultaneously, the covert apparatus designed to counteract the impact of those "active measures" began to draw on elements of the CIA, the National Security Council and the State Department.

What had begun as an apparently legitimate law enforcement campaign to protect the country from the threat of terrorism by monitoring the flow of refugees across the southern borders of the United States, had become, by late 1983, a war over the control of reality. The vital component was control of information.

The Reagan Administration's secret dissemination of its own brand of propaganda and disinformation was a quantum leap beyond the traditional use of the presidency to promote Administration policies and goals. As a covert campaign of domestic propaganda and disinformation, it constituted a basic attack on the collective sense of reality of the citizenry.

Taking Aim at *Hard Times News*

For Varelli, the message of the Quantico Conference earlier that spring was clear: the White House had given its total support to the efforts of the FBI's counter-terrorism unit. The President's mandate to the Bureau was unequivocal: hit as hard as possible at all potential avenues of the communist terrorist-propaganda offensive within the United States. That translated into orders to step up the investigation of CISPES and other Central America groups. Hit them hard. Penetrate to the root of their apparatus and learn everything possible about their operations.[13]

The same message had been repeated in May by Ron Davenport who, according to Varelli, told counter-terrorism agents at a regional conference: "Don't worry overmuch about the Attorney General's guidelines and other constraints under which the Bureau formally operated. This was an operation directly aimed at the protection of the national security. That was our overriding concern. And it was equally clear that Davenport's message was, in effect, a message from Revell. And that meant it came from the highest levels of the FBI," Varelli recalled.[14]

To the members of the Dallas office, the message translated into a redoubling of efforts to ferret out the elusive terrorists embedded in the CISPES organization and to come up with hard evidence that would justify a total bust of the organization. As a result, Varelli and the FBI set their sights on Gene Lantz who, along with his wife, Elaine, was a major actor in the left-wing activist community.

"Lantz's FBI file was as big as an encyclopedia," Varelli recalled later. "He was suspected of being a major strategist in the anti-war movement. He was known to have published clandestine newspapers. Anyone who got close to him would be able to learn the secret operations of the National Resistance movement—the movement that included many of the true, hard-core leaders of most of the country's left-wing political groups. Lantz, who had emerged from the Socialist Workers Party, had a reputation in the Bureau as a real heavyweight. So did his wife, Elaine," Varelli said.

But it wasn't only information about Lantz that the Bureau wanted, according to Varelli. If "Gilberto Mendoza" could win Lantz's confidence, and gain access to Lantz's operations, he would be in a position to mount a secret campaign to sabotage Lantz and discredit his work. At the time, Lantz published a newsletter called *Hard Times News,* which went to a number of organizations—the Peoples Anti-War Movement, the War Resisters League, CISPES and the John Brown Anti-Klan Committee, among others.

Before June 1983, Varelli had known Lantz only from a distance. He had seen the energetic organizer at a number of CISPES meetings, but had never had occasion to become close to him. That month, however, the situation changed. The opportunity presented itself courtesy of the Ku Klux Klan. The Klan had already staged several marches in South Texas, especially in San Antonio and Austin, where Klan rallies earlier that year had led to some street violence between the Klan and other groups opposing its message. It was at a CISPES meeting in early June that CISPES organizers learned that the KKK had requested permission to mount a demonstration in Dallas the following month. The news triggered a mobilization of a number of left-wing groups—black activists, peace organizations and Central America groups—under the umbrella of the Dallas Anti-Klan Coalition. To Varelli, the Dallas coalition was, in fact, an umbrella group of militant, radical organizations with ties to groups like the May 19th Communist Organization, whom the FBI had suspected of violent activities.[15]

Sisters Linda Hajek and Patricia Ridgeley, and others at the CISPES meeting, agreed unanimously that CISPES must be represented at the Dallas Anti-Klan Coalition—especially since the Klan presented as much of a threat to the safety and security of Salvadoran refugees as it did to poor blacks and Chicanos in the Dallas area. Because of his previous anti-Klan experience, Gene Lantz was a natural selection for CISPES representative to the coalition. The other person chosen to attend—not least because of his eloquent stories of horror and repression in El Salvador—was Gilberto Mendoza, the poor, disaffected Salvadoran who had, by this time, managed to insinuate himself deep into the confidence of CISPES leaders in Dallas.

When Varelli reported the development the following day to Flanagan, Evans and Parks Stearns, the assistant Special Agent in Charge of the Dallas FBI office, they were very concerned. Previous Klan events had turned violent. If the Dallas situation blew out of control, it could at the very least end up compromising Varelli's cover. The coalition, moreover, included representatives of several groups which the FBI saw as potentially violent, including the Black Liberation Army and the Jewish Defense League.

The Dallas press, aware of the Klan's history of violence and the fact that its members were heavily armed, immediately focused its attention on the Dallas police. Were they prepared for the violence? How would they handle the situation? As a result, the handling of the marches was a matter of high priority to law enforcement personnel.

The first meeting of the Dallas Anti-Klan Coalition took place around June 13, almost a month before the Klan rally which was scheduled for July 16. Varelli went with Lantz to the Martin Luther King Center in Dallas to participate in the planning meeting.

Lantz was the first organizer to address the meeting, telling the assembled representatives of various groups about the previous history of Klan rallies and explaining that the Coalition was preparing a counter-march to neutralize the impact of the Klan.

At that point in the meeting, Lantz asked the other representatives to identify themselves and their groups and opened the floor to a discussion of the upcoming rally.

Varelli was conscious of the mission that Flanagan had drilled into him. His job was to attract attention, gain confidence and get himself included in the elite steering committee so he would be at the nerve center of the group's operational plans. Of special importance to the FBI was the route the Anti-Klan Coalition would follow. Evans had told him that, even though the Coalition had to specify its route in its application for a march permit, they had frequently in the past changed the route at the last minute. The Dallas police wanted to cordon off streets and close businesses on the route used by the marchers in order to minimize damage in case of a riot. "Gilberto's" mission here was to find the true route the marchers would be using.[16]

As the thirty-odd people at the meeting rose, one after another, to identify themselves, the focus moved to the rear of the room. Varelli stood and identified himself as "Gilberto Mendoza" from CISPES. Starting tentatively, he explained he was a Salvadoran refugee whose family had been wiped out by death squads. Gradually, he sensed a gathering of people's attention and, as his confidence grew, he fell into the cadences he had used six years earlier as an Evangelical minister in El Salvador. "I must tell you that this situation with the Klan makes me very sad," he told the group, "because it reminds me of situation that I have been forced to flee. We, too, have groups like the Klan in El Salvador who terrorize us and push us around. At first, we didn't pay them any attention. We didn't protect our rights. We didn't resist them. And, because of that, they gained in strength. And later, when they had become strong, they started to kill us and there was nothing we could do since they had seized control of the city government, the district government and, finally, of the national government. And now they have killed 50,000 people. This Ku Klux Klan is exactly like the right-wing death squads in El Salvador. Let me tell you my personal story."[17]

Mendoza explained that his parents had been killed by the National Guard because his father was an activist in the labor movement. "He wasn't anybody of importance. He didn't have a high position. My father had simply been a man who wanted to better himself and family, wanted better wages, wanted better working conditions, wanted more opportunities. But one night the National Guard came in and killed my family.

A sister also and my cousins. I was the only one to survive—and only because I managed to get myself to the United States."

The room had long since fallen silent. There were tears in some eyes. There was great sympathy on all faces. The only sound was the rolling intonation of his compelling, Salvadoran voice.

Varelli recalled subsequently that part of his effectiveness came from watching an interview with the Greek actress Melina Mercouri which he had seen on *60 Minutes*. The interviewer had asked her if she could cry for him on camera. She did. When the interviewer asked her how she did it, she explained: "I only have to think of sad episodes in my own life and that makes me sad. For that reason, my tears are genuine." The lesson was not lost on Varelli. When he spoke to the gathering of the death of his family at the hands of the death squads, he was really thinking of several close right-wing friends of his in El Salvador who had been killed by the FMLN. "I was thinking of their deaths, recalling how they died. So like Mercouri, my emotions were genuine."[18]

When Mendoza stopped speaking, there was a long moment of silence. And then, an eruption of applause as the entire meeting to a person stood up and applauded this poor, but so very inspirational, Salvadoran refugee. Mendoza's mission was accomplished. After the meeting broke up and a small cadre of people stayed to plan the march, Mendoza stayed with them into the wee hours of the morning, contributing his opinions on the planning of the entire event.

While the group wanted Mendoza to address the anti-Klan rally, an airtel from Headquarters vetoed the idea, saying that Varelli was too valuable to risk exposure to any potential violence. Permission to speak at the demonstration was denied. But the Bureau's denial left him in a difficult situation. At the next Anti-Klan meeting, Gilberto informed Lantz and the others that he had to decline their invitation to speak at the rally, despite the fact that it was a wonderful honor to be invited. His boss, he explained, was a real son of a bitch who was an enthusiastic supporter of the Klan. He had seen Gilberto passing out anti-Klan literature and threatened him to stop such activities immediately. Not only did his boss refuse to give Gilberto the day off to attend the rally, but he threatened that, unless Gilberto stopped his anti-Klan activities, he would fire him and report him as an illegal worker to Immigration authorities. The group was disappointed, but they saw no alternative for Gilberto except to skip the march and rally.[19]

Still, Varelli had learned from organizers that, in fact, the route of the counter-demonstration was going to be changed. Partly as a result of Varelli's intelligence, which was passed to the Dallas police, the rally took place without serious violence. While the FBI's assistance was not publicly acknowledged, Varelli and the rest of the Dallas office received a teletype from Headquarters the following Monday congratulating them all on a job well done.

His moves on Lantz had also worked like a dream. The organizer was so impressed by Gilberto Mendoza that he subsequently published a profile of Gilberto Mendoza in his publication, *Hard Times News*.[20] But, according to Varelli, the real mission of the Lantz operation—gaining control of his printing press to disseminate disruptive and incriminating material on his letterhead —never materialized.

Reconaissance in Houston

Shortly after the successful conclusion of the Klan—Anti-Klan demonstrations, Varelli traveled to Houston —the first of two trips in the summer of 1983—to provide assistance to Special Agent Jack Sheridan who was in charge of the CISPES investigation of the FBI's Houston office. First, Varelli was to scout out the Salvadoran community in Houston and prepare a profile for Sheridan and his agents to use in tracking potential terrorist activities in the Houston area—the scene of a large and growing community of underground Salvadoran refugees.

In addition, Varelli was to help the FBI agents in Houston recruit several Salvadorans in that city to penetrate CISPES and other left wing groups hostile to the Reagan policies in Central America.

The third—and by far the most sensitive—purpose of Varelli's trip was to step up monitoring operations for both the FBI and the Salvadoran National Guard of refugees who were being deported back to Central America.

After his first trip to Houston that June, Varelli wrote a report for Flanagan which sheds light on the energy with which he approached his missions—and the extraordinary conclusions he drew from his reconaissance.

"On Friday the 10th, around 8 a.m. [Special Agent] Jack [Sheridan] called and told me he wanted to meet with me at 9 a.m. He came by my motel room with another agent and thanked me for coming to Houston to help them. He told me that they didn't have anything going as far as Salvadoran groups were concerned...I turned the radio on and I found four radio stations that transmit in Spanish...In Radio La Tremenda at 8 p.m. every day they have "La Hora Salvadorena," the Salvadoran Hour. One of the announcers is ARMANDO SALAZAR who is in charge of the news during the Salvadoran hour. Another announcer is EFRAIN ME-

DINA. Both of them are Salvadoran and the whole flavor of this program is left-wing, Anti-American...These four radio stations work during the whole day in a systematic, organized propaganda and agitation against the US. They work in the following manner: 1 - They educate politically and ideologically the masses; 2 - They promote the organization of the conscious people among the masses; 3 - They promote the mobilization of the masses. 4 - They promote the communication principle with the purpose of the cohesion of the Hispanics against the "gabachos" (white Americans.) 5 - They educate the masses to a readiness to combat injustices against their own particular interests.

"At 7:30 p.m. I parked in front of the Nuestra Senora de Guadalupe Church - Our Lady of Guadelupe at 2405 Navigation. The church is a poor one that ministers in a poor neighborhood. The people that went in were only poor people and, based on my experience and knowledge of Communist strategies, I feel that in that church they are developing a Community Base with the purpose of indoctrinating and selecting leaders for the mass fronts. The main thinking body is located in another place with intellectuals directly involved in the direction of it...Two kinds of people are needed in Houston in order to infiltrate the terrorist groups. One that could go into CISPES and other organizations in which university students and college level people are involved. Another person that could get into the peasant, labor-type organizations. On the 11th I called several places and told them I was a Salvadoran running from the authorities of El Salvador and of the U.S. The following are the names of the organizations that offered help. 1) Houston Human Rights League - 523-6969. 2) Catholic Charities Refugee Halfway House 526-5192. 3) Holy Ghost Catholic Church - 668-0463. 4) Lutheran Refugee Services - 521-0110. 5) Nuclear Weapons Freeze Campaign of Houston - 522-2422. 6) Ripley House - 923-2661.

"In all these places, they offered more information if I could come personally, but they say that more sanctuary and refugee centers are being created. The centers in Houston are more disseminated than the ones in Dallas, but the same churches, organizations are involved in the terrorism network of the US..."

The entire next page is blacked out except for the following final sentence on the page: "I recommend another trip to consolidate the mission...Franco [one of Varelli's code names], Dallas, 16 June, 1983."[21]

The Taca Connection

The "mission" which Varelli mentioned to Flanagan involved the third purpose of Varelli's trips[22] to Houston: arranging for an expedited flow of information from the FBI and the Immigration and Naturalization Service to the Salvadoran National Guard.

During his visits to Houston, Varelli called on a couple he had known from his days in San Salvador. The man, Miguel, was the son of a former president of El Salvador. His wife, Alicia, was, at the time, working for Taca, the Salvadoran airline, which had its main office in Houston. (Neither Miguel nor Alicia are their real names). As a Taca employee, Alicia had access to a type of information which was valuable to both the FBI and the National Guard in El Salvador: the flight manifests, including passenger lists, of every Taca plane that flew between San Salvador and Houston, Los Angeles and New Orleans.

Over drinks one night, Varelli explained to the couple his work with the FBI, letting them know that the Bureau could benefit greatly from the assistance of someone like Alicia with direct access to the Taca passenger computers. Both Miguel and Alicia understood the value of her work and, by the end of the evening, she had agreed to an arrangement whereby she would get copies of the passenger lists for Taca flights and forward them to the Houston FBI office. With her help, Varelli was able to identify a helpful employee at the Taca office in Los Angeles who made a similar arrangement with the Los Angeles FBI office. Following Varelli's second visit to Houston, she arranged for an employee of the FBI's Houston office to get a job surreptitiously in the Taca office. The result was a steady flow of passenger and flight information to the offices of the National Guard.[23]

Shortly thereafter, Varelli alerted agents in the FBI's Los Angeles office that Eduardo Valenzuela (not his real name), a distant relative who worked in the Salvadoran Consulate in Los Angeles, had a particular fondness for expensive clothing and fine wine. Varelli suggested that a covert approach to Eduardo could yield unforeseen benefits for the Bureau. Again Varelli's information proved good when the consular official agreed, according to Varelli, that, in return for periodic payments, he would provide the FBI office with the names of American activists who applied to the Consulate for visas to visit El Salvador. And, like the arrangement in Taca, the names of those activists were shared with both the FBI and the National Guard.[24]

Varelli explained that only selected names were forwarded to El Salvador—names of known leftist activists both from the US and El

Salvador. "We didn't alert the National Guard to the names of everyone being deported. That would be a waste of time and money. If someone being deported had admitted or confessed to being a member of the FDR-FMLN, or if we had evidence of such membership, we'd call the Guard. Mostly the National Guard would surveil and follow them after they landed in El Salvador in order to locate terrorist cells in the country. If the Guard stopped them at the airport, they wouldn't learn anything. It was better to surveil them and learn their contacts, networks, cells and structures."

Did Varelli feel that as a result of his calls people were killed by Guardsmen on their arrival? "I don't know of any who were directly assassinated because of my forwarding the lists. But I would not be surprised if, of the many names that were checked, some ended up dead. Remember, the country is in a state of war. But I, personally, never marked anyone for assassination. When I did call down there, I did express my own feelings about people. But it was always to set them up for surveillance.

"The only names that were supposed to be on the lists that went from the FBI to the National Guard were of people who were known to have been related to the FMLN. Sometimes, the National Guard never even acted on those names. In the cases of some of the big fish, they did meet them at the airport. At first, I believe the Guard did act responsibly."

But during the ensuing years, the Guard's treatment of returning refugees was less selective, according to numerous reports by human rights organizations in El Salvador and elsewhere. Unfortunately, there are no comprehensive figures on the fates of Salvadoran refugees who were denied political asylum in the United States and returned to El Salvador. The task of such tracking, given the lack of cooperation from the Salvadoran authorities, is difficult under any circumstances. That difficulty is compounded by the fear of Salvadorans of speaking out, the use of false names by refugees and the problem of inaccurate record keeping by the U.S. Immigration and Naturalization Service.

One study, however, by the Political Asylum Project of the American Civil Liberties Union Fund, provides a sense of the proportion of refugees who found imprisonment or death awaiting them on their return to El Salvador. That study focused on a sample of 154 refugees who had been deported in 1983 and 1984. Of the 154, 52 returnees were killed. Seven were arrested. Five were jailed as political prisoners. Another 47 were captured and disappeared under violent circumstances.[25] Whether the Salvadoran security forces had been alerted by the FBI to the return of any of the refugees included in the sample could not be determined.

U.S. left-wing and liberal activists who traveled to El Salvador were also on the lists that were passed to the National Guard. "Many times, they'd have a hard time. Their luggage would be searched, they'd be detained. They'd encounter difficult bureaucratic problems. Especially later, after the FBI put their own woman into Taca, she'd give Jack Sheridan at the Houston FBI office the lists. She included members of left-wing US groups—members of NACLA (the North American Congress on Latin America), WOLA (the Washington Office on Latin America), and IPS (the Institute for Policy Studies.) Groups like that. When you give names like those to the National Guard, you know they'll be waiting for you down there. Unfortunately, the operation hurt more good people than communists."

What most angered Varelli in retrospect was the denial by FBI officials, including Revell, that the FBI did no trading of information with the National Guard.

"When Revell told Congress the FBI did not trade information, he was absolutely lying. He knew I called the intelligence unit of the Guard day and night. Sometimes there were five and six calls a day. He also knew that the FBI alerted the National Security Agency about the calls, knowing they would be monitored by electronic satellites. If those calls had not been approved directly by FBI Headquarters, Villacorta would have been killed as a spy and I would have been busted by the National Security Agency. The FBI knew about every damn call I made."[26]

An Explosion of Names

At 10:59 on the night of November 7, 1983, a tiny wristwatch timer hidden in a crevice of a second-floor window of the United States Senate ticked off the last 60 seconds of its functional life.

A minute later, a clap of thunder echoed out across Capitol Hill. The explosion splintered the doors to the Senate Chamber, some 30 feet away. A hole fifteen feet high and several feet wide appeared in the wall of the ornate, ceremonial Mansfield Room. Debris and plaster dust filled the nearby Republican cloakroom. A rare 1815 Grandfather clock lay in pieces. Portraits of Henry Clay, Daniel Webster and John C. Calhoun were reduced to strips of torn canvas.[1]

The bombing of the Capitol—climaxing, as it did, a chain of similar, unsolved attacks over the previous year and a half—provided the Bureau with an extraordinary opportunity.[2]

On one level, a break in the bombings would go far to restoring the FBI's image as an effective and dependable guardian of the nation's domestic security.

More significantly, the bombing of the Capitol sounded a starter's gun for the FBI to dramatically expand and intensify its next round of intelligence gathering activities on virtually every liberal and left-wing political group in the country.

While the FBI's public information office had portrayed the bombings as relatively insignificant events perpetrated by small, isolated groups of radicals, the more zealous agents in the counter-terrorism unit believed that assessment was designed to serve the political needs of FBI director William Webster. Webster had declared three years earlier that the FBI had "broken the backs" of such revolutionary groups as the Weather Underground and the Puerto Rican FALN. But to many agents in the foreign counter-intelligence and counter-terrorism units, Webster was seen as the ultimate bureaucrat, the kind of man who would go along to get along. In Ronald Reagan's America, it was not good form to indicate that there was substantial discontent within American society. An admission of a domestic terrorist threat would focus attention on discontent.

But agents like Davenport and Flanagan knew that there was discontent. The evidence lay in the dramatic growth and spread of groups like CISPES which were bitterly critical of U.S. foreign policy. And they knew that the best way to neutralize those groups and silence their expressions of discontent would be to connect them to the string of bombings that had been reported in the press as relatively insignificant events committed by a small splinter group of isolated revolutionaries. Any concrete link between the bombers and the network of highly visible Central America political groups would completely vindicate all the FBI's investigations of groups opposed to Reagan Administration policies in Central America. Such a connection would prove that groups like CISPES, the Inter-Religious Task Force, the Nicaraguan Network and the Central America Solidarity Association were all part of a larger terror network, with links to international terrorists.

Such a break could lead at least to a federal conspiracy indictment, with all its attendant publicity. Even more important in the minds of the more zealous agents, it would, once and for all, generate the public revulsion needed to put a stop to the propaganda and disinformation these "active measures" organizations were using to pollute the public discussion of U.S. policies in Central America.

But it was obvious that any investigation aimed at linking highly visible political groups to an international terrorist network would involve extensive domestic intelligence gathering. And that was something with which Webster did not want to be associated. With his blessing, Oliver Revell, at the time the head of the FBI's criminal investigative division, took on the job of overseeing the Bureau's counter-terrorism apparatus. It was a way for Webster to be assured the job was being handled—but without any of his fingerprints, lest the campaign of domestic surveillance be discovered down the line. It was the kind of plausible deniability that enabled Revell to tell a Senate committee in 1988 that Webster did not authorize the CISPES investigation, nor was he informed about developments in the probe—although it lasted at least five years and involved every FBI field office in the United States.[3]

Operating ostensibly behind the back of Director Webster, the FBI stepped up its intelligence gathering activities to a feverish pitch following the bombing of the Capitol. "The Bureau used the bombing as a pretext to gather every possible bit of intelligence on every group they had identified. It was an opportunity to rebuild and reconstruct legally the FBI files on domestic activists that had been ordered deactivated by the Church Committee," Varelli recalled later. "The Bureau exploited the bombing like hell. It triggered a nationwide intelligence gathering mobilization. It was used to the maximum."[4]

Officially the FBI indicated it was most concerned about the emergence of a secret, armed terrorist group which included members from various organizations but which was traceable through none. The fear the FBI expressed in classified briefings to overseers in Congress was that CISPES and a host of other groups, many reincarnations of groups born in the 1960s, were all part of a terrorist infrastructure which drew support and direction from the Cuban intelligence agency as well as the KGB and the International Department of the Central Committee of the Soviet Communist Party.

If members of that hidden network could bomb the Capitol with impunity, what did that mean for the upcoming Republican National Convention in Dallas or the summer Olympics in Los Angeles? The FBI asserted that the spate of bombings could be the signal for a full-blown terrorist offensive in the United States. Whatever damage the bombings might inflict on innocent individuals and private property, moreover, would be dwarfed by the psychological victory of demonstrating to the world the weakness and vulnerability of the nation's law enforcement agencies.

Privately, however, FBI's intelligence contained precious little information to suggest that a coordinated network was actually planning a nationwide campaign of armed violence. And even if such a network of the most hard core groups—those with histories of violent activities —had such plans, it had virtually no public support. The country was in no imminent danger of a mass uprising led by an advance guard of the revolution.

More to the point was the fact that FBI officials had determined the identities of the suspected bombers even before the next round of political intelligence-gathering, under the cover of a terrorism investigation, was underway.

Within days of the bombing, Headquarters officials advised the various field offices that the bombing was the work of a splinter group that the FBI suspected was connected to the small May 19th Communist Organization.[5] The near-instant identification of the suspects came from evidence which had been gathered from the string of bombings over the previous year in New York, where bombs had damaged the Bankers Trust Building, the offices of IBM, the South African airline office, and police and court buildings in New York City—and in Washington, where bombs had exploded at Fort McNair and the Washington Navy Yard.

In the case of virtually every bombing, callers claiming responsibility indicated that they acted on behalf of either the Puerto Rican FALN, the PLO, the Salvadoran FMLN or two hitherto unknown groups, the Armed Resistance Unit or the United Freedom Front. But from forensic evidence and discoveries of explosives and plans, the FBI learned that the bombers were part of the Armed Resistance Unit, a tiny offshoot of the May 19th Communist Organization—with no known connections to the FMLN or any of the domestic Central America groups.

Nevertheless, despite the Bureau's almost immediate identification of the bombing suspects, the FBI used the occasion for a massive intensification of the probe of hundreds of left-wing and liberal groups.

(The Bureau subsequently secured a federal grand jury indictment against seven radicals in connection with the string of bombings: Alan Berkman, Timothy Blunk, Marilyn Buck, Elizabeth Duke, Linda Evans, Susan Rosenberg and Laura Whitehorn. Four of the defendants—Blunk, Buck, Evans and Rosenberg—were already serving jail terms for weapons and explosives charges. The indictment cited, among other evidence, a file containing notes and documents related to a number of the bombing targets as well as explosives and weapons found in the possession of some of the defendants. Except for the defendants' general sympathies with the Salvadoran guerrillas, no links to groups like CISPES were found to exist. On September 7, 1990, Buck, Evans and Whitehorn pleaded guilty to the Capitol bombing and to conspiring to set off explosions at seven other locations. Evans said at the time that the bombing of the Capitol was done to protest the U.S. invasion of Grenada. At the same time, the government dropped its charges against Berkman, Blunk and Rosenberg—who were already serving long prison sentences—because their further prosecution would have been dismissed on grounds of double jeopardy, according to government sources.)[6]

Intimations of Surveillance

It was around the time of the Capitol Bombing—in the fall of 1983—that attorneys at the Center for Constitutional Rights in New York began to hear the first of a series of very disturbing complaints by Central America activists who found themselves the objects of surveillance by agents of an unknown branch of government, of death threats, mysterious break-ins and thefts of files—of a string of intimidating and terrorizing encounters which, from a few early reports in 1983, cascaded into a torrent of such episodes over the next few years. One early report involved an elderly Northern Virginia woman involved in refugee assistance.

Ruth Fitzpatrick, a Catholic woman active in the fight for the rights of Central American refugees and a vocal opponent of the Reagan contra policy in Nicaragua, should have become accustomed to bizarre and mysterious intrusions in her life. But, for some reason, Fitzpatrick, who lives in the Washington suburb of Fairfax, Virginia, kept pushing the events out of her mind.

The first had occurred around 1981 when she participated in a demonstration outside the White House to oppose the Administration's support for the Chilean dictator Pinochet. "During the demonstration, a man carrying a tape recorder sidled up to me and said he was a reporter with the *Washington Post*. He asked my name and address, inquired about why I was demonstrating and engaged me in a discussion of my politics. All of this, he said, was for an article in the *Post*. He recorded the entire conversation. At the time, I thought some of his questions were strange—but my suspicions didn't really surface until the next day when I saw that the *Post* didn't publish any article on the demonstration. In retrospect, I strongly felt the man was an intelligence agent.

"A week or two later—it was about 8:30 in the morning—I came downstairs to my living room to see a man standing behind my car photographing my license plate. A brown Datsun was parked in the driveway. For some reason, I was terrified. I stood there for a moment just trembling. Then I got angry. I grabbed a yellow tablet, slammed open my door and strode toward the man. He ran to the bottom of the road and disappeared into the woods with his camera. When I walked to his car, I saw a parking sticker for Arlington Hall—a major Army Intelligence facility in Northern Virginia.

"The next episode occurred around 1982. One evening, we had a meeting of the Oscar Romero Coalition, a small group with representatives of different organizations. At the time, we were planning a demonstration outside the State Department to protest the contra aid policies. It was a loose group of good-hearted people who hosted house meetings. Occasionally, we had speakers at the meeting. One I remember was a priest who had been tortured by Salvadoran security forces. On this particular evening, we looked out of the living room window and saw a couple—a man and a woman—writing down license numbers. We should have confronted them and asked them what they were doing. Instead, we just laughed and continued with the meetings. But it kept nagging at me after that.

"The next episode occurred in the summer of 1983. Coincidentally or not, it was the day my husband left for a trip to Nicaragua. John is a retired Army colonel who was an adviser in Vietnam in the early 1960s. He knows all about guerrilla warfare—and the need for popular support for guerrilla operations. In 1983, he became curious about the situation in Nicaragua and decided to visit the country to learn the truth about Nicaragua for himself.

"The day of his departure, my son and I returned from the airport to find that our house had been broken into. There was no forced entry, but the louvered glass window on our kitchen door had been unscrewed. I couldn't find whether anything was missing. But I strongly suspected that a bug might have been placed in our home. At first I didn't want to believe it. But when I called the police, they said it was clearly a surreptitious entry. Nothing seemed to have been stolen, but it seemed clear that the house had been examined. Had it been a street criminal, they could have broken an adjoining window and reached in and opened the door. I don't know what they were looking for—and whether it concerned my own political activities or John's trip to Nicaragua. But I must tell you. It's a very unsettling and frightening experience.

"For several years, I was an area representative of the National Association of Religious Women. When we learned that the FBI had infiltrated the organization, I found out it was the Washington Field Office of the FBI that had been watching our group. That means they were watching me. Was that surveillance connected to the break-ins and the other episodes? I don't know. But, if you were me, what would you think?"[7]

A Call to Washington

The day after the Capitol bombing, Varelli received a call from Flanagan. A communication had just arrived from Headquarters instructing the two men to prepare to go to Washington to take part in a special undercover operation to determine who was behind the bombings.

Flanagan explained that Varelli's role, as part of the Capitol Bombing Task Force, would be to determine the involvement of Salvadorans, Sandinistas or other Central American operatives who could have participated in the bombings and whatever links they might have to groups like CISPES, the Nicaragua Network, the Institute for Policy Studies, the Inter-Religious Task Force or other groups opposed to U.S. policies in Central America.

Several days later, agents in Washington reported a development which reverberated in the Dallas office like a God-sent answer to a long-ignored prayer.

On November 12, five days after the bombing, CISPES members distributed leaflets during a demonstration in Washington which contained the same language used by the so-called Armed Resistance Unit, a previously unknown group which had claimed responsibility for the bombings. Some of the CISPES leaflets even contained copies of the ARU's communique which justified the bombing as an act of "solidarity with the people of El Salvador," as well as with oppressed peoples in all corners of the globe. The communique declared: "We are acting in solidarity with all those leading the fight against U.S. imperialism—the peoples of Grenada, Lebanon, Palestine, El Salvador and Nicaragua—who are confronting direct aggression—and those, like the people of Chile and the Philippines, who are struggling to free their nations from U.S. puppet regimes." The document concluded: "U.S. military out of Grenada, Lebanon and Central America. Defend the Grenadian and Nicaraguan Revolutions. Victory for the FMLN/FDR. Support the Lebanese National Movement and the PLO. FIGHT U.S. IMPERIALISM. BUILD A REVOLUTIONARY RESISTANCE MOVEMENT."[8]

Flanagan and Varelli were jubilant. This might be the connecting piece of evidence that would finally knit the entire investigation together. To FBI agents in Dallas, the information fit hand-in-glove with a report which had been issued in late October from the the CIA station in Mexico. The Agency had passed along to the Bureau communications, intercepted by the National Security Agency, which had been sent to a meeting of the International Solidarity Front in Mexico City. The intercepted material included messages from Iran's Ayatollah Khomeini and Libya's President Moammar Khadaffy urging terrorist operatives in Mexico to expand their operations into the United States and begin targeting its citizens. Varelli had learned at a CISPES meeting that the conference had been attended by several CISPES officials.

"The intercepts created an enormous state of alert in the law enforcement community. Every red light was blinking. It was unbelievable. The tension had increased since the previous solidarity conference in Libya when there were telexes warning that Libyan hit men could be entering the U.S.. It was a high state of alert for everyone," Varelli recalled.

To prepare for their trip to Washington on December 12, Flanagan and Varelli worked feverishly reviewing forensic material compiled by investigators at the scenes of the bombings. They reviewed CIA and FBI intelligence material on the Libyan and Iranian threats. They pored over voluminous memos from the counter-intelligence division of the Washington Field Office. They reviewed material from the National Security Agency, the Washington, D.C., Police Department's Intelligence Unit, and, especially, from the New York field office which had compiled the most extensive material on the May 19th Communist Organization.[9]

There was, they reported to counter-intelligence superiors at the Washington Field Office, strong reason to believe that left-wing Salvadorans in the Washington area, in league with the Salvadoran FMLN guerrillas, were linked to the May 19th Communist Organization which, itself, was known to be an offshoot of such radical groups of the 1960s as the notorious Weather Underground.[10]

Varelli recalled that at the counter-terrorism seminar at the FBI Academy in Quantico nine months earlier, agents had focused on several groups, including the May 19th Communist Organization, the John Brown Anti-Klan Committee, the Black Liberation Army and the Puerto Rican FALN—hard core groups whose members definitely had the potential for violence. All of them, moreover, were the 1980s reincarnations of organizations which had been undeniably implicated in armed and violent activities in the 1960s.

"Everyone present at Quantico was certain that CISPES and the other apparently harmless protest groups were connected to the violent groups of the 1960s. They traced a number of individuals active in the earlier groups to their involvement with groups like CISPES. That is something we all believed," Varelli explained.

The Mysterious Washington Safe House

After checking into a hotel near Washington's National Airport on Sunday, the day before the first Task Force meeting, Varelli went directly to the home of Francisco, an old acquaintance from El Salvador who had lived in Washington for more than 10 years and who had a number of contacts in Washington's Salvadoran community. The tall, chunky 40-year-old man had indicated in a phone call to Dallas a few weeks earlier that he had some information which might be useful to the Bureau.[11]

He invited Varelli into the living room which was dotted with Nazi-type artifacts, including several books on Hitler and the Third Reich. He put a piece by Wagner on the stereo to mask the conversation. In a hushed voice, Francisco explained to Varelli that he had accidentally stumbled on a terrorist safe house in Washington. Francisco, who, at the time, managed a coffee shop, explained that a cab driver he knew had

recently driven a group of Salvadorans, armed and apparently dangerous, to a house a few blocks southeast of DuPont Circle.

In that house, he said, half a dozen Salvadorans—some of them
wearing FMLN t-shirts—lived with four or five Iranians. Francisco (not
his real name) had confirmed their presence, and the fact that they were
armed, with some other cab drivers and Salvadorans living in the
Columbia Road area.

Varelli's ears perked up. Salvadorans and Iranians were worlds
apart culturally. The only reason they would be sharing living arrangements is if they had a common political purpose.

At that point, Francisco produced a copy of a radical Spanish-language newspaper, *Nosotros,* which, he said, was published in the same
house, known as Casa El Salvador Farabundo Marti.

When Varelli read the issue of *Nosotros,* he was deeply troubled.
It was written in a Spanish style that, by its idioms and expressions, was
unmistakeably Salvadoran. It contained the kind of rhetoric that, in El
Salvador, had to be taken very seriously. When the FMLN had issued
similar communiques in San Salvador threatening bombings or assassinations, they were not idle threats. The attacks almost always followed
the publication. Varelli noticed that page 8 of the paper contained a
virtual declaration of terrorist warfare. The article declared: "The FMLN
warns the government of the United States that the FMLN wants peace
negotiations. If the U.S. prefers war, there will be war. The decision will
be made right here in Washington. And Washington is where war will
be carried on."

What most alarmed him were the threats contained in the paper.
The authors threatened the members of the Salvadoran National Guard.
They threatened the lives of U.S. government officials. In fact, they
threatened the very life of President Reagan. In one article, the National
Guard was described as a "death squad working for the White House."
The authors added that "we will kill Guardsmen the same way they have
killed the children, wives and relatives of 30,000 Salvadoran campesinos.
And we will do the same to U.S. government officials to see how they
will feel."

The warnings in *Nosotros,* Varelli felt, were real. They could well
be the beginning of a campaign of bloody terrorism in the very heart of
the United States of America. And, even if they were empty rhetoric, they
certainly would help Davenport and his colleagues in FBI Headquarters
to build a case for CISPES' support of terrorism.[12]

Confusion in the Field

But while Varelli, Flanagan, Davenport and others in the chain of command of the FBI's counter-terrorism unit had no doubt about the purpose of their mission, a variety of teletypes, released under the Freedom of Information Act, reveal that many FBI agents around the country were very confused about both the mission and the justification of the investigation.

In the fall of 1983, for example, Headquarters requested the Phoenix FBI office to investigate the Tucson Committee for Human Rights as a possible terrorist organization. On November 9, the Phoenix office reported: "...the Tucson Committee for Human Rights in Latin America has always been a non-violent organization which has been utilized as a forum in the Tucson, Arizona area for dissemination of information regarding Latin American affairs. In view of the above, it does not appear that further investigation regarding the Tucson Committee For Human Rights in Latin America is warranted. The case is therefore being closed."[13]

The very next day, by contrast, agents in the New Orleans field office sent the following teletype to Headquarters: "(BLANK) It is imperative at this time to formulate some plan of attack against CISPES and, specifically, against individuals (BLANK BLANK BLANK) who defiantly display their contempt for the U.S. government by making speeches and propagandizing their cause..."[14]

The confusion of agents in the field is understandable, given the mixed signals emanating from Headquarters. In the case of the decision by the Phoenix office to close its probe of the Tucson Committee for Human Rights in Latin America, Headquarters responded with the following teletype:

"Re: Bureau communications advised that CISPES offices were often contained in, or operated from, offices of other similar type organizations or front offices. Based on the information contained in referenced Phoenix airtel, Phoenix should consider the possibility that the Tucson Committee for Human Rights may be a front organization for CISPES...Before closing this investigation, Phoenix will submit available information regarding the TCHR to Dallas, Houston and San Antonio (BLANK)."[15]

While people in the Justice Department apparently understood the subtle distinctions between communist "active measures," international terrorism and the legitimate exercise of free political speech, it is clear from declassified teletype traffic that those distinctions were lost on many agents in the field. The teletypes between the field offices and Headquarters betray enormous confusion on the goals of the investigation, the methods to be used and the distinction between legitimate free speech and terrorism.

One of the more cogent rationales for the investigation is contained in a teletype from the Louisville Field Office sent at the end of November 1983. In an extensive airtel recapping the results of the Louisville investigation to date, the Special Agent in Charge of the Louisville office wrote:

"It is noted that the foregoing information has been included herein to provide background data concerning local origin of captioned organization only and should not be construed as an effort to investigate the exercise of First Amendment rights of individual CISPES members who politically oppose U.S. policy in El Salvador and Central America. Said data does serve, however, as a data base to begin the process which is intended to ultimately ferret out the identities and activities of those members who are knowingly supporting Salvadoran guerrillas in the U.S. and Central America and furnishing financial and material support to the guerrillas."[16]

But while Louisville noted that the probe "should not be construed as an effort to investigate the exercise of First Amendment rights," agents in Mobile, Alabama, had no such qualms. In January, 1984, an agent in the Mobile FBI office monitored a two-hour radio program on WKRG, featuring a discussion by Dr. Steve Schaeffer, a professor of pharmacology at the University of South Alabama Medical School. The two-page single-spaced communication recounts the following statements by Schaeffer: "He advised the [Salvadoran] guerrillas want negotiations with the United States and that they are tired of the current oppression. He advised that they are just another liberated group and movement who want their freedom and that they, CISPES, have nothing to do with nor want anything to do with Communism. He advised that the CISPES group does desire land reform and wants to be used as a tool so that the United States can save face and open negotiations with the El Salvadorian [sic] guerrillas...Mobile division will continue attempts to develop information as to location, leadership, and activities of the above group."[17] In other words, for its advocacy of land reform and the opening of negotiations with the rebels, and despite its renunciation of communism, CISPES gained the continued attention of the Mobile FBI office as a possible terrorist organization.

Meanwhile, agents in Louisville were apparently still struggling to understand their marching orders relative to CISPES as late as March 1984. A teletype from Louisville explained: "Purpose of investigation is to identify organizational activities and members who knowingly support Salvadoran guerrillas in the U.S. and Central America by furnishing financial and material support to guerrillas, and not to impede or interfere with First Amendment rights of CISPES members who politically oppose U.S. policy in El Salvador and Central America."[18]

The confusion was evident to Headquarters as late as July 1984, when officials at the Bureau sent yet another teletype to the field offices to clarify the guidelines and goals of the investigation. After two pages of deleted material, the document notes:

"Based on the above, there is sufficient grounds for this investigation. It must be noted, however, that many of the people and groups involved with CISPES do so for political, emotional, or sociological reasons and are not aware of or involved in the CISPES covert activities enumerated above. Therefore it is imperative that these investigations are closely monitored to ensure our investigations do not infringe upon the rights of those individuals or groups protected by the Constitution."[19]

Nevertheless, Headquarters had still failed to clarify matters for agents in the field, as evidenced by the two following teletypes received from the New Orleans and Denver Field Offices the following month:

"New Orleans agrees that maximum efforts must be exerted in order to ensure the protection of Constitutional rights (BLANK BLANK BLANK) New Orleans would appreciate knowing if other offices are experiencing the 'umbrella insulation' of CISPES members through their affiliation with various legitimate organizations."[20]

Several days later, the Special Agent in Charge of the Denver office wrote Headquarters:

"Denver concurs with New Orleans that, in spite of attempts by the Bureau to clarify guidelines and goals for this investigation, the field is still not sure of how much seemingly legitimate political activity can be monitored."[21]

Two weeks later, on August 27, 1984, the Special Agent in Charge of the Chicago office wrote:

"Chicago investigation has revealed that Chicago CISPES membership, approximately 300 paid individuals, is made up to a large extent of the 60's activist type who is often described as 'A rebel looking for a cause.' These individuals indeed surround themselves in more than one activity or organization which has the look of legitimacy. Chicago has not investigated the organizations that appear legitimate."[22]

Headquarters made yet another effort to clarify the purposes of the probe in an October 1984 airtel: "In response to reference to teletypes and other communications forwarded by other field offices, FBIHQ is setting forth this information, and these instructions to assist recipients in their investigation of captioned organization and related investigations.

"Perhaps the best beginning of understanding under what parameter and methods this organization must be investigated is to first realize the possible violations involved and the goals of these investigations." Unfortunately, the core of the Headquarters clarifications is not available since the rest of the document has been blacked out.[23]

But whatever the instructions of Headquarters, the investigation proved a major source of confusion to FBI agents around the country. Perhaps they were confused by the fact that, despite Headquarters' repeated assertions that CISPES was providing illegal material support to the Salvadoran rebels, no such violations were ever found. Perhaps they were confused by the assertions of FBI officials that CISPES was a "terrorist" organization, despite the fact that no links between known terrorist organizations and CISPES were ever discovered. Most likely, they were confused by the lack of distinctions between Bill Casey's concept of "Soviet active measures," which the FBI considered a form of international terrorism, and Thomas Jefferson's concept of constitutionally protected free speech. The distinctions are virtually invisible to this day.

It is clear, however, that at least in the Dallas office, FBI officials were aware of the potential illegalities of the FBI's CISPES operation. In the margin of a 1983 teletype a supervisor in the Dallas office wrote the following note: "Stress this with o/a [operational asset]—we're all going to be writing depositions for the litigious vampires at the next swing of the pendulum."[24]

A Death Threat and Intercept

Around the same time that Flanagan and Varelli flew to Washington, the New York *Daily News* ran an editorial cartoon. One panel showed several men in Latin American military uniforms with smoking guns and several dead nuns on the ground. It was captioned: "Death Squads Western Style." A second panel depicted a group of Soviet leaders standing in a row atop Lenin's tomb in Moscow under the caption: "Death Squads Eastern Style."

For some reason, the cartoon offended the sensibilities of David Lindorff, a New York-based free-lance writer. Lindorff sat down and wrote a short letter to the *Daily News* saying that, since the United States government and the CIA were training and encouraging Central American death squads, the cartoon should have showed the White House and the Politburo. "It would have been a more accurate parallel," Lindorff wrote. To his great surprise, the normally conservative *Daily News* ran his short letter on the paper's editorial page on January 12.

Around 1 o'clock the following morning, Lindorff was awakened by the telephone. Although his answering machine was on, he was afraid the late night call might be occasioned by some family emergency. By the time he got himself out of bed and over to the telephone, the message machine had already kicked on. "I stood at the phone and heard a breathy, creepy voice. 'Hello Dave,' the voice said. 'We read your letter in the *Daily News*. So you don't like death squads? Well, when we were in Nam, we had death squads and that's how we dealt with communists and people like you. Now we're back here protecting democracy in America. We have death squads here, too, Dave. You're number nine on our list. I can't say when we'll get you, but we will.'"

Lindorff had no idea of the identity of the caller. He thought it might be just an idle drunk. But there were no party noises or bar noises in the background. Just the breathy stage-whisper of what sounded like a very intimidating white North American male. He dismissed the call as a crank and went back to bed. It wasn't until the next morning, when he was about to leave his apartment, that Lindorff became worried. "I know there are lots of nuts in New York. But nevertheless I felt kind of weird—a little shaky—going out the next morning."

Lindorff forgot about the episode until several months later. At that point, he had occasion to call a CISPES office in connection with an article he was writing. When he dialed the number, it was answered by an operator who announced "Intercept." Lindorff asked whether this was the CISPES office and whether he had dialed the correct number. The operator abruptly hung up.[25]

The Heart of the Terror Network

By 6 Monday morning, Varelli found it impossible to sleep any longer. This morning, December 12, was the opening meeting of the Capitol Bombing Task Force and he was too charged up even to stay in bed any longer. By 7, he was at the Twin Bridges Marriott Hotel near National Airport where Flanagan was staying—nearly two hours before the meeting of the Capitol Bombing Task Force was to convene.[1]

Around 8:30, Edmundo Mirelles and his partner, Tim Weber, both counter-intelligence agents from the FBI's Washington Field Office arrived at the hotel. They were followed by two members of the intelligence unit of the Washington Police Department and, in turn, by two Secret Service agents who introduced themselves and explained they were attached to the National Security Council. In all, there were about a dozen people present. When Manny Johnson, a black FBI supervisor from the WFO introduced himself, Flanagan quietly told Varelli to ignore whatever he said. Johnson was there, Flanagan added, as part of the quota system.

Varelli recalled later that he felt guilty at not responding to Johnson—a soft-spoken, well-educated agent. But he was under orders from Flanagan, who displayed the kind of racism Varelli had seen frequently at the Bureau.

There was some small talk, including references to the Soviet shootdown the previous month of KAL flight 007. The task force meeting came to order when Ron Davenport, Headquarters' man in charge of the El Salvador Terrorism investigation arrived with a huge stack of files and photographs.[2]

The short, stocky Davenport emanated a strong sense of personal command. With his conservative suits, his straight-back hair and his occasionally sarcastic tone, he always seemed to evoke instant attention from the agents he worked with. But despite his no-nonsense demeanor,

149

Davenport also commanded a great deal of loyalty from his people. Six months earlier, when Davenport had flown to Dallas to attend a regional FBI meeting, he praised the assembled agents for their work on the CISPES and El Salvador Terrorism investigations. "Things will change for the better soon," he had told them. "If we stick together, we'll all make it big. If I make it, you'll make it too. We'll all be in good shape." It was clear that Davenport expected the investigations to win him a promotion—perhaps to be the new head of the FBI's Global Counter-Terrorism Unit.

He also had a reputation as one of the FBI's more dedicated anti-communists. One veteran in Headquarters, who accorded him something less than ringing respect, once said of Davenport: "If he entered a room and saw a man standing over a corpse with a smoking gun, the first thing he'd do is look behind the curtains for Communists."[3]

But that attitude apparently endeared Davenport to Revell. And Varelli noticed that when Davenport referred to the FBI's executive assistant director, he almost invariably called him "the Director." Flanagan apparently noticed it too. He talked to Davenport more than to anyone in the Dallas office. Varelli was surprised at the closeness between the two men. But he attributed it, in large measure, to Flanagan's keen sense of bureaucratic politics. When Davenport had told Flanagan and others the previous May to "stick with him," most of the agents responded with a guarded silence. Flanagan alone had responded "Amen."[4]

After coffee was brought into the room, each agent introduced himself and the unit he represented. Agents from different units presented reports on the status of various groups and activists they had been monitoring.

A number of the groups were known to have had close contact—and, in some cases, virtual sponsorship—by various liberals in Congress. The discussion led into a reading by Davenport and others from the FBI's files on those legislators.

Varelli had known the Administration considered the legislators threats to the security of the country. In fact, he learned from his Salvadoran contacts that Otto Reich, the head of the State Department's Office of Latin American Public Diplomacy, had put out the word through COPREFA, the public information arm of the Salvadoran Armed Forces, that the dozen or so legislators were either confirmed communists or, at least, active supporters of the communist cause. During the morning session, one agent referred to the Congressional liberals as Lenin's "useful idiots" who provided platforms for propaganda and disinformation to forces hostile to the United States. Other agents spoke mockingly of their politics. During the meeting, Davenport read from file information on the legislators, including transcripts of wiretapped telephone conversations.

Ostensibly the legislators were subject to FBI investigation because of their contacts with representatives of foreign governments. That was the hook in the FBI's guidelines that permitted the Bureau to investigate them. But Varelli knew the real reason lay in their sympathy with groups or movements that were clearly "communist-inspired." In fact, the FBI had been monitoring the legislators less to find out what kind of information they were passing to Salvadoran communists and members of the Nicaraguan Sandinista government than to determine how and to what extent they were being used as "agents of influence" by those enemies of the United States.

Sen. Christopher Dodd, (D-Conn.), for instance, was suspected by the Bureau of having clandestine ties to some Sandinista leaders. The FBI knew that Bianca Jagger, a journalist and the former wife of the Rolling Stones' Mick Jagger, had close ties to the Sandinistas. Dodd dated Bianca Jagger, although the FBI believed that was a cover to conceal his true political agenda which was to promote the Sandinista cause. Material in FBI files indicated that a number of Dodd-Jagger meetings were actually working sessions to arrange plans for demonstrations or for Dodd's promotion of the Sandinista regime on the floor of the Senate, according to Varelli. At the very least, the Bureau concluded, Dodd had made himself a willing target for cultivation by the Nicaraguans as an agent of influence in a textbook "active measures" operation.[5]

Rep. Michael Barnes was generally despised in the Bureau as a vigorous and outspoken opponent of Administration policies in Central America. Moreover, Barnes, along with Conyers, Dodd, Dellums and Solarz, sponsored a number of rallies against the Reagan Administration which were orchestrated by groups strongly suspected by the FBI of being part of the terror network.

Rep. Ron Dellums was suspect because of ties between his staff members and the late Grenadian leader Maurice Bishop. Don Edwards, the California Democrat who had oversight over the FBI through his chairmanship of the House Judiciary Subcommittee on Civil and Constitutional Rights, had recently met several years ago with a visiting Soviet delegation to a World Peace Council conference.

Rep. John Conyers of Michigan, another outspoken opponent of Reagan foreign policies, came under FBI suspicion because of his refusal (along with one other legislator) to condemn the Soviet shootdown of

Korean Air Lines flight 007. In addition, Conyers was known to have made overtures to Yasser Arafat, reviled by the Administration as one of the world's foremost practitioners of terrorism. Several months earlier, Conyers wrote to an organizer of the United Nations Conference on the Question of Palestine. In the letter, he conveyed special greetings to the PLO's delegate to the UN, as well as to Arafat, adding: "I urge you to continue your struggle on behalf of peace and to remember there are those of us within the U.S. who represent a broad coalition which supports you. We represent another America, a rainbow coalition dedicated to changing the direction of our country."

The agents read file reports on about a dozen legislators altogether, including Senator Thomas Harkin and Representatives Conyers, George Crockett, Mervin Dymally, Mickey Leland, George Miller, Stephen Solarz, Gerry Studds and Ted Weiss—all of whom had known contacts with people high up in one or more leftist political groups and all of whom had opposed Reagan Administration policies in Central America.

The next order of business was the perusal of hundreds of photographs from the files of the Washington Field Office. As Davenport laid out the folders full of photographs, Varelli and the others looked them over.

"We were trying to look through thousands of pictures of demonstrations and individuals and trying to figure out who they were. You could see that in some cases the photos were taken from vans parked nearby. Some were shot from above from buildings. Some photos of individuals were close ups, as though taken inside a store. But the FBI didn't know who many of the people were," Varelli said.

One photo, he noted, was of the front of a building that housed the International Center for Development Policy, a leftist non-profit organization headed by Robert White, the former U.S. Ambassador to El Salvador. Three years later, in 1986, people at the Institute would develop a great deal of damaging information about the secret contra-aid operations of Oliver North, and the involvement in those operations of the CIA. In November 1986, the Center would be the object of a break-in that has never been solved.

Following the review of the photographs, Davenport told Varelli that his foremost responsibility that week was to learn anything he could about the involvement of Sandinista or Salvadoran terrorists—and especially their U.S. support groups—in the bombings.

Secondly, according to Varelli, Davenport asked him to conduct several reconaissance operations. Using a cover, he was to enter the national office of CISPES, as well as the offices of the Institute for Policy

Studies, a left-liberal think tank which might have ties to the terrorists, and Epica, a left-wing publisher. Once inside, his job was to case the offices—to memorize their layouts, security systems, exits, alarms and locations of file cabinets, Varelli said, adding his recollection of this conversation was especially clear.

When Varelli looked quizzically at Davenport he was told: "This operation has the backing of the White House. It has been fully authorized by the National Security Council."[6]

Francisco Chickens Out

After Flanagan told the group about the house with the Salvadorans and Iranians, Varelli mentioned that Francisco was eager to help the FBI. Davenport told him to go get Francisco and bring him to the motel. But, as Varelli recalled later, "one thing went wrong. Francisco chickened out. When I brought him into the hotel room, and he saw that this was a real operation, he backed off.

"The day before, when I asked him for help, he talked very tough, very patriotic. I told him this wasn't for me—this was for the United States of America. He said he didn't want money, that he'd assist us out of pure patriotism. I think he felt that if he scored some points with the Bureau, he might be able to get something from them in return.

"But it didn't work out that way," Varelli said. "When we brought Francisco into the meeting, I introduced him to the agents there and said he would take us to the house where the Iranians and Salvadorans were living. The other agents showed Francisco pictures of the demonstrators and asked him to identify any local Central Americans he recognized. Then I saw his jaw drop. He realized he was in deep shit. He didn't have guts to admit he recognized people in those photos. When it became evident he wasn't going to help, Flanagan told me to take him home.

"On the way back, I said, 'Francisco, you don't realize what you've done. You told the FBI you know where there are terrorists. On top of that, you now know the identities of a bunch of agents who are involved in a very secret operation. You're in trouble. It would have been better if you'd never said this stuff.' "

Francisco decided on a compromise. While he was too frightened to take the agents to the house himself, he gave Varelli the addresses and names of several Salvadorans he said who might know more about them. He also gave Frank several issues of *Nosotros*.

When Varelli returned to the Task Force meeting with the newspapers, the other agents were appalled by the kind of threats they contained. Immediately Mirelles and his partner, Weber, from the Washington Field Office, drove back to Francisco's house. They took him to FBI Headquarters to interrogate him where he confirmed everything he had told Varelli. "They scared the shit out of him so he completely spilled his guts," Varelli recalled.

The next day, agents from the Washington Field Office put a wiretap on the telephones at the house to learn what they could about the group and its ties to domestic political organizations. While Varelli was concerned about the residents of the house, he had serious doubts about their connections to such high-profile groups as CISPES and the Institute for Policy Studies. "These were very secret, isolated individuals—almost like a terrorist cell. They carried weapons. They appeared violent. Some of the things in their newspaper made it seem like they were almost looking for a shootout," he recalled.

Following the meeting, Varelli decided to learn what he could about the group from other Salvadorans in the Columbia Road area in northwest Washington. He would start with a Salvadoran shopkeeper he knew who reputedly sold dope as well as dry goods. He went into a number of bookstores, where he purchased leftist newspapers and magazines. He entered the shop of his acquaintance, but found a group of hostile looking Salvadorans in FMLN t-shirts acting suspiciously like bodyguards. He left without making contact. He spoke to a number of people in the neighborhood, some of whom hinted they thought the Salvadorans at Casa El Salvador Farabundo Marti might be a splinter group which had broken from the ERP, a violent, Maoist faction of the FMLN coalition which had been involved, earlier that year, in the unsuccessful kidnapping of the wife of a former Salvadoran ambassador in Miami. But nothing he learned connected the group to any of the large liberal or left-wing Central America organizations.

Into the Nerve Center of CISPES

Varelli woke up Tuesday morning with a rush of adrenaline even before the 6:30 alarm went off. His pulse was racing. Today was the day he was going to penetrate the heart of the enemy. It was one thing to hang around with the CISPES people in Dallas. He had become used to them. It was easy to be friendly and personable with Linda and the others. But here in Washington was the center of the whole operation. Any real terrorist operations would be run out of the national office. And, ironically, the CISPES headquarters was a mere block away from FBI Headquarters on Pennsylvania Avenue.

Like other members of the Task Force, Varelli was tantalized by the recent distribution by CISPES members of leaflets containing the same language used by the Armed Resistance Unit which had claimed credit for the Capitol bombing. He knew that no one had uncovered a link between CISPES and the violent factions involved with the bombings. If such a connection did exist, the evidence would exist most probably at the national headquarters of CISPES.

Varelli's apprehensiveness was compounded by his fear that he might be recognized by some Salvadoran in the CISPES office. Just six years before, Varelli, then an ordained Baptist minister, had mounted a major religious crusade in San Salvador. Posters containing Varelli's picture had been plastered all over the city. Some 300,000 leaflets containing his photograph had been distributed. There was a good chance he would be recognized—and his cover blown —by someone recently arrived from El Salvador.

Later, Varelli would liken his assignment to the FBI sending a case of nitroglycerine into the CISPES office. "I was very inflamed. I was still thinking like a Salvadoran. I would have interpreted any unusual act by them as hostile and dangerous. I've had more real experience with terrorists than anyone else in the Task Force. I've been face to face with terrorists. I've been shot at by them. In situations like that you shoot to kill, not wound. I had hollow point bullets in my 9 millimeter pistol. If I got inside the CISPES office and they put a hand on me, I would have killed them all. In retrospect, I can't believe how irresponsible the Bureau was, telling me to go in there armed. I wonder how many other people they use that way. Some day it's going to blow up in their face."[7]

That morning, Varelli, Flanagan and the other members of the Task Force convened again at the hotel. The main order of business was arranging backup for Varelli in case anything went awry during his visit to CISPES. He was to spend only 15 minutes inside CISPES headquarters, they agreed. If he needed help, he was to fire his gun one time.

After logistics were arranged, Flanagan drove Varelli by the CISPES building, wished him luck and dropped him off at the end of the block.

Varelli entered the old building, found the CISPES listing, and took the old elevator up to the third floor.

"I was really in a state of high alert. I expected to find heavy security, people with weapons. I was half prepared to call in backups to confiscate weapons and raid the whole place."

But what startled Varelli most was his discovery, on emerging from the elevator, that the office housed not only CISPES but also the Nicaraguan Network and the Guatemalan Network. Stepping into the hallway,

Varelli saw three huge flags —the Sandinista FSLN flag, the Guatemalan EGP flag, and the flag of the Salvadoran FMLN.

"When I saw there were Sandinistas there, I can't describe the feeling. It was almost like coming face to face with Danny Ortega or Shafik Handal [the Salvadoran Communist Party leader]. My whole body tensed and I came within one click away from acting. I could have handled it better if FBI told me other groups were there. I wasn't quite so afraid of CISPES people since I'd been with them. But I didn't know if there were active Sandinista agents there."

Realizing that his agitation might make it impossible to maintain his cover, Varelli turned and walked back down the hall into the bathroom. There he popped a valium and sat on a toilet for a few minutes for the valium to take effect before entering the office.

The first person to greet him in the hallway outside the suite of offices was Manuel Pedrosa. Pedrosa, a short clean-shaven Salvadoran, seemed immediately suspicious of Varelli. He introduced himself in Spanish to Pedrosa, explaining he was Gilberto Mendoza, an illegal alien, from Dallas. He had come up from Texas, he said, to visit a friend in Alexandria, and had taken a bus into Washington that morning.[8]

Since he was here, he said, he wanted to visit the national head-quarters of CISPES, the group that was doing so much to help his people, and to get the latest issue of their newsletter, *El Salvador Alert,* to show to his friends and relatives who wanted to learn how to help get the Reagan-sponsored U.S. forces out of El Salvador.

But he was not sure how this act was playing with the suspicious, dead-pan Pedrosa. The short man in the plaid short-sleeve shirt stared at Varelli relentlessly. "He was reading me real, real hard," Varelli recalled later. While he chatted with Pedrosa, he again flashed on the crusade leaflets with his photograph in El Salvador. It was much easier to deceive a gringo than to try to fool another Salvadoran.

Although he was extremely courteous, Varelli could tell that Pedrosa was extremely wary. Periodically, the man touched his black wavy hair or put his hand to his chin as Varelli spoke. He listened virtually without response, as though the silences in the conversations might contain land mines into which Varelli might stumble and blow his cover.

The tension was broken when another CISPES official, Bob Ostertag, came out of a second door and joined the conversation. Ostertag looked to Varelli like a young German man. His short hair and rimless glasses gave him a very serious air. Varelli thought Ostertag looked like someone who was into computers or who was always worrying about nuclear war. "He looked harmless, even nice, but I considered him very dangerous. I knew he had been at the Solidarity Conference in Mexico City," Varelli recalled later. "He was one of the heavy ones."

Varelli looked over Ostertag's shoulder back into a room where he heard the sounds of a teletype machine clicking away as well as a mimeograph machine churning out pages. He acted impressed. "Do you do your own printing here?" he asked. "Oh, absolutely," Ostertag answered enthusiastically, ushering Varelli into the mimeograph room where he showed him shelves full of fliers, posters, bumper stickers and publications.

In response to several questions, Varelli told the two men about his work with CISPES in Dallas. He mentioned Sister Linda Hajek, the nun who had befriended him in the Dallas chapter.

Moments later, Pedrosa wandered away into a room off the adjoining office. From the corner of his eye, he watched Pedrosa sit down at a desk to make a telephone call. From a few snatches of conversation, Varelli could tell that he was phoning the CISPES people in Dallas to verify his identity.

As he was talking to Ostertag, Heidi Tarver, a founder of CISPES and a long-time target of the far right, came out of a side room into the office. "She looked like an ordinary dumb American. But I felt she's real dangerous. She was very sweet. But I remembered not to fool myself. These people could smile as they put a knife in your back."

The tall, heavyset woman with the blond pony tail was delighted to meet Gilberto Mendoza. While Varelli chatted with her about conditions in El Salvador and the work that CISPES was doing, he noted that Tarver fit the mold of CISPES women to a T. She was wearing a plain skirt and blouse that was undeniably K-Mart quality. She also wore rimless glasses, he thought, "like all the communists."

While the three talked, Varelli pulled out a roll of bills which he had prepared in advance—all fives and ones. "I handed her this batch of bills, which looked like a lot more than the $40 it was. She and Ostertag looked excited. That broke the ice."

Throughout the conversation, Varelli kept scanning the office. There was precious little security for the office. All he could see was one self-contained alarm on one exterior window. And that could be rendered useless simply by removing the pane. He counted the desks in the office—four—and noted a bank of six telephones in addition to two single phones. Only two of the desk drawers were locked, indicating, perhaps, that they contained money.

As they talked, Varelli moved toward the phones, memorizing the two main numbers and six extensions "just like snapping photographs in my head."

The task was not new to Varelli. He had trained his memory through hours of practice—looking briefly at a room and then closing his eyes and forcing himself to remember every detail he could.

Looking out the window, he noticed that he could see the antennas atop the FBI Hoover Building from the CISPES office. From the roof of the building, Varelli imagined, one could look straight in through the windows of the FBI building.

At one end of the room, his attention was riveted by a large steel cabinet, about six feet high and four feet wide. Just large enough to hold a large gun rack. He noticed the metal doors of the cabinet were secured by a huge padlock. There was no question in Varelli's mind that if CISPES did have an arsenal, that cabinet contained at least part of it.

He also noted that the suite of offices, dense with desks, filing cabinets and office equipment, was far too crowded with furniture to be used as a meeting place. If agents in Washington wanted to infiltrate CISPES, they would have to find out where the meetings were held. The main office was clearly not the meeting place.

Abruptly, Varelli checked his watch. Nearly twenty-five minutes had elapsed since Flanagan had dropped him off. They had agreed the visit would last only fifteen minutes. It was time to leave.

"Gilberto" told his hosts he had to go and thanked them profusely for all the good work they were doing for his country.

Ostertag told him to help himself to any literature he wanted. He took a stack of newsletters and notices, mentally planning to forward them to different FBI offices to keep agents abreast of the names of officers of various chapters, various resolutions passed at different regional meetings, and information about new chapters of the organization. He took an armful of posters.

He took a bunch of buttons which said "I am In Solidarity with the People of El Salvador", as well as a handful of bumper stickers ("U.S. Out of El Salvador") for other FBI agents to use in surveillance and infiltration operations.

As he was leaving, Tarver, obviously moved by the effort of this poor Salvadoran so far away from home to visit CISPES, approached Varelli and gave him a big hug.

For a moment, Varelli forgot who he was. "They all seemed so appreciative of my coming. Then she hugged me and her feelings seemed very real," he recalled. "When someone hugs you in pure, good faith, it's very easy to forget your true role and why you're there—and to get swept up in the emotions of the moment."

But Flanagan had trained Varelli well against moments like this.

"Dan would always ask me how I felt about the CISPES people in Dallas. One time, I mistakenly told him they really seemed to like me. All he said was, 'Let's have lunch together today.' Inside the restaurant he really let me have it. 'Your mission,' he told me, 'is to protect the security of the United States. You are an important part of that mission. You must remember that at all times—whenever you're dealing with people in CISPES or any other group you're infiltrating. Remember always that their kindness is directed toward the person you're pretending to be—not the real you.'

"When Heidi Tarver hugged me, I made myself remember that. The real me is ideologically repulsive to them. If they knew the real me, they'd blast me. They only like who I was pretending to be. If I were naked of that personality, I would be alien to their system of being and belief."[9]

By now, Varelli was beginning to panic about the time. The last thing he wanted was for Flanagan and a group of agents to barge in to the office and blow his cover.

He thanked Pedrosa, Ostertag and Tarver, promising that he'd return, and telling them how much his friends and relatives would appreciate the literature. He left the office and entered the elevator with a stack of papers so high he could barely carry them.

As he left the building, a police officer began to follow him. Varelli's initial wariness melted a moment later when he realized the man was part of his backup. As he reached the corner, Flanagan grabbed him by the jacket and pulled him into the waiting car.

The two men drove away quickly. They rode in silence until Flanagan parked the car near Lafayette Park, a small grassy area behind the White House. Then they walked to a nearby park bench where they were joined by Mirelles. Flanagan opened a notebook and took notes as Varelli briefed him on everything he saw and learned inside the office. He sketched the layout of the office while Varelli pointed out the locations of the desks, the files and the suspicious vertical cabinet.

After the 30-minute debriefing, Varelli went to the car and gave Mirelles some buttons and bumper stickers for use by the agents in the Washington Field Office.

Next Stop: Institute for Policy Studies

When Mirelles left, Varelli let his head fall back and gazed at the grey, leaden sky. As he felt the refreshing cold air on his face, he realized the operation had left him emotionally exhausted. But the workday was still young. Next stop, the Institute for Policy Studies.

When they arrived at the IPS off DuPont Circle, Varelli recognized the building from a photo he had been shown at the motel. He recognized the door he was supposed to enter.

"The best way to get anywhere with a liberal is to pretend to be a wetback," Varelli recalled. "I don't know if it's guilt, or whether they're just trying to show how liberal they are, but if they see you're poor and sort of helpless, they'll help you in the street. They'll tell you everything you want to know."

The door to the Institute for Policy Studies was locked, so Varelli began to bang on the door when a man opened it and asked, "Can I help you?"

"Yes," said Varelli, acting lost. "Is this the attorney's office?" "No," the man responded, "this is Instituto de Studios Politico."

Varelli noticed the type of locks at IPS and the kind of alarm system on the door. He looked over the man's shoulder and saw on a bulletin board that the local chapter of CISPES had scheduled a meeting for seven the next night downstairs in the same building.

Bingo! Just an hour earlier, he'd been worrying about where CISPES held their meetings in Washington. He had no idea it was the IPS. He was on a roll.

Next, he and Flanagan drove to the National City Christian Church at 14th St. and Massachusetts Avenue. They parked next to the church which housed a center for Central American refugees.[10]

While Flanagan sat in the car, Varelli entered the church pretending to look for someone among the Hispanic men and women entering and leaving the building. Inside the vaulted lobby, he spotted a visitors' book. Scanning the pages, he noted that a delegation from Waco, Texas, was attending a conference there. He drew out his notebook and wrote down every Hispanic name from Texas that he saw. He also entered every name that was accompanied by a listing of a Central America or refugee-assistance group such as CASA, the Inter-Religious Task Force and Caracen.

When he returned to the car, he told Flanagan to note in his book that the church had an electronic alarm system that could only be deactivated by the control box inside. Otherwise, one had to cut off the electricity or use a glasscutter to open the doors.

Stuffing the Files

The next two days seemed aimless and anticlimactic to Varelli. On Wednesday, he and Flanagan drove around the city, checking out a number of bookstores and other places.

That evening, when Varelli dropped Flanagan off at his hotel, he mentioned that he might swing by later on for a drink after scouting the Salvadoran area some more. Flanagan begged off. He had some friends coming up from Quantico, he explained. Why didn't Frank just keep the car and pick him up in the morning?

That night, when Varelli had an opportunity to study the material he took from the CISPES office, he realized what a windfall the visit had yielded. While it might not appear particularly dramatic to an untrained eye, he realized that information, especially in *El Salvador Alert,* added a number of critical pieces to the terrorist network they were slowly and painstakingly tracing.[11]

First he noticed that the CISPES newspaper, for the first time, declared that CISPES supported the FMLN-FDR. This was the first time CISPES acknowledged openly its links to the military arm of the Salvadoran revolutionaries. Previously the group had claimed only that it supported the FDR, the political arm of the Salvadoran rebels. But now, in black and white, it proclaimed its support of the armed forces.

A second item of signficance was the identification of CISPES with the FSLN, the ruling Sandinista party of Nicaragua. CISPES had never before extended its embrace to the Sandinistas.

Scanning the addresses of the CISPES regional offices listed in the paper, he noticed that, yet again, the organization kept changing the addresses of its locations. That meant yet another group of telephones to tap and another U.S. map redrawn to indicate changes in the CISPES regional structure.

The newspaper noted that CISPES had now grown to 300 chapters. That meant a new round of work for the FBI, Varelli thought, since only a portion of the chapters used the name CISPES. The field offices would have to be notified to spread their nets even wider to keep up with the growing and constantly changing network.

Armed with a notebook and yellow highlighter, Varelli proceeded to read each article from beginning to end.

"It was an absolute rule that every single name in the newspaper, everyone quoted as saying things against the Administration or in favor of CISPES or the FDR-FMLN, went into the computers, into the terrorism files. There were no exceptions," he noted.

He knew the FBI already had an extensive file on Jesse Jackson. So when he read an article on the Nov. 12 CISPES demonstration, his eyes widened when he saw a quote from James O'Dell, of Jackson's PUSH organization in Chicago. "For Operation PUSH, the demonstration is part of the confrontation of the history of our country in relation to Central America," O'Dell was quoted as saying, adding he condemned the U.S. policy of "intervention and chauvinism." Varelli entered O'Dell's name onto his growing list.

Similarly, he added the name of Esmerelda Brown, a member of the United Methodist Church, also quoted in the article.

One article in the newspaper dealt with the life and death of a Honduran priest, who died while working with Honduran guerillas. At the bottom of the article, Varelli read a tagline: "Much of the above is based on a story by Robert L. Koenig which appeared in the *St. Louis Post Dispatch,* Sept. 25, 1983. For more information, contact the Honduran Information Center, 1151 Massachusetts Avenue, Cambridge, Ma., 02138." The article generated airtels to the Boston FBI office to check on the Honduran Information Center. It also generated an airtel to the St. Louis field office, requesting any information on Robert Koenig, the *St. Louis Post Dispatch* reporter.

In another article, this one on the support of American blacks for the Sandinista regime in Nicaragua, Varelli read: "In 1969, 10 years before the Sandinista victory, the FSLN published the 13 articles of its program. Article 11 states: 'It will support the struggle of the Black people of the United States for an authentic democracy and equal rights.'" To Varelli, that underscored the fact that the same revolutionary elements of the Black Panthers and Black Liberation Army of the 1960s and 1970s were still alive and vital.

The newspaper also contained a profile on the Austin, Texas, chapter of CISPES. Varelli made a note to forward the Austin material to special agent Jack Sheridan in Houston. The article noted that the chapter was restructuring its organization by consolidating three committees in a larger outreach committee.

Sheridan later secured good intelligence on the chapter. His information showed that people had branched out and created a phone tree that covered not only parts of Texas but also Oklahoma and Arkansas. Later, Varelli put his own name and number on the phone tree. Each time there was a mobilization, "Gilberto" got a call and would proceed to call four other members.

In addition, the FBI put a mail cover on the CISPES post office box in Austin. The Bureau focused on a list of foreign students who were CISPES members, many of whose parents were involved in some way or other with the Salvadoran left. Varelli was certain that some of the students were conduits for money which eventually made its way to the FMLN. The chapter held a number of events at which they auctioned items like hammocks and hats from El Salvador. But the FBI was never able to definitively trace the flow of cash back to El Salvador. The foreign students who traveled to Mexico or Central America never had much cash with them. And other money raised by CISPES ended up being sent to political research groups as NACLA, WOLA and IPS in Washington and New York. "After awhile, the money disappeared into their accounts and we never learned exactly how it got back to El Salvador," Varelli said.

Besides the names that were entered into FBI files, the newspaper contained a number of photographs of rallies and demonstrations. Later, the FBI's photo lab blew up each photograph so that every member of the crowd could be placed on a separate piece of photographic paper. The photos were distributed to the various field offices for identification.

The final item in *El Salvador Alert* that captured his attention dealt with a series of demonstrations on the West Coast timed to coincide with the Nov. 12th Washington rally, five days after the Capitol bombing.

"The initiative emanated from Mexico, where activities in support of November 12th are planned in Mexico City and northern towns. The West Coast rally is sponsored by the Nov. 12th Coalition and the U.S.-Mexico Border Commission in Solidarity with the People of El Salvador," the item said.

For Varelli, this notice proved foreign control of domestic political demonstrations in the U.S.. The initiative, he figured, originated with Salpress—the press office of the FDR-FMLN leftists in Mexico City. The people in Salpress were trained propaganda and disinformation specialists. He was positive they were behind the initiative.

The material may not have netted the FBI a smoking gun, Varelli thought. There was nothing they learned that could justify any arrests yet. But every piece of data fit like a brick in a building. Slowly and surely, they were building an unassailable case to prove the secret terrorist support structure that he believed was so deeply embedded in the CISPES network.

In any case, the FBI was sufficiently impressed with what Varelli saw as the sinister nature of some of the material he gathered from CISPES that they passed it along to the Secret Service, according to documents on file.

Flanagan's Mysterious Ride

Around 11 Thursday morning, Varelli knocked on Flanagan's hotel room door. Dan obviously was suffering from a serious hangover. He asked Varelli to take a ride with him, but his manner made it clear he wanted no questions. Flanagan drove along the Potomac toward Alexandria, then turned inland. At length, he came to the large Landmark shopping center. He drove to one store, left Varelli in the car, came out a few minutes later empty-handed. Then he drove to another area of the shopping mall and repeated the performance. For two hours, Flanagan criss-crossed the shopping center, going in and out of various stores. He offered not one word of explanation to Varelli. Around 2 p.m., he asked Varelli if he wanted a hamburger. "Sure," Varelli answered. Flanagan pulled up in front of a restaurant, but made no move to leave his car. When Varelli closed his car door, Flanagan told him to go inside, get lunch and wait there until he returned. Varelli obeyed. About 30 minutes later, Flanagan joined him at the table.[12]

"To this day, I don't know what he was doing," Varelli recalled. "Except for one thing. He made it obvious that, all of a sudden, he had no more money problems. After all his complaining about being squeezed, having to support two families, always being behind on payments, always apologizing for shorting me on my reimbursements, all of a sudden he had no money problems."

After lunch, Flanagan took Varelli into an electronics shop. He spent twenty minutes looking at a very expensive watch with a tiny television screen before deciding not to buy it. He bought a number of gifts for his wife. "It was weird," Varelli said. "Just two days before, he was so broke he chewed out a poor cab driver who had overcharged him by two dollars."

Later that day, the two men drove back to Flanagan's hotel where they prepared a 20 page report, much of it based on the material Varelli had taken from the CISPES office.

A Pickup at Western Goals

The next morning, Friday, Varelli took his aunt with him on a tour of several bookstores where she purchased some leftist books and periodicals for him. She accompanied him into a plush Alexandria office when he made his first stop: the office of Western Goals.[13]

Flanagan had told Varelli to go to Western Goals to pick up some material that had been ordered by the FBI. Wearing his coat and tie and newly-shined shoes, Varelli approached the secretary, identified himself as an FBI employee from Dallas and asked for Linda Guell, executive director of the foundation. When the secretary brought Guell to the reception area, she was very courteous and businesslike. Varelli identified himself again as an FBI representative, adding he had been told that Guell had material for the Dallas office. He mentioned to Guell the types of groups the FBI was investigating, and gave her his post office box number to arrange for future shipments of material from the organization.

Guell, a short, attractive, well-dressed woman with curly black hair and a slight Southern softness to her speech, produced a package of Western Goals material, most of it compiled or edited by John Rees, some of it containing names of opponents of Administration policies, some of it containing intelligence material that supported the Reagan Administration's activities in Central America. Varelli paid Guell for the material, waited while she wrote out a receipt and left.

The following week, when he brought the material back to the Dallas field office, agents xeroxed every book and pamphlet from cover to cover for their own files. They returned the originals to Varelli, telling him to use it in his work. It had to be done that way because FBI guidelines prohibit the Bureau from purchasing and filing political material. But, under the guidelines, the FBI is permited to file such material if it is in photocopied, rather than in original, form, and if it is not solicited by an official FBI agent.

Varelli was rocked, when they returned to his aunt's home, by a furious phone call from Mirelles of the Washington Field Office. "Where in the hell was Flanagan?" he wanted to know. Dan was supposed to have met with Johnson and Mirelles to review the report. He never showed. Where was he? Varelli had no idea.

The next morning he met Mirelles and Weber, ironically at the same shopping center where he had spent much of Thursday with Flanagan. Mirelles explained that he had scheduled a Friday morning briefing of the whole Task Force and Flanagan never showed.

Mirelles asked Varelli where they had been on Thursday. But Flanagan had ordered him to keep his mouth shut about their ride. So he fudged, telling the two Washington agents they had cruised around. Varelli added that he would send them a full report from Dallas as soon as he returned.

"They thought I had conspired with Flanagan to screw them. I told them it was absolutely not true. I felt very bad for both Mirelles and Johnson. Both of them were gonna be chewed out good for this and there was no way I could help them," he explained.[14]

Losing Faith

On his flight back to Dallas on Sunday, Varelli was confused and deflated. He was bewildered by the mysterious ride with Flanagan on Thursday afternoon. And he was suspicious of Flanagan's sudden and newfound affluence. He was confused by the initial burst of activity—followed by two half-lackadaisacal days which, to Varelli's mind, were wasted. If the terrorist threat was so serious, why weren't they doing more about it?

Certainly the trip was not a total bust. They had learned from the telephone taps on the Casa house that none of the Salvadorans or Iranians there had any contact with people from CISPES, the Institute for Policy Studies, Epica, or any of the other visible leftist political groups. They had confirmed that the group was a small remnant of the ERP, a group of Salvadoran Maoist terrorists, that had largely disintegrated in the past few years. The people in that house were now the responsibility of the Washington Field Office. But they had been discounted as having any relationship to the ongoing investigation of CISPES, the Nicaragua Network, the Inter-Religious Task Forces on Central America, or other groups that were subject to surveillance or penetration. Still the material he obtained from the CISPES office had yielded a number of new and revealing clues.

But something was happening within the FBI, some shifting of ground under Varelli's feet that he didn't understand. Was the Bureau losing interest in the investigation altogether? That didn't explain the enthusiasm and energy that Mirelles, Weber and some of the other field agents displayed.

On the other hand, the work of the first couple of days had barely scratched the surface. Varelli, alone, had gathered at least 20 leads worth pursuing. But Flanagan had seemed not to care. Varelli found himself totally frustrated by the refusal of Davenport and others to authorize arrests of people who were involved in forwarding money to the rebels in El Salvador. They could have used technicalities of the Immigration and Naturalization Service laws to question a number of Central Americans, but, again, the supervisors turned thumbs down.

The following week, when Varelli confronted Flanagan about this disappearance, all Flanagan said was "I don't give a fuck." Flanagan said he had sent a copy of the report to Davenport Friday morning and it was up to Davenport to share it with the Task Force or not. Personally, he repeated, he didn't give a fuck.

He knew that Flanagan had a streak of cynicism in him, that occasionally his enthusiasm flagged for operations which did not directly bring him personal credit. But Dan's erratic moods did not explain this strange week, which began in a burst of intense and highly focused activity only to trail away into apathetic routine and time-killing diversions.

He knew Flanagan was aware of what was happening. And if Flanagan knew, Davenport did too. And if Davenport knew, then Revell would know.

Varelli recalled that over the previous couple of months he had been fighting to suppress a growing feeling of skepticism about the FBI's real intentions. But now, he could no longer push the question away. He had to admit that while the Bureau justified its investigation of hundreds of new groups opposed to the contra policy by citing their links to CISPES and the terrorist network, it was clear that the investigation had turned away from the hard core terror network. Instead, the Administration was using the CISPES investigation as a cover for its attempt to neutralize opponents of the contra policy.

In fact, Varelli let himself entertain the possibility for the first time that the entire FBI counter-terrorism operation was, itself, merely an elaborate cover for another effort: neutralizing the Administration's political enemies.

Recently it seemed to him almost as though Flanagan and Davenport had come to think of the investigation as a game. It was not that they resented Varelli's pointing out the mistakes, misunderstandings and the cultural ignorance of many FBI agents he had worked with. It was more that they had listened, agreed—and then dismissed them as irrelevant to the real task at hand.

Varelli was still not certain. But the possibility was beginning to dawn on him in a sickening way. Was the FBI simply using the investigation as an excuse for a political campaign that came down from the top? Was he, himself, with his extensive knowledge of terrorist organizations, their genealogies and methods of operation, being used for one purpose—an investigation of international terrorism—which was, itself, only a front for an operation that had as its true mission the protection of the President's political agenda rather than the rooting out of terrorists? It was a realization whose implications he did not want to acknowledge. But it was also one he could no longer ignore.[15]

Epilogues of a Reconaissance

Several months after the formation of the Capitol Bombing Task Force, both the Institute for Policy Studies and the headquarters of CISPES were broken into by unknown intruders.

Files had been rifled and copied, but nothing of value was stolen, except one camera which was taken from the IPS office.[16]

The Honduran Information Center located in the Old Cambridge Baptist Church in Cambridge—the source of one of the articles in *El Salvador Alert*—was the target of several of 11 break-ins at the Church between 1984 and 1988. The FBI has refused to investigate the break-ins. It has also refused to turn over its files on the church, saying that to do so could result in compromising a confidential source of the Bureau.[17]

The following year, 1985, the apartment of Esmerelda Brown, one of the people mentioned in *El Salvador Alert* whose name Varelli had entered into the FBI's terrorism files, was broken into twice. Brown, who worked for the United Methodist Church's United Nations office, specializing in Central America affairs, said intruders rifled her files and stole several documents.[18]

Passing The Torch: From the FBI to the NSC

One of the great unsolved mysteries of the assault on left and liberal activists during the Reagan Administration lies in the covert tangle of byzantine arrangements and underground contacts for the exchange of information between law enforcement and intelligence agencies and collaborators in the private sector. Data gathered by private spies ends up in FBI files. Information gathered by the Bureau has surfaced in all sorts of publications disseminated by private right-wing lobbying and educational organizations. Information held in FBI files is leaked to sources who publish it in open literature which the FBI then cites as justification for its own policies and campaigns. Like the secret files of the Salvadoran security forces, which were snatched away by renegade officials only to be circulated in the private sector and covertly returned to the security forces, the flow of information about individuals, groups and institutions opposed to Reagan Administration policies resembles an elaborate and extremely complicated information-laundering operation.

On January 4, 1983, a small part of the secret public-private information exchange surfaced into public view. Jay Paul, a detective in the intelligence division of the Los Angeles Police Department, had inadvertently attracted the attention of police investigators who learned that Paul was taking large amounts of raw political intelligence material out of the department.[1]

Acting on a tip from another detective, police investigators visited Paul's home, searching both the house and a garage on the property of his wife's law office in Long Beach. There they discovered 180 boxes of police intelligence files on West Coast political activists—environmentalists, opponents of nuclear energy, advocates for increased civilian controls over the police, members of left-wing political groups, as well as reports on politicians, judges and members of the Los Angeles Police Commission.

Paul's removal of the material from the police files was not an idle exercise. Investigators learned shortly thereafter that the files were being transmitted via a transcontinental computer hookup into the database of the Western Goals Foundation, which was controlled by John Rees.

As the investigation unfolded, it turned out that Rees had received about 5,000 police files on activists from Paul. Another official in the Los Angeles police department testified subsequently that Paul's activities had been approved by a former captain of the department. Among the material that Paul supplied to Rees were lists of demonstrators arrested in Florida and California, as well as a confidential LAPD domestic security report.

Some material provided by the Los Angeles detective was subsequently published in a Western Goals publication and in Rees' own *Information Digest.*[2]

One upshot of the revelation of the data-exchange between Western Goals and the LAPD was the payment by the city of $1.8 million to satisfy a lawsuit brought by the American Civil Liberties Union on behalf of a group of plaintiffs whose names appeared in the stolen files.[3]

Another upshot is that some of the methods employed by Rees—as well as some connections between the Western Goals operation and the private network run out of the National Security Council—were unearthed by detectives in the Department's Internal Affairs Division who were charged with investigating the scandal.

The Internal Affairs detectives, in a confidential report to the Los Angeles Police Chief, noted that Rees used his own information-laundering scheme to conceal the sources of illegally obtained information. According to their report: "Rees' own publication, *Information Digest,* could be used to conceal the identity of sources of information that was illegally obtained. This was accomplished by first printing the information in the *Information Digest* and then quoting from the *Information Digest* in subsequent publications of Western Goals. Using this procedure, [Rees] was effectively able to assert a First Amendment privilege to [conceal] the identity of its sources." Rees has insisted that, as a journalist, he has a right to protect the privacy of his sources. "Like any journalist, I talk to people, including police. If someone is arrested, I try to find out why," adding his relationships with police constitute purely "journalistic activity."

But Rees' contention seems gratuitous in view of one finding of the LAPD investigators. A 1981 Western Goals publication on domestic security indicated, "This report is prepared by Western Goals for the use of government and law enforcement officials." The Internal Affairs investigators, however, found that the report duplicated a confidential "Domestic Security Report" prepared by the department's Anti-Terrorist Division.[4]

After the LAPD investigators identified the source of Rees' information, they discovered a direct link between the Western Goals operation and the private network which worked in the shadows to promote the cause of the Administration's Central America policies.

The investigators came upon a memo from Rees to Larry McDonald, at the time president of Western Goals. According to the memo: "Jay Paul, John Rees and members of the Western Goals advisory board would determine the groups, political or social movements, issues or individuals to be targeted for collection."[5]

At the time, the 25-member Western Goals advisory board included a number of figures who would subsequently become known for their activities in what has come to be characterized as Oliver North's private network. Chief among them was John Singlaub, the Administration's point man in raising money for weapons for the contras from private sources.[6] Singlaub's connections went to the center of the clandestine "private network." He served under CIA director Bill Casey during World War II when Casey was stationed in London for the OSS. Singlaub, moreover, boasted publicly that Casey's office door was always open to him. Following the disclosure of the Iran-Contra scandal, Singlaub acknowledged to Congressional investigators in the summer of 1987 that, through his position with the World Anti-Communist League, he had worked to support anti-communist resistance fighters in five countries in addition to Nicaragua. A former president of the League, Singlaub was closely allied with the Rev. Moon organization, the Korean CIA and elements of South Africa's security forces, as well as with reputed Guatemalan and Salvadoran death squad leaders, including Roberto D'Aubuisson.

In 1985, Singlaub proposed to Casey a plan to get Soviet-made weapons to anti-communist rebels in Angola, Afghanistan, Cambodia and Ethiopia through an "off-the-shelf" operation which bypassed both Congress and the State Department. And while the proposal was apparently never implemented, Sen. Paul S. Sarbanes (D-Md.), a member of the Iran-Contra committee, called the plan "as serious a concern as anything I have seen that has come before us in these hearings."[7] In the case of left-wing and liberal activists inside the U.S., it was Singlaub, among others, whom Los Angeles detectives learned would help determine the "targets of collection" of data by the private right-wing Western Goals foundation.

Until it came under public scrutiny with the Jay Paul revelation, the Western Goals operation, in tandem with Rees' private publication, *Information Digest,* was embedded in an incestuous information exchange circle. Western Goals material was sent to members of the John Birch Society and other conservative activist groups, as well as to a number of local and state police departments, the Federal Bureau of Investigation and the Central Intelligence Agency.[8]

Moreover, Rees himself was identified as a paid FBI source by an Assistant U.S. Attorney. According to a 1982 affidavit, "Some federal agencies received information…from John Rees or S. Louise Rees [Rees' wife], sometimes in the form of issues of *Information Digest,* and from time to time they were compensated by the FBI for furnishing information."[9]

Some of the material which was gathered on liberal and left-wing groups by Rees, Singlaub and others—and which was disseminated to conservative activists and law enforcement agencies—consists of disinformation, character assassination and scurrilous accusations. In a 1985 issue of *Information Digest,* for example, Rees focused on the movement of some 200 churches and synagogues to provide sanctuary for Central American refugees: "The 'Sanctuary movement' is an outgrowth of long-standing organizing…by radicals who want to [open] the borders to the totalitarian left." The article added that a lawyers' group sympathetic to the Sanctuary movement has filed lawsuits "of direct benefit to…the Sandinistas, Cuba and the Soviet Union," as well as a "Communist Party front." The article includes the names, addresses and phone numbers of 21 Sanctuary leaders and organizations around the country. Several of those individuals suffered break-ins and other forms of terrorizing harassments.[10]

Western Goals fell into disarray at the end of 1983, with the death of Larry McDonald. The organization was subsequently taken over by Carl Channel and used as a financial conduit to launder secret payments to the Nicaraguan contras. By that time, Rees had left the organization following a dispute with its executive director Linda Guell.

But Western Goals was only one of several organizations that directed considerable energy, manpower and financial resources to "neutralizing" liberal political and religious Central America groups with a flood of disinformation, red-baiting and character assassination. Early in 1984, a number of private right-wing groups stepped up their own attacks on groups opposed to Reagan Administration policies in Central America.

For instance, reports accusing CISPES of supporting terrorists by both the Young Americas Foundation, a right-wing group with two White House advisers on the board, and by J. Michael Waller, of the ultra-conservative Council for Inter-American Security, were circulated among FBI field offices and retained in the FBI files.[11]

The YAF report cited the fact that CISPES had helped raise money for a shoe factory in El Salvador as evidence it was supporting the armed guerrillas, since combat boots, which could have been produced at the factory, are, according to the report, a form of military assistance.

The Waller reports, moreover, were financed by the ubiquitous State Department Office of Latin American Public Diplomacy—the office set up by Casey to orchestrate domestic propaganda.[12]

Other FBI documents indicate that members of CARP, the campus arm of the Moon's organization, spied on meetings of left and liberal Central America groups and passed their reports to the FBI. Frank Varelli, moreover, has said that the Moonies were on the payroll of the FBI in Dallas. Their purpose was both to spy on the Central America groups and to create disruptions whenever CISPES or other groups held rallies, marches or other events. Varelli said his knowledge of Flanagan's payments to the Moonies was reinforced in 1984 following revelations that Flanagan had withheld money from Varelli, as well as other sources. At that point, Special Agent Jim Evans, in the FBI Dallas office, went to the Moon organization to verify Flanagan's payment vouchers, Varelli recalled.

"Your Cover is Blown!"

But as the private activity of right-wing activists escalated, a mysterious and bizarre event put a premature end to the role of the FBI's Dallas Field Office in the Bureau's CISPES investigation. Early in 1984, after Flanagan and Varelli had returned from Washington, the Dallas Field Office received a teletype from Headquarters requesting an update of the CISPES investigation at an upcoming terrorism conference at the FBI's Academy at Quantico. Unlike the seminar the previous year, however, Flanagan, rather than Varelli, would address the FBI counterterrorism specialists. In late March, Varelli compiled a full updated report of the CISPES investigation for Flanagan's presentation. Flanagan arrived in Washington around April 6, two days before the conference. He carried with him two briefcases of top-secret material—including the CISPES investigation report and the FBI's security arrangements for the protection of President Reagan at the Republican National Convention which was to be held that summer in Dallas. The CISPES report, in particular, contained the code numbers and identities of a number of sources working for the FBI's terrorism and counter-intelligence units— including the true identity of a Dallas-based infiltrator who used the name of Gilberto Mendoza. The report, additionally, contained a number of charts, a code book, and some correspondence about the CISPES investigation between Special Agent Sal Escobedo, in the San Antonio office, and Special Agent Jack Sheridan, of the Houston office.

What happened next is still a mystery. Flanagan later told investigators he parked his car near the Potomac River in Washington in order to take a walk by the river and admire the cherry blossoms. When he returned to the car, he later told FBI superiors, he found the car had been broken into. The two briefcases of classified documents were gone —along with Flanagan's gun and his FBI badge.[13]

The next day, Jim Evans, a special agent from the Dallas Office, called Varelli at home: "Lie low," he told Varelli, "there has been a serious security breach. Dan's briefcase was stolen. Your cover is blown. Stay low. We'll contact you later." The following day, Flanagan, speaking without a copy of the CISPES report, so botched the presentation that Davenport took him off the podium and asked Special Agent Sal Escobedo to take over the session.[14]

In short order, the FBI flew Flanagan back to Dallas where he was suspended and removed from internal security work. In fact, his FBI superiors found Flanagan's account of the burglary so incredible that they began an espionage investigation of the 16-year FBI veteran who had come to speak fluent Russian during his previous assignment covering Soviet representatives to the United Nations.

After Flanagan returned to Dallas, Varelli was told to report directly to special agent Jim Evans. It was during this period that Varelli learned that Flanagan had withheld a number of FBI payments to him and, additionally, had collected expense money by turning in vouchers, attributed to Varelli, for expenses which Varelli had never incurred.

Late one afternoon, after Evans had confronted Flanagan about the money, Flanagan flew into a rage at Varelli, telling him, "This whole goddamned thing is all your fault." Varelli, who had considered Flanagan one of his closest friends, felt suckered. When Flanagan had come forward as a witness at Varelli's naturalization ceremony in 1982, for instance, he wrote a card of congratulations which said, in part: "Franklin, I want you to know how proud I am…You have proved that your ideals and sense of justice are strong…You will always have a friend in me, and call upon me for any reason, Dan Flanagan." The following year, Flanagan gave Varelli a gold watch for his birthday. It was only after Flanagan's loss of the documents, when Varelli learned that Dan had deducted the cost of the watch from his payments, that Varelli began to realize how Flanagan had cheated him.

After the long, heated argument in Flanagan's office, the life seemed to evaporate from Flanagan's body. He slumped down in his chair. He confided to Varelli the fact that the previous night he had come within a hair of killing himself. "I know I've let you down, and I've let the Bureau down as well," Flanagan said. He recounted the bitter break-up of his first marriage and the financial problems that had plagued him for the last several years. And then, in a burst of penitence, he promised to repay $400 which he had withheld from Varelli's last payment. True to his word, Flanagan pawned several items of jewelry and repaid Varelli the next day. In retrospect, Varelli said, he was deeply saddened by Flanagan's fall. "He was a good friend and a good agent. If he had only asked me, I would have let him keep the money."

Several weeks later, the FBI ordered Flanagan to report to Washington for a polygraph examination. Shortly thereafter, Thomas Kelly, the special agent in charge of the Dallas office, told Varelli that Flanagan had failed the test and that he was being allowed to resign. But as the FBI's Revell noted in 1988, the Bureau did go as far as to make a presentation to a U.S. Attorney to prosecute Flanagan for both the security breach and the withholding of money from Varelli.[15] (Varelli subsequently recovered about $7,000 of the $65,000 he said the Bureau owed him when a federal Claims Court in Washington, D.C., ruled in his favor.)[16] Apparently, the Bureau was persuaded that Flanagan had not, after all, sold the documents to the Soviets. In fact, the Bureau has maintained, in the wake of Flanagan's resignation, that he was probably telling the truth about the car break-in—and that the documents were probably tossed into a dumpster in some Washington alley by street thieves who had hoped to find money or valuables in the briefcases.

There are other speculations as to what happened to those documents which Flanagan lost and which he has refused to discuss ever since.

"I never thought Flanagan gave the material to the KGB," Varelli said. "What I really think happened is that Flanagan passed the material to the National Security Council and, from there, it began to be distributed to the right-wing operatives who spied on Central America groups."

A Federal Catalog of Leftists

While Varelli's suspicions about the vanished FBI material are nothing more than speculations, they do fit one teasing, but unprovable, scenario which involves the recycling of the FBI material through the State Department's Office of Public Diplomacy—the State Department office which was controlled by former CIA propaganda chief Walter Raymond from the National Security Council—and which had been established at the suggestion of CIA director Casey.

Six months after Flanagan lost the CISPES files, William Perry, a staff member of the Office of Public Diplomacy (OPD), left the office to set up an ad hoc three-person institute to do a survey of public opinion on Central America.[17]

The survey, which took three months to compile, was done by Perry and two colleagues on a grant from the OPD. The book, entitled *The Latin Americanist Establishment: A Survey of Involvement,* was ostensibly intended to help the State Department sell its Central America policies to the American public by identifying every activist group involved in Central America issues.

But to Varelli, the similarity between some of the material in the book—and material he had seen in the terrorism files of the FBI—was striking. After reviewing portions of the book, he noted that it contained a number of the same names and organizations that the FBI had entered into its files in the course of the CISPES investigation.

"It's absolutely amazing—some of the material in that book. There are names of people—not prominent or visible people—not people who would be generally known—but names that we put into the FBI's terrorism files. Those names are in this OPD book. It's very possible they could have gotten them from the report that Dan reported stolen," Varelli speculated.[18]

The book, itself, is a model of the type of material generated by the Office of Public Diplomacy. In an introductory section, the authors noted: "In political terms, one cannot help but be struck by the concentrated numbers of institutions ... which rest on the left of the ideological spectrum...(By our own thumb-nail reading of the program descriptions, we found that well over ninety percent of those demonstrating a clear political orientation are of the leftist bent.)" Later in the introduction, the authors add that: "The premises from which the majority of [Central America-oriented] groups work include a...distinct sympathy for left-wing movements in Latin America and a strong proclivity to be critical of current (and perhaps any conceivable) U.S. policy toward the region."[19]

"This situation," the study concluded, "obviously complicates the policy-making process of the U.S. government…Under current circumstances, an active and well-endowed Public Diplomacy program is clearly necessary for the U.S. government. However, such a program is, by itself, insufficient…It should not be imagined that the current Latin Americanist establishment will be convinced by public diplomacy, or that the U.S. Government alone can match the human and material resources which this establishment has mustered. The key must be to enlist new elements into the currently unequal contest…."

The next section of the book identifies virtually every Central America group in the United States, including the names of their directors, addresses, phone numbers, types of activity and, if available, sources of funding. Another segment of the book consists of 15 single-spaced pages of names of activists from various political and religious Central America groups around the country.

A section of the manual titled "Additional Comments" includes a number of descriptions of Central America groups which echo characterizations found both in FBI files and in the publications of a number of activist conservative organizations.

For instance, the report notes of the American Friends Service Committee that it "played a leading role in organization support for armed struggle by leftist guerrilla groups in Central America." The report describes one group called the Coalition Against U.S. Intervention in Central America and the Caribbean as a "front" of the "Soviet-directed Communist Party, USA." Its entry on the Institute for Policy Studies reports that: "IPS fellows and speakers have included members and close friends of a variety of radical organizations, including the Communist Party, USA, the Trotskyite Communist Socialist Workers Party, and the radical Students for a Democratic Society…IPS fellow Saul Landau is well-known as a pro-Castro propagandist." The North American Congress on Latin America (NACLA) was noteworthy, according to the report, for its "dedication to 'anti-imperialism' and the political use of information for openly Marxist-Leninist goals." Even as apparently benign a group as Oxfam, America—a group devoted to the eradication of world hunger, becomes, in the OPD report, a group that "has been working firmly on the side of the revolutionary left in Central America."[20]

Putting aside the question of whether the manual contained FBI material gained through the Flanagan "security breach," the financing and dissemination of such scurrilous characterizations by the U.S. government casts some light on the domestic propaganda apparatus established by the director of the Central Intelligence Agency.

In fact, the source who provided a reporter with the manuscript of the book—and who was, himself, a member of the private contra-support network which reported to Oliver North at the National Security Council—hinted strongly that the book may have been actually compiled as a handbook for perpetrators of break-ins at Central America organizations.[21]

Perry, in a brief phone conversation, defended the book as a legitimate survey of public political opinion. Ultimately, questions about the book's sources of information, as well as its intended uses, come down to bare speculation.

Whatever happened to eradicate Flanagan's chronic financial problems three months before he lost the documents—as well as the fate of the documents themselves—will probably never be known.[22]

What is known is that the period of the book's compilation—beginning late in 1984—marked the beginning of a terrorizing and infuriating string of break-ins, death threats, ransacking of offices, thefts of files, torching of homes and abductions of activists that marked the second and most covert phase of the assault during the administration of Ronald Reagan on groups of citizens who found the President's Central America policies repugnant to their own conception of the role of the United States as a vanguard of democracy.

Giving the Lie to the Polygraph

By the late spring of 1984, the counter-terrorism unit in the FBI's Dallas Field Office—the FBI's Office of Origin for the entire CISPES investigation—was beginning to fall apart.

Shortly after Flanagan was ordered to go to Washington for questioning about his loss of the documents, as well as his badge and gun, Varelli received a call from Special Agent Sal Escobedo. Escobedo, who was assigned to the San Antonio office, was flying to Dallas and wanted to have dinner with Varelli. When he learned that Varelli had originals of FBI and CIA teletypes in his home, his jaw dropped. He told Varelli he had to return the material to Tom Kelly, the Special Agent in Charge of the Dallas office. When Varelli called Kelly, he and Drew Clark, another FBI agent in Dallas, drove to Varelli's apartment.[23]

When Clark saw the classified, top-secret documents, he flew into a rage. Varelli had no right to retain such sensitive material at home, he said. But Varelli told him he had taken the material home to work on at

Flanagan's order. At that point, Kelly slammed his fist down on the table: "I told Parks Stearns to keep an eye on Flanagan. I told him to keep him on a leash, damnit!" Stearns, at the time, was the Assistant Special Agent in Charge of the Dallas office.

As their anger drained away, both men grew very quiet. They said that what Flanagan had done was embarrassing—even humiliating—to the FBI. They lamented the breach which could cost the FBI four years of work. And they told Varelli that, except for the documents which they were removing, to destroy every bit of evidence that could link him to the Bureau. The following day, Kelly called Varelli to tell him that Flanagan had flunked his polygraph exam in Washington. "Dan is no longer with the FBI," Kelly told Varelli, adding that in the middle of his lie-detector test, Flanagan interrupted the questioner and said that Varelli's account was true.

Meanwhile, Varelli had become increasingly concerned about the upcoming Republican National Convention which was scheduled to be held in Dallas that August. After one of his right-wing contacts had given Varelli a book on the Kennedy assassination, Varelli was struck by a number of peculiar events that had preceded the murder of the young president. And he was becoming concerned by some uncanny parallels he detected in 1984. For one thing, Varelli had on several occasions told Flanagan and Davenport that he wanted to alert the Secret Service that CISPES was planning to disrupt the convention. While the group's plans were not yet formulated, it was clear to Varelli that, at the very least, they were planning to block the President's motorcade and spray red paint on his limousine to draw attention to the atrocities in El Salvador. But both Flanagan and Davenport had blocked Varelli's attempts to reach the Secret Service at every turn.[24]

Varelli at first accepted the fact that the FBI was trying to conceal Flanagan's security breach. But, since one of the briefcases he lost had contained the security codes for the protection of President Reagan at the convention, Varelli felt strongly the Secret Service should be notified of Flanagan's loss. His fear was increased by a flow of teletypes warning the office that the CIA was concerned that a Libyan or Iranian hit squad might attempt to assassinate the president. On top of that, some 200 rocket launchers had recently been stolen from the National Guard Armory in Austin, Texas.

To Varelli's mind, it would be duck soup for a Libyan or Iranian to infiltrate CISPES. Then, piggybacking on the plan of CISPES leaders to block the President's limousine, they would have had a clear window of opportunity to fire a mortar at the President's car during such a disruption. This the Secret Service had to know.[25]

But before Varelli would be permitted to talk to the Secret Service, he would have to undergo an FBI lie-detector test himself. On June 7, Varelli met with two FBI agents in the Double Tree Hotel in Dallas. In a room, one wall of which was covered by a mirror, Varelli sat down to answer the examiner's questions. One set of questions dealt with whether Varelli had approached a mercenary in the Dallas area about a contract to assassinate Jose Duarte, the president of El Salvador. Varelli laughed and told the examiner that the man had approached him in 1981 and that, moreover, he had made a complete report about the incident to Flanagan. He, himself, Varelli emphasized, had no interest in seeing Duarte assassinated. But when the examiner asked who had raised the subject on a second occasion—Varelli or the mercenary—Varelli conceded he could not recall. The examiner noted that Varelli had failed that question.[26]

The examiner then asked Varelli two more sets of questions, all of which dealt with his activities for the FBI. He asked whether Varelli had been in contact with foreign agents, whether he had sold or given sensitive information to the KGB, who else knew he worked for the Bureau. To all these questions, Varelli answered straightforwardly. The examiner noted in his report that Varelli had answered all these questions without deception. Toward the end of the long session, the examiner told Varelli: "Confess. We know you're lying. You'll rot in jail anyway, so you might as well confess."[27]

The high-strung Varelli became terribly agitated. He jumped up and tore the wires off his body. He threw a pile of papers at the examiner and told him to go to hell. At one point, he picked up his gun and told the examiner that this kind of harassment could provoke him to an act of violence. At that point, the examiner apologized. Extending his hand, he told Varelli: "You did just fine. Congratulations. You've passed with flying colors."

Several weeks later, the examiner would report to Washington that, with the exception of one question about the second 1981 conversation about Duarte, Varelli had shown no deceptions in any of his responses.[28] The following month, the FBI's technical review team declared that: "A technical review of the polygraph examination...of Frank Varelli on 6/7/84 has been completed. This review disclosed that the examination is satisfactory in all aspects and review personnel concur with the results of the examination."[29]

Two months later, after meeting with the Secret Service and outlining his concerns,[30] Varelli quit the FBI—broke, disillusioned and determined to avenge his wounded Salvadoran honor. The extent to which that honor had been brought into question by the FBI would not become clear until 1988—when William Sessions, the new Director of the Bureau, told Congress that the entire CISPES investigation had been a terrible mistake—and that it was all the fault of one Frank Varelli.

In the summer and fall of 1984, the Dallas office sent a number of teletypes to headquarters requesting that the FBI change the Office of Origin to Washington, noting that as far as the investigation of CISPES nationwide, "Dallas no longer has coverage in this area."[31]

It was not until three years later—when Varelli attempted to go public with allegations of FBI misdeeds before a Congressional committee in 1987—that someone at FBI headquarters retroactively decided that he had not told the truth to the examiner.[32]

When Congressional staff members began to question FBI officials about Varelli's allegations, they were shown the recently-altered polygraph results, and warned not to trust Varelli because he had flunked the lie-detector. Said Daniel Alcorn, Varelli's attorney who had won release of his FBI files: "This is a glaring attempt by the Bureau to rewrite history three years after the fact."[33]

The damage, however, had already been done. Varelli's credibility was in shambles. As far as Congressional investigators knew, he had failed his polygraph exam and that was reason enough to dismiss everything he had to say.[34]

The FBI and Oliver North's "Private Network"

It was in the spring of 1984, around the time that Special Agent Dan Flanagan lost two briefcases full of top-secret FBI documents, that the attention of other elements of the federal intelligence bureaucracy began to focus on the growing movement in opposition to President Reagan's policies in Central America.

And over the next two years—between early 1984 and the summer of 1986—a series of secret contacts took place between Oliver North and officials of the FBI—that would give the lie to the contention of William Webster and his number two man, Oliver Revell, that the Bureau's campaign against dissenting citizens was strictly a non-political matter of counter-terrorism and foreign counter-intelligence.

According to a number of documents, as well as testimony given to the Iran-Contra Committee, a number of contacts between North and the Bureau appear to have been blatantly political in nature. One strand of a covert NSC-FBI operation which concealed the illegal contra supply effort apparently reached the office of Vice President George Bush. Documents involving a second strand of that relationship, aimed specifically at discrediting Jack Terrell, a former member of the contra supply team who turned "whistleblower," reached no less a personage than President Reagan himself.

The Congressional Burial of Rex 84

Toward the end of 1983, it was becoming clear to Administration leaders that a growing number of Congressional representatives were becoming disenchanted with the Administration's Nicaragua policies, which had actually dated back to 1981 when William Casey had granted

CIA approval for training of the Nicaraguan rebels by members of the Argentine military. A number of legislators were becoming similarly skeptical of the Administration's growing commitment of military aid to El Salvador.

Around the same time that the Office of Public Diplomacy was gearing up for its CIA-inspired covert disinformation and propaganda campaign, Lt. Col. Oliver North was working with officials of the Federal Emergency Management Agency—an obscure agency which had traditionally overseen relief planning for disasters—to draw up a secret contingency plan to surveil political dissenters and to arrange for the detention of hundreds of thousands of undocumented aliens in case of an unspecified national emergency. The plan, part of which was code-named Rex 84, called for the suspension of the Constitution under a number of scenarios, including a U.S. invasion of Nicaragua.

The strongest objection to the plan within the administration came from William French Smith, at the time President Reagan's Attorney General. In a strongly worded letter to National Security Adviser Robert MacFarlane in August 1984, Smith wrote: "I believe the role assigned to the Federal Emergency Management Agency in the revised Executive Order exceeds its proper function as a coordinating agency for emergency preparedness." According to *Miami Herald* reporter Alfonso Chardy, Smith's letter added: "The [Justice] Department and others have repeatedly raised serious policy and legal objections to the creation of an 'emergency czar' role for FEMA."[1]

The plan, which was modeled after a plan that Reagan and Edwin Meese had developed in California to deal with black activists, anti-war protesters and members of the student Free Speech Movement, involved the cooperation of a number of agencies, including the Immigration and Naturalization Service which took steps to establish a network of detention centers capable of holding thousands of undocumented aliens.

The number of U.S. activists targeted by the preliminary plans for Rex 84 was never disclosed. But in addition to groups opposing United States policies in Central America, the FEMA plan reportedly included environmental activists, opponents of nuclear energy and refugee assistance activists. In addition, the plan reportedly called for the establishment of 50 State Defense Forces, to be composed of members of local law enforcement and military reserve agencies, who would implement the plan at a local level.[2]

The fate of Rex 84 has never been definitively explained. Nor has the plan's development been thoroughly explored. During the Iran-Contra hearings in the summer of 1987, Rep. Jack Brooks (D-Tex.) attempted to raise the issue during an open session of the committee during the appearance of Oliver North.

Brooks: "Col. North, in your work at the NSC, were you not assigned, at one time, to work on plans for the continuity of government in the event of a major disaster?"

Sen. Daniel Inouye (Co-chair): "I believe that question touches upon a highly sensitive and classified area so may I request that you not touch upon that."

Brooks: "I was particularly concerned, Mr. Chairman, because I read in the Miami papers and several others that there had been a plan developed, by that same agency, a contingency plan in the event of an emergency that would suspend the American Constitution. And I was deeply concerned about it and wondered if that was the area in which [North] had worked. I believe that it was, and I wanted to get his confirmation."

Inouye: "May I most respectfully request that that matter not be touched upon at this stage. If we wish to get into this, I'm certain arrangements can be made for an executive session."[3]

That was the beginning and the end of any Congressional discussion of the plan. Apparently, there was no follow-up executive session in which committee members tried to learn just how extensive and well-developed was this plan to surveil and imprison large numbers of citizens and refugees who might object to the United States invading Nicaragua or becoming embroiled in armed hostilities in other parts of the world. But, as researcher Diana Reynolds and others have noted, "It is clear that the FEMA contingency plans to round up political dissenters was related to the FBI's investigation of political dissidents."[4]

A Private Eye of the Private Network

In the summer of 1984, North was reassigned from domestic crisis planning to managing the covert and largely privatized effort to support the Nicaraguan contras. But while his new role emphasized the coordination of the Nicaragua initiative, it is clear that North still kept his eye on domestic developments. His relationship with Philip Mabry, a private investigator in Fort Worth, Texas, is a case in point.

In late 1983, Mabry, a former CIA contract agent who works as a security consultant in the Fort Worth area, wrote to Edwin Meese that he wanted to help the cause of the "freedom fighters" in Nicaragua. Meese responded with a letter advising Mabry that his name had been given to the "appropriate people." Shortly thereafter, Mabry said, Meese's secretary, Dee Kuhn, put him in touch with Wilma Hall, a secretary at the National Security Council who, in turn, put him in contact with North. Her daughter, Fawn, had recently begun a job as North's secretary. At North's encouragement, Mabry set up a small organization called Americans for Human Rights and Social Justice. And while the group, which consisted of the 49-year-old Mabry and his associate, Randy Pearce, a young, entrepreneurial auto mechanic, operated on a shoestring budget, it was quite successful in gaining access to local newspapers and television stations to counter the growing demonstrations against United States policies in Central America.[5]

(Mabry gained inadvertent notoriety during the Tower Commission hearings when the commission unveiled a hand-drawn diagram of a number of interlocking private foundations and conservative organizations involved in the contra support operation. While the commission initially attributed the schematic to North, it was later learned that the diagram was made by Mabry on a memo which later turned up in North's files.)

In a series of interviews, the short, balding, pipe-smoking South Carolina native—whose telephone bills show more than 40 calls to North's NSC office in 1984 and 1985, and whose name pops up frequently in North's diaries[6]—explained that North gave him a list of individuals and organizations opposed to U.S. policies in Central America. "Ollie suggested to me very strongly —I think his exact words were, 'A good way to get these assholes is to let the FBI check them out. This list includes pro-Marxists, communists, traitors.'" Mabry said that North instructed him to write to the FBI, requesting that the Bureau investigate the groups—and asked Mabry to arrange for a number of other conservative activists to send similar letters to the FBI all citing the names of the same liberal and left-wing activists and groups. "Ollie explained that if the Bureau got a bunch of letters from different sources all citing the same people, that would be enough for the FBI to have a legal mandate to investigate those groups," Mabry recounted.[7]

Writing under the letterhead of his organization, Americans for Human Rights and Social Justice, Mabry addressed his letter to William Webster, then FBI director. In the letter, Mabry wrote: "In the interest of justice...and our U.S. National Security, we respectfully request an investigation of the following protest groups and individuals that are in our opinion...pro-marxist and...a threat to our national security and vital interest in [Central America.]"[8]

The groups cited in the list included the National Network in Solidarity with the Nicaraguan People, the Nicaragua Exchange Office, the Central America Peace Campaign, the Inter-Religious Task Force on Central America. The individuals Mabry cited in the letter include Robert White, former U.S. Ambassador to El Salvador; Elaine and Gene Lantz (the same activists Varelli cultivated in order to obtain access to Lantz's printing press); and Hollywood personalities Arthur Gorson, Sean Daniel, Michael Douglas, Martin Sheen, Vonetta McGee, Susan Anspach and Susan Sarandon. (Sarandon was active in a group called Madre, which provides literacy, parenting and nutrition assistance to poor women, especially in Central America. The group suffered two mysterious break-ins several years later.) In addition, Mabry listed 10 members of Congress, including former Speaker Jim Wright, who had signed a conciliatory letter that year to Nicaraguan leader Daniel Ortega.

On December 27, 1984, Mabry's letter received a response from none other than Buck Revell, at the time assistant director of the FBI's criminal division. Revell assured Mabry that "your concerns and comments will be carefully reviewed."[9] Reflecting on the response, Mabry said later that North must have known at the time about the FBI's probe of Central America groups. "It's very strange that Revell, himself, responded to my letter. He had to be aware that it was coming in. Otherwise, the letter would have been answered by a clerk, not an assistant director of the Bureau."

Mabry sent copies of his FBI letter—together with the list of groups and individuals to be targeted—to about a dozen other conservative organizations. Among others, he wrote to J. Michael Waller, whose reports subsequently turned up in the FBI files where they were used, presumably, to build the case against CISPES as a terrorist organization.[10]

In addition Mabry wrote to his long-time friend, Linda Guell, who was executive director of Western Goals, as well as to CAUSA, a political arm of the Rev. Sun Myung Moon's organization. (A photocopy of a 1985 check for $1,000 indicates that the Moon organization helped Mabry bankroll his small, pro-contra organization in Fort Worth.)[11]

Mabry said that, at North's request, he monitored the activities of a number of Central America groups. A 1985 list in Mabry's possession—under the heading of "Liberal Pro-Nico Groups Monitored for North & State"—includes CISPES, the Christic Institute, the International Center for Development Policy, the Inter-Religious Task Force on Central America, New El Salvador Today, the Nicaragua Network, the Fort Worth Nuclear Freeze Campaign, the Ft. Worth Alliance for Justice, the Ft. Worth TCU Students for a Democratic South Africa, St. Phillips Presbyterian Church (Sanctuary), Casa Oscar Romero, Committee of Concern for Central America, National Network in Solidarity with the Nicaraguan

People and others. "I also photographed demonstrations in front of the Federal Building in Fort Worth and got on the mailing lists of some 30 or 40 organizations. Much of that material I forwarded to Fawn Hall," Mabry said. "I never asked Ollie what he did with these photos and other material, and he never volunteered any information to me except to tell me to keep up the good work," Mabry recalled. At one point, Mabry was asked by another member of the North network if he would be willing to consider a break-in at the Christic Institute. But he stressed that he wanted no part of any illegal activities.[12]

In the spring of 1985, just before a major Congressional vote on contra aid, Mabry received the following letter on National Security Council stationary.

"Dear Phil and Randy: Just wanted to drop a note for 'good luck' before the vote. We are, as always, grateful for the work you do to communicate the President's policy in Central America. We are all working tirelessly to educate the American people on why it is so important to help the Nicaraguan Freedom Fighters.

"There are many people who believe in the cause of freedom and democracy, but far fewer who are willing to act to support it. Your dedication and ambition are much appreciated....

"Thank You—God bless you! Fawn"[13]

The FBI and Iran-Contra

It is not known how the FBI used Mabry's letters (or letters sent to the Bureau from other groups at Mabry's request) asking the Bureau to investigate members of Congress as well as Central America political activists. But it is clear from Mabry's narrative and documents that the FBI was receiving encouragement, if not direct support, from private groups in Oliver North's contra support network.

Mabry said he never heard any more from the FBI after the first response from Revell. But he said he sent copies of Revell's response to North, to Otto Reich, at the Office of Public Diplomacy, and also to Bill Casey. "When Ollie saw that, he said it was super. He was very pleased I had gotten the other groups to write in to the Feebies," Mabry added.

What did become clear during the Iran-Contra hearings was Revell's familiarity with Mabry. In October 1986, when the Sandinistas shot down a contra supply plane and captured Eugene Hasenfus, there was talk of Mabry going to Nicaragua to arrange to get Hasenfus released. The plan never materialized. But during Revell's deposition before the Iran-Contra committee, one staff member asked him about an October memo captioned: "RE: PHIL MABRY." Revell noted that the document, which was routed to the FBI's Floyd Clarke, bore a notation from another FBI official, Bob Ricks, who wrote: "Floyd, the real problem would be the potential discovery if a special prosecutor is appointed." Revell said he asked Ricks what the notation meant. Ricks' response, according to Revell, was: "If Oliver North became the subject of an independent counsel investigation, then it might reveal what is blacked out here, which is the method and source of intelligence."

Q: "And this is on the Mabry matter?"

Revell: "This is where the information came from."[14]

The documents appear to show that the then-Vice President was much more knowledgeable than he ever admitted about the private network of Oliver North. Bush's inclusion in the North "loop" may also have been known, as well, to William Webster, former director of the FBI, and a successor to both Bush and Casey as Director of Central Intelligence.[15] As Revell pointed out to the Iran-Contra investigators, the airtel referring to sources of intelligence whose potential exposure concerned FBI officials bore not his initials but those of Webster.

The FBI-NSC Connection

While the documentary evidence linking North to the FBI's sweep of Central America groups is more suggestive than conclusive, it is clear that the former lieutenant-colonel used the FBI to go after Administration critics who were threatening to expose the illegal contra support operation he coordinated. In fact, a body of clues points to a back-channel relationship between the NSC and the Bureau far broader than anyone in Congress or the FBI has acknowledged.

For one example, Allan Bruce Hemmings, a 17-year CIA official, has said that the FBI knew about the Administration's secret weapons shipments to Iran as early as the fall of 1985. But the Bureau never undertook an investigation based on that information.[16] Hemmings added that FBI agent Randall Boone in fact called the CIA to ask if an American airplane, spotted in the Iranian city of Tabriz in October 1985, was an Agency plane. Boone was told the plane might be part of a "White House operation" and, as a result, he never pursued the matter—despite the fact that it was his job to investigate violations of export control laws, of which the arms shipments to Iran were a flagrant example.[17]

Hemmings, who served as a CIA contact person for the FBI, added that he received information from the FBI about U.S. shipments to Iran through 1986, including information on the visit in May 1986 of North and National Security Adviser Robert MacFarlane to Iran.[18]

On the other front of the Iran-Contra scandal, FBI documents indicate that the Bureau was aware of the illegal transport of weapons to the Nicaraguan contras as early as the fall of 1984. In July of 1985, moreover, North told Special Agent James Kramarsic of his activities in helping arm the contras—during a period when such activity had been forbidden by act of Congress. (The FBI subsequently explained that that particular piece of information never got to Headquarters because of a foul-up with a teletype machine over which the material was allegedly transmitted to FBI Headquarters.)[19]

FBI documents secured by attorney John Mattes on behalf of his client Jack Terrell indicate that the FBI conducted interviews with key players involved in contra training and weapons-supply operations in October and November of 1984 and in January and February of 1985. By April of 1986, the documents show, the FBI had obtained detailed statements from at least 12 active participants on the illegal contra supply operation and its ties to the National Security Council.[20]

Ollie's Enemies

There are indications, as well, that the FBI also cooperated with North in his efforts to spy on and sabotage the work of domestic critics who were trying to unravel the cloak of secrecy surrounding his operations.

The FBI's Revell, for instance, told a Congressional committee that North had asked him to order the FBI to investigate the funding sources behind a suit brought by two journalists, Martha Honey and Tony Avirgan, who were being represented by the Christic Institute in a lawsuit against members of North's private network. But, Revell added: "I told [North] that is what the FBI didn't do."[21]

Revell's response, however, was less than candid. The relationship between North and the FBI was far more extensive than Revell acknowledged. And it did involve, among other efforts, an FBI check on Daniel Sheehan, the lead attorney for the Christic Institute, as well as the surveillance of Honey and Avirgan, the plaintiffs in the Christic lawsuit. On another front, the FBI also assisted North in his efforts to neutralize Jack Terrell, the former member of the private contra operation who turned whistleblower.

A key to the relationship between North and the FBI lies in a 14-month series of contacts by phone and in person between North and

Special Agent David Beisner, an FBI foreign counter-intelligence agent assigned to the same Washington Field Office that was involved in the first CISPES investigation and that was central to the Capitol bombing investigation in which Varelli participated.[22]

In mid-May 1985, according to North's calendar, he had lunch with Beisner, who had recently been reassigned from a surveillance operation involving Vietnamese refugees to matters involving Central America.

A cryptic notation in North's notebook for May 8, 1985 indicates that his approach to the FBI may have involved Casey. The notation reads: "11:10 talk to Beisner—recontract formalities—direct to DCI. Lunch May 14." It is unclear whether Beisner, himself, learned of North's role in the illegal contra-support operation during those conversations. But, shortly after meeting with North, Beisner put North in touch with a second FBI agent, James Kramarsic, who testified that North did tell him about his activities in violation of the Boland Amendment.[23]

In the spring of 1986, Beisner began to meet with Jack Terrell to try to get Terrell to gather intelligence on liberal activists in the Washington area.

Several months earlier, Terrell had provided the FBI with copies of the notes of conversations between Honey and Avirgan and their confidential sources in Central America who alerted them to the alleged role of narcotics traffickers in the secret contra supply apparatus. Those notes were later released, under a Freedom of Information Request, from the FBI's Washington Field Office.[24]

By the time Beisner approached him, Terrell, who had previously worked as an informant for the FBI's New Orleans office, had become disillusioned with the secret contra aid apparatus and had begun to work with investigators at the International Center for Development Policy, a liberal think tank, to unearth details of the roles of the NSC and the CIA in the illegal contra operation.

Terrell recalled that Beisner asked him to "obtain copies of...all files of funders and information from [the Center] to give to the FBI." Through an FBI spokesman, Beisner confirmed to journalist Jeffrey McConnell that he had encouraged Terrell to obtain computer disks containing the names of donors to the Center, which was headed by former ambassador Robert White. That office would become, in the fall of 1986, the target of yet another unsolved break-in. Staff members at the Center, including Terrell, were also working with the staff of Sen. John Kerry (D-Mass.), which was investigating the involvement of narcotics traffickers in the contra supply network.

Beisner told Congressional investigators that he spoke with North on numerous occasions in 1985 and 1986. Shortly after his meeting with North in May 1986, Beisner requested FBI and CIA checks on Sheehan, the Christic Institute attorney who was representing Avirgan and Honey. A June 2, 1986, notation in North's calendar, moreover, refers to a conversation with Beisner and bears the notation: "Looking at what can be done to expand surveillance activity of Avirgan and Honey."

The following month, after learning of Terrell's assistance to liberal and left-wing groups, North told Revell that Terrell might be involved in a plot to assassinate President Reagan. Revell assigned the case to Beisner, among others. But it appears fairly clear that the investigation of Terrell as a possible presidential assassin was not taken at all seriously inside or outside the FBI. For one thing, the FBI's questioning of Terrell involved material such as a book proposal by Terrell and accounts of his work with the left-wing and liberal watchdog groups, according to Terrell's attorney, John Mattes. The operation resembled an attempt to intimidate Terrell and take pressure off the contra operation much more than one designed to protect the President.

In a memo for President Reagan, prepared by North and forwarded over the signature of National Security Adviser John Poindexter, Terrell was described, in July 1986, as: "An active participant in the disinformation/active measures campaign against the [contras]. Terrell has appeared on various television 'documentaries' alleging corruption, human rights abuses, drug running, arms smuggling and assassination attempts by the [contras] and their supporters. Terrell is also believed to be involved with various Congressional staffs in preparing for hearings and inquiries regarding the role of U.S. Government officials in illegally supporting the Nicaraguan resistance."

In a subsequent portion of the presidential memorandum, North noted: "The Operations Sub-Group of the Terrorist Incident Working Group has made available to the FBI all information on Mr. Terrell from other U.S. Government agencies...The FBI is currently consolidating this information for their investigation.

"The FBI reports that Terrell went to Miami coincident with your visit on Wednesday. The FBI, in concert with the Secret Service, has Terrell under active surveillance. [Next sentence is deleted].

"It is important to note that Terrell has been a principal witness against supporters of the Nicaraguan resistance, both in and outside the U.S. Government. Terrell's accusations have formed the basis of a civil law suit in the U.S. District Court in Miami and his charges are at the center of Senator Kerry's investigation in the Senate Foreign Relations

Committee. Since it is important to protect the knowledge that Terrell is the subject of a criminal investigation, none of those with whom he has been in contact on the Hill have been advised."[25]

With the possible exception of a single deleted sentence, there is no reference to Terrell's threat as a potential assassin, except a note that he was in Miami on the same day as President Reagan. The rest of the memo, as well as several others concerning Terrell, make it clear that, FBI denials aside, the Bureau targeted him for surveillance at North's request because of his potential to expose a secret political operation being run out of the National Security Council.

It was also during this same period of time, the FBI surveilled David McMichael, a former CIA analyst who was also working at the same International Center for Development Policy. McMichael had previously resigned from the Agency because he claimed the CIA was supplying phony intelligence material to the White House to support a claim by the President that the Nicaraguan Sandinista government was providing a substantial flow of weapons to the Salvadoran rebels.[26]

Simultaneous with the Bureau's surveillance of McMichael and Terrell, according to documents released by the Iran-Contra Committee, the FBI also conducted brief investigations of three Congressional opponents of Reagan Central America policies. The Bureau conducted probes in May and June of 1986 of Sen. John Kerry (D-Mass.), Sen. David Durenberger (R-Minn.) and Rep. Lee Hamilton (D-Ind.) to determine whether their opposition to Administration policies in the region was being assisted by intelligence agents of the Nicaraguan government. [27]

Shortly thereafter, Glenn Robinette, a former CIA wiretap specialist who was the security chief of North's "enterprise," met with Terrell to discuss a possible business deal. In reality, Robinette was attempting to learn what Terrell knew about the progress of North's opponents.

That summer, during a meeting with Beisner, Robinette, the former CIA agent, insisted: "I am not a plumber." (The term "plumber," meaning political burglar, was made famous by a group of break-in specialists in the Nixon White House who burgled the Democratic Party's office in the Watergate Hotel as well as the office of the psychiatrist of Daniel Ellsberg, a major figure in the anti-Vietnam War movement.) Later when Revell was questioned by reporters about the Bureau's dealings with North and Robinette, the FBI's executive assistant director conceded that he was concerned, given the involvement of Robinette, "that we had a plumbers' operation on our hands." He added that the concern was significant enough that the FBI was considering giving Robinette to a lie-detector test.[28]

But, for reasons which have never been explained, "all our suspicions were allayed," according to Revell, and the FBI never followed up on an investigation of a possible plumber's operation run out of the White House.

While the Iran-Contra Committee never undertook to explore what linkages may have existed between North and the FBI's massive investigation and harassment of political groups opposed to the President's policies in Nicaragua and El Salvador, an appendix to the Committee's final report, authored by Representatives Peter Rodino, Dante Fascell, Jack Brooks and Louis Stokes, concluded that in the fall of 1986:

"Members of the House Committee on the Judiciary wrote to the Attorney General requesting a preliminary investigation [regarding allegations] that North, Poindexter, Casey and others illegally assisted the contras...Attorneys [in the Justice Department] canvassed the FBI and Customs to determine what investigations involving the contras were pending. Neither the FBI nor Customs revealed their numerous contacts with North in various criminal investigations. It is a question the appropriate committees of Congress should pursue more fully."[29]

Such pursuit never materialized in the rush of Congress to put the half-explored Iran-Contra scandal behind the country.

More to the point, a staff member of the Iran-Contra committee said angrily: "There's one troubling thing about all this. [Former FBI Director] William Webster assured Congress that the FBI had provided an account of all of the Bureau's contacts with North. But the meetings between Beisner and North were not among them."[30]

A final note on the mystery surrounding the relationship between North and the FBI's CISPES investigation. It is documented that Revell sat on several inter-agency committees with North, including the Operations Sub-Group. At one point, Revell was asked whether he had discussed the CISPES investigation with North. He conceded that the CISPES probe would be a topic for coordination by the group, but refused to elaborate, stating only: "We don't comment on specific cases."[31]

"Oh God, Contragate!"

Sometime over the long Thanksgiving weekend in 1986, burglars scrambled over a rooftop next to the International Center for Development Policy in southeast Washington and hurled a brick through a second-floor window at the Center. The Center had been the focus of one of the photographs studied by members of the Capitol Bombing

Task Force in the winter of 1983. Bypassing thousands of dollars worth of computers and other office equipment, they rifled through more than 20 filing cabinets. Papers and files were scattered throughout the three-story building. When an investigating detective from the Washington police arrived on the scene, he said: "This must be political." When he was told the focus of work going on at the Center, he added: "Oh, God. Contragate."[32]

The following week, as the staff sorted through the wreckage of papers, the object of the break-in became clear. While thieves had taken a letter from South Africa's Nelson Mandela, as well as a report by a Korean dissident, the most crucial theft involved a file on Southern Air Transport, a CIA proprietary airline which was involved in the illegal ferrying of weapons to the Nicaraguan contras. Despite the fact that members of the Center were working with a Senate Foreign Relations Subcommittee investigating the illegal arms supply operation and the possible involvement of drug traffickers, the FBI insisted it had no jurisdiction to investigate the break-in. After two months of public pressure, the Bureau reluctantly agreed to investigate the issue of whether the Center's right to petition Congress had been violated.

Some weeks later, a photojournalist who lived next door to the Center called the FBI. The photojournalist, Jeffrey Heimers, told an agent that the day before the break-in, he had spotted three men on the roof of the building next to the Center. The men, he said, wore paramilitary-type outfits with combat boots. When he went up on the roof to question the men, they told him they were thinking of buying the property and wanted to look it over. The photographer said he found both their explanation and their conduct highly suspicious. The agent responded: "Don't take this too seriously. This particular break-in may have been political, but I wouldn't make any connection between it and all the other break-ins at political groups that are being reported. Between you and me, most of those break-ins are self-inflicted."[33]

But apparently the FBI felt the same way about the burglary at the Center. As Lindsay Mattison, executive director of the Center, subsequently told a Congressional committee, the FBI clearly did not dig in any meaningful way to solve the mysterious break-in. "Press reports which say the Bureau is investigating our break-in are not accurate," he said.[34]

An Epidemic of Terrorism: Continued

In February 1985, a woman approached the Rev. Donovan Cook, pastor of the University Baptist Church in Seattle. The woman, who said she had been very moved by a talk given by a Salvadoran refugee, offered Cook the birth certificate of her deceased son, telling him he could use it to help a Salvadoran refugee gain entry into the U.S. Cook, concerned about the illegal nature of the offer, discontinued the conversation. Several weeks later, a Latin man, with small tears tattooed under his left eye, entered Cook's office and offered him counterfeit birth certificates and Social Security cards. Again, Cook, who had recently been named as an unindicted co-conspirator in the trial of eleven Sanctuary movement workers, declined to avail himself of the illegal opportunity to help refugees.

In July 1985, the offices of Cook's church were broken into. While nothing of value was taken, the keys to the rooms where six Central American refugees were staying were taken. The intruders also examined legal files, as well as a file containing a list of supporters of the church's Sanctuary effort. Cook said that shortly before the break-in, church workers observed a man in a parking lot across the street carrying a walkie-talkie. When Cook approached the man, he left. Following several more incidents of intimidation, including the painting of swastikas on the church's doors and the smashing of a stained-glass window, Cook received a letter from the company that insured the church, stating: "There is clearly an increase in hazard to our insured's property caused directly by their involvement in the [Sanctuary] movement and by their providing sanctuary to refugees...As long as our insured allows their premises to be used as a sanctuary to the refugees, the increase in hazard will exist. As an insurance company, we cannot accept this exposure.

Only if the insured agrees to do away with the exposure now and in the future will we be able to continue insuring them..."

In retrospect, Cook said, the break-in and several other harrowing experiences "had a chilling effect on the congregation. But it also had the consequence of deepening our commitment. But initially it was very chilling. It created suspicion among the congregation. It put an edge on our conversations. During the period of 1985 and 1986, it was pretty tough around here."[1]

Unknown to Cook, his experiences in Seattle had been foreshadowed by eerily similar events at University Lutheran Chapel in Berkeley, California.

According to Rev. Gustav Schultz, a provincial bishop of the church, in January a woman called the church to offer the Social Security card and birth certificate of her deceased husband for use by Central American refugees. Shultz, fearing entrapment, declined the illegal offer. The following month, a Hispanic man, dressed in a t-shirt and leather vest, with teardrops tattooed under his left eye, offered a member of Shultz's congregation blank birth certificates to help the refugees. Again Schultz declined. Then, on the evening of March 8, intruders entered the church, rifled the church's files, and attempted unsuccessfully to enter the pastor's study and other offices on the church's second floor. Nothing of value was taken during the break-in. Schultz, who testified about the incidents at a 1987 Congressional hearing, introduced himself by noting: "I am the pastor of the University Lutheran Chapel in Berkeley, California...I am also the chairperson of the National Sanctuary Defense Fund and a founder of the East Bay Sanctuary Covenant. All of the above organizations have been involved in providing advocacy, protection and support to Central American refugees or in providing legal defense for members of religious groups who do provide such support to refugees. The other thing that the above groups have in common is that they have all experienced break-ins at their offices..."[2]

In June of 1985, the staff of the Los Angeles office of Amnesty International discovered a list of 1,500 donors missing from their files. The list profiled Amnesty "celebrity" supporters, many of whom were active in Central America issues.[3]

In September 1985, the office of David Myers, a Jesuit priest who also works as an attorney on political asylum cases, was burglarized. A file box marked "cases on appeal" was missing. Myers said he suspected the break-in was done with the cooperation of one or more federal agencies, but added he had no proof of such involvement. [4]

On October 25, 1985, the office of the Central America Refugee Project in the American Baptist Church in Phoenix was broken into on two occasions over one weekend. Attorney Susan Giersbach, who worked on refugee immigration cases in the church, noted that during the initial break-in, an intruder pried away several wrought iron bars, breaking a window and gaining access to the office. Files, some smeared with blood, were strewn about the room. Phone logs and client files appear to have been copied. During the second break-in, a number of files, some of them containing the names of undocumented aliens seeking legal help, were examined. Tellingly, an envelope containing $500 for bond money was examined—but not stolen.[5]

The following month, Michael Lent, the national program coordinator for CISPES, received a series of strange phone calls. Each time he answered the phone, the person on the other end hung up. Then, toward the end of November, his apartment was broken into. The thieves did not touch $160 in cash, an airline ticket or a television set. But the intruders opened a suitcase full of CISPES documents and other files and scattered papers around the apartment.[6]

Around the same time, CISPES members in Florida and New Orleans reported receiving death threats—while a Tennessee chapter of CISPES learned that it had been infiltrated by members of Civilian Military Assistance, an Alabama-based mercenary group that later worked for Oliver North in a covert program to train the Nicaraguan contras. Several months earlier, a man identifying himself as Jim Brockey volunteered his services to CISPES in Washington, offering to do artwork for the group's publications and newsletters. When a CISPES staff member called the artist's apartment, the call was answered by a man who said: "Intelligence Division, Metropolitan police."[7]

In November 1985, a volunteer at St. Williams Catholic Church in Louisville, Ky., entered the church to find that the apartment of the Rev. James Flynn in the church's rectory had been entered. Drawers were opened, a stack of slides from Nicaragua lay scattered around the room, and files were in disarray. The intruders left a letter from a Salvadoran refugee applying for sanctuary on top of the desk under a lamp, where it had apparently been photographed. But the intruders did not take either an electric typewriter or some cash which had been left on top of the desk. Fr. Flynn had been especially visible in the Louisville area due to his speaking and his placing of op-ed pieces critical of U.S. policies in Central America.[8]

The following month, intruders used an electric saw to make three large holes in a wall of the Pico Rivera Methodist Church in California.

Files were rifled, desks searched and the church's membership list and tax records examined.[9]

In April 1986, two instructors at the Massachusetts College of Art were preparing for a cultural exchange program with Nicaraguan artists. One evening, the Brookline, Mass., home of Dana Moser, an instructor at the college, was broken into. While his filing cabinets were rifled, the intruders did not touch a collection of expensive video and film equipment. Rachel Weiss, coordinator of the college's visiting artist program who shared the apartment with Moser, noted that a number of computer disks were stolen as well as a beeper used to retrieve messages from her answering machine.[10]

The following month, the offices of the North American Congress on Latin America, located on 19th Street in Manhattan, were burglarized and the office ransacked. File cabinets were opened and the files of the group's Central America research staff were examined and scattered about. Electronic typewriters, calculators and portable computers were untouched. At the time, the liberal research organization was producing a report on Oliver North's coordination of a private network supporting the contras.[11]

That summer, in August 1986, a fire broke out in the home of Mary K. Espinoza, one of the defendants in the Sanctuary trial. Espinoza was working at the Sacred Heart Church in Nogales, Ariz., when the fire was detected. By the time firemen arrived, the entire house had been burned. Only the four walls remained intact. According to fire investigators, the fire was set by intruders who ignited the living room sofa. The family dog—a boxer named Macho—was found dead nearby. An autopsy performed on the dog revealed it had been poisoned. One neighbor said she saw two men in the home shortly before the fire. Both men wore hunting shirts. One wore khaki pants and a camouflage cap—the uniforms of a mercenary group that was working both for the Nicaraguan contras and to help the Border Patrol by harassing Mexicans who they found entering the country illegally. In the ensuing year, Espinoza's apartment was broken into two more times. Drawers and files were left open, while a television set and a VCR were left untouched.[12]

On October 7, and again on Oct 13, 1986, the office of Stephen Brannon, the director of the Western States Legal Foundation who is also a priest of the St. Edmund's Episcopal Church in Pacifica, California, was broken into. The only items disturbed in both instances were Brannon's files. Two storage boxes under his desk containing legal files were opened and disturbed. In addition to church files, Brannon's files on Central America political asylum cases and on cases involving anti-nuclear weapons protesters were disturbed. Cash, left on the desk, was undisturbed. Three months later, Brannon's office was burglarized again.[13]

In February 1987, the Berkeley, California, home of David Cunningham was invaded while he slept. The thief took a box of three-by-five index cards listing the phone numbers and addresses of members of the Contragate Action Committee of which Cunningham was an organizer. They left behind $4,000 worth of computer and stereo equipment. Two days later, the Oakland home of Bob Mandel, a colleague of Cunningham's, was also the target of a break-in. Burglars climbed a fire escape up to Mandel's third floor apartment. They were frightened away when a tenant on the floor below began to yell at them. The investigating officer said the attempted break looked like the work of government operatives. At the time, the Contragate Action Committee was organizing a protest against the use of a local airport by Southern Air Transport, a CIA proprietary airline which was used to ferry arms to the Nicaraguan contras.[14]

The burglaries at the Contragate Action group were a prelude to a much more frightening string of episodes to the south.

On April 1, 1987, the office of the Interfaith Peace Coalition in San Jose was broken into. Around noon, a staff member discovered the office door ajar. Inside, intruders had rifled files and strewn them around the room. Other files had been stuffed back into filing cabinets in a helter skelter manner, according to Catherine Burke of the Coalition, who added that the intruders had examined every file in the office. She added that the burglars ripped a telephone off the wall. The investigating officer told members of the Coalition it was probably the work of kids. When they raised their concern about political motivations, the officer told them they had been watching too much television. He refused to search for fingerprints, she added.[15]

That April, four cars belonging to CISPES members in Los Angeles were broken into or vandalized. In early April, the car of Hugh Byrne was vandalized while it was parked outside his home. The back window was smashed. But nothing appeared to have been removed. Byrne said that it was the fourth time his car had been vandalized.[16]

The same weekend, the car of a CISPES attorney, Victor Rios, was broken into. Rios parked his car outside his home around midnight. The next morning, he found that the door handles had been broken. His glove compartment had been opened and papers spread all over the car. "There's no question these break-ins are political. It's far too coincidental for four people to have their cars broken into in so short a time in completely different locations around the city. It's hard to know whether it's being done by the police, by state or federal agents, or by vigilantes in contact with government agencies. But it's clear that all of us were followed before the break-ins. There's little question in my mind these are connected with official agencies."[17]

Shortly after the break-ins at Byrne's and Rios' cars, the Center for Constitutional Rights, which had set up a hotline to monitor and verify complaints of political harassment, received a letter from three employees of a San Francisco travel agency, Trips Out Travel. The authors of the letter, Bury Willes, Tina Chan and Allen Thatcher, noted that: "We have had three unusual break-ins in the last six months. Although the building has heavy security, our office has been entered each time. Last week, thieves broke into the office and totally destroyed our safe. Police told us the burglary was the work of real professionals. What is so unusual is that they stole our files of clients who have traveled to Nicaragua and El Salvador—and left $1,500 in cash outside the safe. Since we have been working with Central America organizations, we feel there is a connection between the break-ins and the files."[18]

The Washington-based Coalition for a New Foreign and Military Policy had been an active opponent of Reagan Administration Central America policies since 1981, the year in which Varelli had identified the group to Villacorta at the Salvadoran National Guard. For six months, beginning in October 1986, and culminating at the end of the following April, David Reed, director of the Coalition, had worked ceaselessly to put together one of the largest demonstrations of the decade in opposition to those policies. Working with religious activists, labor organizers, anti-apartheid groups and a host of Central America organizations, Reed was frantic with last minute preparations for the march in Washington. During the last week of preparation, he was annoyed that his telephone had gone dead three or four times. He had noted a crew of repairmen working at the end of his block. Then, on April 27, the Thursday night before the march, Reed went to his garage to find that one of his tires had been slashed. Another organizer, Stephen Slade, returned home from a day of organizing to find that his battery cable had been severed. Both men shrugged off the episodes as street vandalism. It was not until the Monday after the march that Reed returned to his office to find that intruders had broken in. A window which had been painted shut and had never been opened was raised. Files had apparently been studied. "There were definite indications that someone broke into our offices," he said. Reed, whose organization had been the subject of intense red-baiting by several conservative political groups, called the D.C.

police. The investigating officer took down the details of the illegal entry and shrugged. "You're political," the officer said. "You got to expect this kind of thing."[19]

May 17, 1987: A staff member of the New Institute of Central America in Cambridge, Mass., entered the office to find a map of Nicaragua torn off the wall and left, in two pieces, on the floor. Muriatic acid had been poured over 40 computer discs containing information on programs run by the Central America solidarity group, which was housed in the basement of the Old Cambridge Baptist Church two blocks from Harvard University. It was the eighth political break-in at that church since November, 1984.[20]

Many of the incidents listed above were initially reported to the Movement Support Network—an arm of the Center for Constitutional Rights in New York which, for four years, monitored, recorded, verified and tried to publicize the extended campaign of political violence that was directed against opponents of Reagan Administration policies in Central America.

For the last couple of years of its operation, the Movement Support Network was staffed by a 28-year-old woman named Alicia Fernandes. Fernandes, a graduate of Yale University, was born and raised in Argentina. As a high school student in Buenos Aires during the early 1970s, when Argentina had its first civilian government in 18 years, Fernandes became active in high school and national politics. But her career as a political activist was short-lived. In 1976, several members of a paramilitary group showed up at her home asking for Alicia and her sister. The men made it clear they were members of an Argentine death squad. Shortly thereafter, Fernandes left Argentina and enrolled at Yale. It was when she went to work for the CCR and began fielding phone calls from terrorized activists about break-ins, torchings and death threats that a sense of horror began to set in.[21]

"Certainly you can't compare break-ins and death threats to the level of deaths and disappearances we saw in Argentina, and, later, in El Salvador and Guatemala. But the difference is one of degree only. These episodes exist on a continuum of repression. I find them much more ominous and frightening than others who simply say 'Oh, the FBI is up to its old tricks again.'"

It was when Fernandes learned of the abduction of Yanira Corea and the spate of death threats on the West Coast that she suffered a series of nightmares. "I thought I had put my experiences in Argentina behind me. Obviously this has reawakened a lot of fears. But what's important here is to keep things in perspective. The work that needs to be done—providing support to mothers and children in Central America, teaching them basic health and literacy, trying to stimulate the production of decent housing—that's what's important. All these incidents of harassments—both official and unofficial—are off the point. And the reason we've been doing this work at the Center is to permit the other groups—the ones doing hands-on work—to continue to keep their eye on the real goal."

And how effective were the break-ins, the death threats, and the FBI investigations in curtailing the Central America movement?

"It depends on who you talk to. Many American church activists—those who responded out of their hearts rather than out of political ideology—have clearly been intimidated by these activities. The Central Americans up here—Salvadorans and others—who have been the object of these threats have been absolutely terrified. Many have been reluctant to give their names. Others have made us promise never to divulge their identities. They recall the death squads and security forces first hand. Those are the most terrified of all. A lot of Salvadoran groups were so freaked out they simply stopped functioning.

"On the other hand, many North Americans, especially those who have worked as activists before, are better able to cope with this sort of thing. For many, it only strengthens their resolve. On the other hand, we've gotten a number of calls from church groups who want to know how to deal with their congregations. They feel, in some cases, they have to find a way to prove they're not communists. In several cases, congregations have been split by internal dissension and fear. Look at Old Cambridge Baptist Church. The FBI refused to release their files on the church on the grounds that it could compromise the identity of a confidential informant. Can you think of any better way to turn a congregation against itself with suspicion and intimidation? The issue of informants inside a congregation or a group is very divisive, very destructive. The FBI could not have found a better strategy."

Theories about the perpetrators of the break-ins abound. But nothing is proved. FBI documents released under Freedom of Information requests indicate the cooperation of local police intelligence divisions in a number of cities. Varelli has said that when he entered a church in the Dallas area to gather literature, two members of the Dallas police acted as lookouts outside. One person who slept overnight in an office of the Cambridge church said he saw two members of the Cambridge police rifling through drawers. But the person refuses to come forward. The evidence is scarcely credible—and certainly not proof of the participation of local police in illegal break-ins.

Nor is there evidence that the FBI, itself, committed the break-ins. Varelli accused members of the Dallas office of committing two break-ins at the homes of CISPES members. But an internal FBI investigation concluded there was no evidence to support his claim.

The modus operandi of the intruders, moreover, has varied from one break-in to another. In several cases, thieves used crowbars to pry out locks or break down doors. In other cases, sophisticated lock-picking equipment was used. Some of the suspects observed around the scene of a break-in prior to the event seemed to be white Anglo men dressed like mercenaries in combat boots and army fatigues. In other cases, group members recalled seeing Hispanic-looking strangers near the site. Still other victims of break-ins have reported prior surveillance by people who appeared to them to be government agents.

What we do know is really a negative. The FBI has consistently declined to investigate virtually all of the reported incidents. Since there is no evidence they involve government agencies and, moreover, since the monetary value of the stolen material is so low as to fall into the misdemeanor—rather than the felony—category, the Bureau has decided that each break-in properly falls within the jurisdiction of local police. And those police departments, overtaxed by high rates of violent crime, drug traffic, homicide and robbery can be forgiven for not deploying massive resources to solve an isolated break-in and theft of files from some obscure political organization.

In the Era of George Bush

Four years after the CISPES investigation was officially closed, two years after Rep. Don Edwards (D-California) held Congressional hearings on the break-ins, and a year after FBI Director William Sessions apologized to two Congressional committees for the FBI's campaign, the civil war in El Salvador again gained major prominence in the North American press, first with the arrest in San Salvador of church worker Jennifer Casolo and, shortly thereafter, with the brutal murders of six Jesuit priests in San Salvador on November 16, 1989.

About a week before Casolo's arrest, Sean Conway, a longtime friend of Casolo, returned to his Long Island, N.Y., home to find that an intruder had broken a glass door, entered and taken some Salvadoran currency from a bowl on his living room table. The following week, after the Salvadoran security forces announced they had found a cache of weapons buried outside Casolo's home, Conway, a carpenter, asked a client in Easthampton if he could use the phone to call El Salvador. Two days after the phone call, the client's home was also broken into. Nothing was taken, but drawers had been opened and examined. "I have strong suspicions of a collaboration between the Salvadoran secret police and our own. But I certainly can't prove it," Conway said.[22]

On November 24, shortly after the murders of six priests and two women workers at the University of Central America, Rev. James Flynn, whose apartment at St. Williams Church in Louisville had been broken into in 1985, received a photograph of the slain priests torn from the previous week's edition of *Time* magazine. The photo was accompanied by a note which read: "Jim, here are some of your left wing buddys. Your next, Jimmy." In a phone interview, Flynn said: "I absolutely think this is the work of someone working for the CIA or some other clandestine group. It is clearly part of a larger pattern of break-ins all over the country that must be coordinated somewhere."

Three days after Flynn received the photograph of the slain priests, intruders broke into the office of the Valley Religious Task Force on Central America in Phoenix. Coordinator Ferd Haverly said that sometime over the weekend, intruders broke a three-foot hole into a wallboard and entered the church. They kicked in the door to the office of the Task Force and pried open a metal filing cabinet. All the drawers were open and files had obviously been examined. The intruders also removed $50 in cash from the cabinet and left it on top in full view. They also left a new computer, a television set, a video recorder and expensive office equipment.[23]

The following day, religious activists in three offices in Los Angeles received death threats, according to Ruth Capelle, an official at the Central American Refugee Center in Los Angeles. Capelle said the death threats were received by Fr. Luis Olivares and Fr. Michael Kennedy, both of whom worked at La Placita, as well as by Fr. Greg Boyle, a pastor at Mission Delores. The letter to the Refugee Center read: "Directed to all those self-proclaimed priests that you're not who you say you are. You're simply disguising yourselves as priests falsely...All of you will die because you are a part of the FMLN. Just like you are being destroyed in El Salvador, in the same manner will you be destroyed here."[24]

On March 9, 1990, the Thomaston, Connecticut, home of Jennifer Casolo's mother was broken into. Intruders ransacked the house, dumping files and paperwork on the floor of Casolo's bedroom. The break-in was discovered by Casolo's mother, Audrey, when she returned from work to find her own night table rifled and a soft drink splashed on the wall.[25]

The following month, the Center for Constitutional Rights in lower Manhattan was broken into. Intruders broke a glass window in the office's outer reception area. They stole an envelope full of keys and entered a room that was used to store the Center's Freedom of Information request files, examining the files as well as a rolodex on a desk. The burglars were unable to enter other offices which were secured by locks.[26]

On April 9, 1990, an office building in the Jamaica Plain section of Boston, which houses the New England Central America Network, the New Institute of Central America and other political groups, was entered. Intruders dumped desk drawers over the floor and rifled files. The building, which also houses several commercial offices, was protected with a modern electric-eye alarm system. Anne Wright, a NECAN member, said that the intruders had disabled the electric eye system for the Central America offices, leaving the rest of the alarm system intact. The wires connecting the alarm systems in the political offices had been neatly cut, taped and stuffed back into a ceiling box.

Three days later, staff members at NECAN discovered that the intruders had also infected their office computer with a computer virus. Consultant Thomas Donnebrink, who was able to excise the virus, described it as a virus known as SCORE, which had been in circulation since 1987.[27]

Completing the Cover-Up

Beginning at the end of 1984, the press carried a few, isolated stories about the break-ins and death threats. But they did little to arouse public opinion. Some members of the public even seemed willing to accept the FBI's assertion that many of the break-ins were most likely "self-inflicted" attempts by activists to gain publicity for their cause.

Nor did Varelli's aborted testimony before Congress in 1987 attract much public attention. When he attempted to detail his knowledge of FBI misdeeds before the House Judiciary Subcommittee on Civil and Constitutional Rights, Varelli testified that during his years in the FBI he never actually saw CISPES members commit any illegal acts. But that testimony was sabotaged when Rep. James Sensenbrenner, a conservative Republican member of the committee, produced a document attributed to Varelli which indicated that CISPES may have been planning to assassinate President Reagan in 1984. Varelli denied making the charge, claiming the document had been altered by a right-wing activist who changed Varelli's assertion that CISPES was planning to "disrupt" the convention rather than "assassinate" the President. But his denial, which seems to be substantiated by a tape recording of his interview with Secret Service officials in Dallas shortly before the 1984 convention,[1] was of no help. The damage had already been done. His credibility, at least in Congress, was in shambles.

It was not until January of 1988, when attorneys at the Center for Constitutional Rights won release of some 3,500 pages of the FBI's files on CISPES, that the scope and extent of the FBI's assault on political activists became known.

Again, however, the public response was minimal and the press essentially treated the revelation as a two-day story, culminating in the selection by ABC News of Margaret Ratner, a lead attorney on the CISPES case, as that news program's "person of the week."

The disclosure of the probe was followed, in March of 1988, by a preliminary report to the Senate Intelligence Committee from Revell, in which the FBI executive assistant director testified that Director Webster did not authorize nor was kept apprised of the progress of the CISPES investigation.

The following September, the new FBI Director, William Sessions, made a full report to both the Senate Intelligence Committee and the House Judiciary Subcommittee on Civil and Constitutional Rights. In an extraordinary public concession, Sessions said that "the CISPES investigation was an aberration...an unfortunate aligning of mistakes in judgment at several levels that cumulatively led to an investigation of which the FBI is not proud." In his presentation, Sessions blamed the affair generally on the Bureau's lax management and inadequate supervision. Sessions also announced he had suspended three FBI officials and censured three others for negligence and mismanagement.

But, in introducing the line which would serve to cover up the FBI's more egregious violations, Sessions laid the blame for the entire campaign on the shoulders of Varelli. "Absent the information provided by Frank Varelli, there would not have been sufficient predication for an international terrorism investigation of CISPES...By the time it was realized that Varelli's information was unreliable, the investigation had been under way for approximately one year. The investigation would not have developed as it did had Varelli's reliability been properly scrutinized at the outset."[2]

While the legislators seemed, overall, eager to accept Sessions' version of events and to put the embarrassing episode behind them, it is clear from a number of documents which were released after his testimony that Sessions lied extensively to the committees. Whether the FBI director (who did not assume the leadership of the Bureau until more than two years after the conclusion of the CISPES investigation) was aware of the untruths he told Congress or whether he was merely repeating what he had been told by his own Inspection Division is not known. But in any case, his testimony—and the ensuing report of the Senate Intelligence Committee—constituted a cover-up of many layers.

The Scapegoating of Frank Varelli

Start with the question of Frank Varelli—the "operational asset" whose credibility was torpedoed by conservative activists in 1987 and who never again was able to persuade Congressional investigators that the story he had to tell was, in essence, a true one.

In the winter of 1988-89, through the efforts of his Washington attorney, Daniel S. Alcorn, Varelli received a windfall of some 4,000 pages of FBI documents as a result of a protracted Freedom of Information lawsuit. Those files documented the truth of Varelli's accounts of numerous FBI operations during the period of his employment by the Bureau.

Even without those documents, however, the FBI's succession of statements about the former asset are, on their face, more contradictory and less credible than the elaborate story told by Varelli.

In 1986, for example, when reporter Christi Harlan of the *Dallas Morning News* interviewed Varelli for an article on Flanagan's loss of the documents, several FBI agents in Dallas confirmed Varelli's account of that incident, assuring Harlan that Varelli was, indeed, telling the truth.[3]

The following year, when Varelli testified before Congress, the FBI claimed he was too low-level and insignificant a source to know what he claimed to have known. Several FBI officials told journalists on an off-the-record basis that Varelli was an opportunist who would say anything for pay. In 1988, however, when the Center for Constitutional Rights won release of 3,500 pages of FBI documents, some of which confirmed Varelli's central role in the CISPES operation, the FBI did an about-face. Bureau officials conceded that Varelli did have access to the most highly classified information. At that point, the same officials, who had previously cast Varelli as a low-level informant operating on the margins of the FBI now suggested on background that Varelli was really a diabolically clever agent for the Salvadoran right wing who had penetrated and manipulated the FBI's counter-terrorism operations. That position was fulfilled by FBI Director Sessions when he essentially blamed the entire five-year, nationwide operation on Varelli.

But Sessions' assessment is contradicted by a number of documents which paint a very different picture of the Bureau's evaluation of Varelli's credibility and value. In June of 1984, after Flanagan lost the two briefcases of FBI documents, the FBI subjected Varelli to a six-hour polygraph examination. At the end of the test, the examiner noted that Varelli had answered truthfully all questions about his work with the FBI. The examiner's findings were endorsed two months later by a technical review team at FBI headquarters who found that the exam "was satisfactory in all aspects."

When Varelli began to go public three years later, however, FBI headquarters officials changed the results of his polygraph examination, explaining they had retroactively discovered "deceptive" answers to several questions involving his work with the FBI. When Congressional investigators raised Varelli's allegations with FBI officials in classified briefings, they were shown the altered results of his lie-detector tests. As a result, Congressional staffers decided they could not rely on any of Varelli's information since he was a demonstrated liar. The Bureau's assassination of his credibility was complete.

When Sessions concluded in 1988 that "By the time it was realized that Varelli's information was unreliable, the investigation had been under way for approximately one year," his statement went unchallenged by the Senators and Congresspeople who seemed relieved to be able to blame the entire affair on Varelli.

But a series of FBI airtels released to Varelli at the end of 1988 showed that the FBI considered him to be credible long after the 1984 date Sessions cited as the time the FBI learned he was unreliable. In fact, Varelli was regarded as a highly prized FBI asset from 1981 until more than a year after he left the Bureau, according to a series of internal FBI documents:

July 13, 1981: "… [Varelli's] true value is in his ability to obtain information regarding El Salvadorian (sic) activities in matter of hours, due to his experience in that country and numerous resources at his disposal in the U.S. and El Salvador."

November 23, 1982: "…captioned source [Varelli], the most knowledgeable and reliable El Salvadorian (sic) asset in the Bureau, was responsible for presenting the threat from El Salvador terrorists to the Bureau…."

May 30, 1984: "FBIHQ intends, after review of polygraph examination results, to provide [Varelli] with a lump sum which may exceed the amount requested in [referenced teletype]…He was tasked to penetrate the inner circle leadership of CISPES locally and furnish info concerning plans and activities…If the source has not compromised his relationship with the FBI through his contacts with Salvadoran government officials, he can be of great benefit to the FBI in the Salvadoran terrorism investigations. The asset appears intelligent and eager to cooperate and work with the FBI. He does need close supervision of his activities and must be given specific tasking and direction to obtain information needed by the FBI in these investigations."

May 3, 1985: "Dallas has no objection to Houston's utilization of [Varelli] and would highly encourage the relationship."

In other words, a year after Varelli had already left the FBI—and two years after the date at which Sessions said the Bureau learned he was "unreliable"—the FBI thought highly enough of his work that it encouraged the Houston field office to re-hire him.

Given that succession of highly complimentary documents in Varelli's personnel file, it is difficult to understand how members of Congress permitted the FBI Director to lay the blame for the entire FBI investigation on Varelli's "unreliability."

But Varelli's personnel file aside, it defies common sense to believe that the FBI would base a five-year nationwide investigation on the uncorroborated statements of one Salvadoran-born asset who clearly had his own political axes to grind.

What emerges from a review of the available material is a different picture than the one painted by the FBI and the Committee—a picture of an innocent FBI being conned by a diabolically clever Varelli. In fact, it was not Varelli's information that both Sessions and the Senate Intelligence Committee called "unreliable." It was the enormous volume of intelligence material forwarded to the FBI from the Salvadoran security forces and death squads—material for which Varelli was merely the conduit, not the author. It was material, moreover, that the FBI actively solicited and disseminated to every field office in the country.

The real secret that both Sessions and the Committee covered up is the fact that the FBI—following the lead of the White House and the Reagan CIA—allowed the direction of its investigation of American liberals to be partially dictated by the Salvadoran security forces, thereby collaborating in the persecution of American citizens with one of the most terrorist governments in the world.

From the time Varelli's central role in the investigation became known, FBI officials on background strongly suggested that Varelli was a "mole," a secret agent of the Salvadoran National Guard who had penetrated to the center of the FBI's counter-terrorism apparatus and manipulated it for the advantage of his true masters, the Salvadoran security forces. But that interpretation is an inversion of the real agenda of this very complex man.

Varelli's history of intimate involvement with the Salvadoran police and military is a matter of record. His father was, after all, director of the National Police as well as Minister of the Interior of that country. Varelli, himself, was a product of the Salvadoran Military Training Academy. His 1977 religious crusade, designed to counter the growing influence of "liberation theology," was actively supported by then-President Carlos Romero. Varelli's involvement with members of El Salvador's Council of Families—people who funded death squads, set up a private intelligence operation in the United States, and, in 1981, discussed the possibility of assassinating Jose Napoleon Duarte in Varelli's presence—testifies to his credentials as a trusted member of the Salvadoran right wing.

Varelli has admitted, moreover, that with the knowledge of his superiors, he occasionally exaggerated, distorted and even fabricated information in FBI files to strengthen the Bureau's case against dissenting United States citizens. (The FBI's Inspection Division found several instances in which Varelli's initial reports were further exaggerated prior to dissemination by Flanagan, probably in the service of his own career ambitions). It is also possible that in his zeal, Varelli may have suggested to FBI superiors, without saying it directly, that CISPES was actually planning to harm President Reagan at the 1984 Republican Convention.

But while Frank Varelli is relentlessly obsessive in his anti-communism—and fanatically tenacious in his vision of a world-wide communist plot behind every development in left-wing and liberal circles—he is also a very intelligent man.

He took pains to assure that his work for the FBI was thoroughly chronicled and fully reported. He assented to, if not initiated, the FBI's request to the National Security Agency to monitor his calls to El Salvador. With the knowledge of the FBI, he provided intelligence to the CIA, ostensibly to help the Agency interpret developments in El Salvador.

In short, his activities for the FBI were open to full scrutiny by members of the Bureau's counter-terrorism and foreign counter-intelligence units. (Coincidentally, that estimation of Varelli's performance—as one which was consistent with the orders and approvals of his superiors —was endorsed by a Federal Claims Court judge in Washington who awarded Varelli a victory in early 1989 in his long-standing claims case against the Bureau.)[4]

The truth about Varelli is that, while his roots and allegiances stem from his Salvadoran anti-communist background, he saw in his FBI assignment an opportunity to serve the interests of both the United States as well as his native El Salvador. He believed Flanagan and Davenport when they told him he was acting as part of a top-secret operation that had the blessings of the President of the United States. Even the FBI was unable to cite to Congress any specific instances of Varelli passing unauthorized classified material back to the Salvadoran authorities. And, given his long-term goal of working for the CIA, it is doubtful that, as an FBI employee, he would have committed any breach that would have called his basic allegiance into question.

Varelli saw basically no difference between the FBI and the National Guard of El Salvador. They were two agencies of the two countries which shared a common enemy and a common mission. Frank Varelli saw himself as serving both at the same time. For him, there was no conflict of purpose, no division of loyalty. The only difference between the two countries was an abstraction which his FBI superiors implicitly assured him was of no relevance to his work: the Constitution of the United States.

In its 1989 report on the FBI's CISPES campaign, the Senate Intelligence Committee indirectly conceded that Varelli was not solely responsible for the Bureau's activities. It noted, for instance, several sources of information other than Varelli who indicated to the FBI that CISPES had ties to the Salvadoran guerrillas, to Middle Eastern terrorist groups and to the Sandinista government in Nicaragua. "Before the FBI investigated CISPES…in 1981, the FBI had opened separate international terrorism investigations of alleged support from other elements in the United States to Salvadoran revolutionary guerrilla activity…During 1982 the FBI received intelligence reports of contacts between persons in the United States and members of the Salvadoran Marxist revolutionary movement…By late 1982, the FBI had opened several international terrorism investigations based on information from sources other than Frank Varelli indicating involvement with Central American terrorism."[5]

In fact, the CISPES investigation was but one of at least a half dozen investigations of U.S. citizens who opposed the Administration's policies in Central America. By burying aspects of the same investigation under separate captions, the FBI in fact investigated thousands of groups and individuals under a number of investigations of which CISPES was only one. Documents on file indicate that the FBI used such captions as "Salvadoran Leftist Activities," "Salvadoran Leftist Activities in the United States," "Nicaragua Demonstrations" and "Central American Terrorism" to surveil, penetrate and possibly disrupt religious and political activists concerned about U.S. policies in the region. Unfortunately, the relevant Congressional committees have not seen fit to call the FBI to account for any of those other investigations.

In its report on the CISPES campaign, the Senate Intelligence Committee essentially endorsed the FBI's version of events. It concurred with Sessions that the problem lay not in a deliberate abuse of political power by the FBI but in lax management by FBI officials at middle and lower levels of the Bureau. While both the Committee and the FBI deny it, it appears that the investigation was known to officials in the Reagan White House and National Security Council. What neither Sessions nor the Committee acknowledged, moreover, is that the investigation was authorized and encouraged by the top level of FBI leadership. Hundreds of documents in the CISPES files, for instance, were initialled by Oliver "Buck" Revell, until recently the number two person at the Bureau. It was Revell, moreover, who authorized the October 1983 order to expand CISPES into a nation-wide investigation.

But five years later, that development would prove the occasion for a curious display of institutional amnesia by Bureau officials. When FBI director Sessions testified before Congress in 1988, he called the October 1983 expansion of the investigation the "biggest mistake" of the whole investigation. During his appearance before Congress, Sessions was asked by one senator why no FBI higher-ups had been punished for their roles in the investigation. Sessions responded that, try as he might, he could find no evidence in the documents to indicate the involvement of higher-level officials. He must not have looked very hard. A copy of the October 28 teletype—directing the nation-wide expansion—was signed by no less a higher-up than Buck Revell.[6]

A Speculative Scenario: The Guiding Hand of the CIA

It is clear from notations on a number of FBI documents that the Central Intelligence Agency was certainly kept abreast of the FBI's campaign against political dissenters. One speculative scenario suggests that the guiding hand behind the FBI's campaign was that of William Casey, the late Director of Central Intelligence.

It was Casey who, shortly after assuming his post in 1981, declared to colleagues that El Salvador had become the latest battleground in the global contest between freedom and communism. It was also Casey who raised the issue of "active measures" as a major threat to the security of the United States. And it was Casey's CIA that identified CISPES, within months of the group's formation, as an "active measures front" of Moscow.

Simultaneous with the production of the CIA study that cited CISPES as an "active measures" operation, the CIA forwarded to the FBI intelligence material that purported to prove that the group was the creation of the Salvadoran leftist guerrillas. That material, which allegedly came from the diaries of two Salvadoran communist leaders, was provided by the Salvadoran National Guard to the CIA, which forwarded it to the FBI.

But, as Senate investigators would conclude eight years later, the FBI, in using that material: "...asserted without documentation that CISPES was composed of groups 'initiated by the Communist Party USA...and Farid Handal'." Calling the diaries "alleged," and "unauthenticated," the investigators concluded: "The FBI's CISPES file does not reflect any Justice or State Department characterization of the nature or reliability of the alleged captured document or any effort to evaluate its bona fides. The [FBI's] Inspection Department was unable to find any information directly corroborating the statements in the purported Handal document."[7]

What is most ironic is that the CIA and FBI, in collaboration with the Salvadoran security forces—the elements that most feared the persuasive power of CISPES' message—were driven to use a disinformation-based "active measures" strategy in their effort to paint CISPES as an "active measures" front group.

William Casey's sensitivity to the threat of adverse public opinion was clearly the motivation behind his initiative in establishing a covert "public diplomacy" operation designed to reach beyond the conservative elements of American society who already supported the Reagan Central America policies.

Finally, as Bob Woodward noted in *Veil,* his 1987 book about Casey's CIA, there was a strong constituency around Casey which favored breaking down the traditional barriers between the CIA and the FBI. That notion was articulated by Kenneth de Graffenreid, an expert on counter-intelligence who was to become a major force inside the Reagan National Security Council. In a study of the country's counter-intelligence needs, de Graffenreid promoted the notion that "[b]ureaucratic barriers needed to be broken down between the FBI, the CIA and the military intelligence agencies...If necessary, a centralized counter-intelligence authority with centralized records should be created. The split of counter-intelligence functions at the U.S. borders (CIA abroad, FBI at home) was artificial. It was a civil liberties bugaboo to worry whether they were joined. It was not a distinction the KGB observed."[8]

Given the extraordinary expertise in the use of disinformation by both the CIA and the Salvadoran National Guard, one can make the argument that, if the FBI was not explicitly "tasked" by the CIA to crack down on political dissenters, it certainly could have been "unwittingly duped" by the Agency into the same operation.

In fact, there is evidence the relationship was more deliberate. One month after the issuance of the President's December 1981 order governing the intelligence operations, Reagan signed a directive authorizing the CIA to "request the FBI to collect foreign intelligence or support foreign intelligence requirements of other [intelligence] agencies..."[9] Given William Webster's statement to Congress in 1985 that the FBI may have been "tasked" by the CIA or National Security Council to interview activists returning from Nicaragua, it seems apparent that such "tasking" had become a routine part of FBI activities by the mid-1980s.

As for the doctrine of "active measures" which was raised to the level of high policy focus by Casey and used by the FBI to justify numerous operations—including a campaign to spy on users of public libraries—it is still the subject of an ongoing inter-agency task force and, as such, can still be used to discredit and investigate law-abiding citizens by labeling them as "fronts" for Moscow, Havana or other purported hostile foreign powers.

As late as August 1989, for instance, the State Department issued a report titled: "Soviet Influence Activities: A Report on Active Measures and Propaganda, 1987-1988." That report, according to its preface, was prepared by an inter-agency Active Measures Working Group which includes representatives of State, the CIA, the U.S. Information Agency, the Arms Control and Disarmament Agency, the Defense Intelligence Agency and the Departments of Defense and Justice.[10]

The speculative scenario, which casts the CISPES campaign as merely one arm of a CIA-directed operation which involved the country's entire national security apparatus, is supported by a good deal of evidence that the FBI did not pursue its investigation of policy foes in a vacuum. Its campaign against political dissenters was paralleled by the surveillance of political activists at the request of Oliver North's National Security Council as well as by the secret domestic propaganda campaign run out of the NSC at the direction of Bill Casey. And the activities of all those agencies—the FBI, the NSC, the CIA and the State Department— were augmented by a network of private individuals and organizations all of whom united under the umbrella of the Administration's foreign policies—especially those in Central America. As former Ambassador Robert White said in response to a question about the CISPES investigation: "You're only looking at the FBI. That's just one piece of it. What Ronald Reagan has done is to mobilize the entire government around his policies in Central America."

Unasked Questions: The FBI and the Disappeared Refugees

The most sinister aspect of the FBI's collaboration with the Salvadoran National Guard may lie in unmarked graves and obscure ravines in the small war-ravaged Central American nation, where refugees, having sought shelter and a safe haven in the United States, were buried after being deported by U.S. officials back to waiting security forces.

One sample of 154 refugees deported in 1983 and 1984, which was reported by the Political Asylum Project of the American Civil Liberties Union Fund, included 52 returnees who were killed, seven who were arrested, five who were jailed as political prisoners, 47 who disappeared (fates unknown) and 43 who were captured and disappeared under violent circumstances.[11] But because of a number of circumstances—including Salvadorans' fear of speaking out, the use of false names by refugees, the problem of admittedly inaccurate record keeping of the Immigration and Naturalization Service and the lack of cooperation by the Salvadoran security forces—it is impossible to document the number of refugees killed or "disappeared" on their forced return to El Salvador. Given the additional blanket of secrecy covering the collaboration between the FBI and the National Guard, it is impossible to estimate the numbers killed by Salvadoran security forces with the cooperation of the FBI.

But if, as Varelli has maintained, "the FBI knew and approved of every damn call I made [to the National Guard]," then the Bureau has on its hands the blood of innocent refugees. And it is remarkable that, in its efforts to call the FBI to account for abuses of lesser gravity, the Congress chose not to question the Bureau about its possible participation in the most grotesque kind of human rights violations.

The Unsolved Break-Ins

From a U.S. standpoint, the most frightening aspect of the assault on dissenting citizens lies in the string of break-ins, thefts, death threats and assaults that stretches forward from 1983 to 1990 like an underground epidemic of low-grade terrorism.

Partly because the FBI has consistently declined to investigate those break-ins—categorizing them as local crimes under the jurisdiction of local police rather than evidences of an interstate conspiracy—we may never know who has planned and coordinated them.

The CIA could well have coordinated a number of private groups, Salvadoran as well as North American, in a campaign of break-ins which it hid under the cover of the FBI's official investigations of those groups. It does not seem coincidental that the majority of break-in victims were also affiliated with groups which were targeted for official investigation by the FBI.

It is equally plausible to speculate that the string of break-ins was coordinated by elements in Oliver North's private network, using lists of targets produced by the FBI, CIA or State Department. When Revell, for instance, said he was afraid that Glenn Robinette, the head of security for North's "private enterprise," may have been running a plumbers' operation, he could have been referring to a campaign of illegal burglaries and harassments that extended far beyond a few groups like the Christic Institute or the International Center for Development Policy, which were working to expose North's illegal operations.

It is also possible that at least some of the break-ins were the work of right-wing Salvadorans and other zealots inside the United States who, by virtue of their earlier information-trading arrangements with the FBI, felt they had the Bureau's sanction in taking the next step and stealing files, trashing offices and terrorizing activists.

Rep. Don Edwards, the former FBI agent who has chaired the House Judiciary Subcommittee on Civil and Constitutional Rights which held hearings on the break-ins in February of 1987, has said he believes the break-ins to be the work of Central American operatives. In late 1987, Edwards wrote an article titled "The Unsolved Break-Ins," in which he stated that "there are two likely sources for these break-ins...[One possibility is that they] may be the work of agents of one or more Central American government or of factions representing the ruling classes in those countries. We know in the past violent government have sent their agents to the U.S. to harass and intimidate their opponents here. The Shah of Iran and Marcos of the Philippines both had active intelligence operations in this country...The right-wing government of Chile was involved in the car bombing in Washington that killed Orlando Letelier. Is history repeating itself? Are foreign agents now carrying out break-ins against sanctuary churches and opponents of the Administration's militaristic policy in Central America?"

"Another possibility," Edwards wrote, "is that the break-ins are the work of [U.S.] right-wing groups who support the contras and U.S. policy in Central America. We know there was a private network established to raise money for the contras. We also know that some members of the network were active in promoting the Administration's views. Is it possible that they were interested as well in frustrating the efforts of groups opposing those views and sought to collect information about them? Unfortunately, we may never know the answers to these questions."[12]

Perhaps the most likely scenario is that the break-ins were coordinated by the CIA, which had (and continues to have) direct lines into both the network of private right-wing activists in the U.S., as well as into the security forces of El Salvador and Guatemala. And while the break-ins may not have been committed by U.S. government agents, there is no doubt they are part of a well-coordinated, centrally-directed campaign to neutralize and intimidate opponents of U.S. policies.

CISPES: The Latest Chapter in an Old History

Whether or not the FBI played an active role in the break-ins—or whether the Bureau was merely a passive accomplice in declining to investigate them—the FBI's operations against liberal and left-wing citizens opposed to U.S. policies beg to be seen in the context of the Bureau's history of abusing its law enforcement powers by persecuting law-abiding dissenters for strictly political reasons.

Given that historical context, the FBI Director's description of the CISPES probe as an "aberration" is indefensible. For the FBI's investigation and harassment of Central America groups in the 1980s is, after all, simply one more chapter in a continuing series of FBI political police operations which date back at least to the 1950s—and which have continued, virtually unabated, to the present.

One contention of numerous experts which is worth noting here is that the FBI, which was established in 1908 as a national law enforcement agency, has never been explicitly authorized by Congress to gather intelligence on political, as contrasted with criminal, targets.[13] In fact, virtually every authorization of the FBI to gather political intelligence and mount political operations against domestic political activists and movements has come in the form of Justice Department guidelines and Presidential executive orders—without passing the test of open public debate.

Nevertheless, dating at least from the McCarthy period of the 1950s, the Bureau has engaged in active investigations of virtually every major dissident political movement in recent American history. Those investigations have involved techniques ranging from file checks to active surveillance to infiltration and provocation to harassments and character assassination to such covert operations as "black-bag jobs," wiretaps and assassinations.

In its report on "Intelligence Activities and the Rights of Americans," the Senate's Church Committee in 1976 cited a series of FBI campaigns all of which were patently political in nature and had little, if anything, to do with the FBI's legal mandate to investigate criminal activities.

According to that report: "Intelligence agencies have collected vast amounts of information about the intimate details of citizens' lives and about their participation in legal and peaceful political activities. The targets of intelligence activity have included political adherents of the right and the left, ranging from activist to casual supporters. Investigations have been directed against proponents of racial causes and women's rights, outspoken apostles of nonviolence and racial harmony; establishment politicians; religious groups; and advocates of new life-styles."[14]

The targets of FBI intelligence operations cited by the Church Committee 15 years ago included participants in virtually every significant political movement.

"The 'Women's Liberation Movement' was infiltrated by informants who collected material about the movement's policies, leaders and individual members. One report included the name of every woman who attended meetings, and another stated that each woman at a meeting had described 'how she felt oppressed, sexually or otherwise.' Another report concluded that the movement's purpose was to 'free women from the humdrum existence of being only a wife and mother....'"[15]

An adviser to Dr. Martin Luther King, Stanley Levison, was investigated on suspicion he was a communist sympathizer. According to a 1964 FBI memorandum which ordered the investigation to continue: "The Bureau does not agree with the expressed belief of the field office that [Levison] is not sympathetic to the Party cause. While there may not be any evidence that [he] is a Communist, neither is there any substantial evidence that he is anti-communist." [16]

The Committee found, moreover, that the Bureau continued to investigate the NAACP for possible communist links for more than 25 years despite an early FBI report that the NAACP had a "strong tendency" to "steer clear Communist activities."[17]

Similarly, the Bureau investigated the Socialist Workers Party for more than 30 years, collecting information on the organization's attitudes toward food prices, race relations and the Vietnam War, despite an FBI finding that the group had committed no illegal acts.[18]

In the case of the small SWP alone, the Bureau employed 1,600 informants in a 16-year-period to infiltrate the group, at an estimated cost of $26 million.[19]

In 1970, according to the Congressional report, the FBI ordered investigations of every member of the Students for a Democratic Society and of every Black Student Union, regardless of "their past or present involvement in disorders."[20] As a former FBI intelligence official told the Committee, the Bureau opened files on thousands of young men and women so that "the information could be used if they ever applied for a government job."[21]

Nor was the Bureau immune to the political bidding of a succession of U.S. presidents. President Franklin Roosevelt instructed the Bureau to open investigative files on citizens who wrote the White House to espouse an "isolationist" policy in opposition to the President's foreign policies.[22] Harry Truman solicited FBI reports on union organizers, journalists and former Roosevelt aides.[23] Dwight Eisenhower received FBI reports on "purely political and social contacts with foreign officials" of Bernard Baruch, Mrs. Eleanor Roosevelt and Supreme Court Justice William O. Douglas.[24] And officials in the Kennedy White House had the FBI wiretap "a Congressional staff member, three executive officials, a lobbyist and a Washington law firm," while Attorney General Robert Kennedy received the fruits of FBI wiretaps on Martin Luther King, Jr.[25] At the request of President Lyndon Johnson, the FBI conducted file checks on various anti-war legislators and compared their statements on the Vietnam war to the statements of the Communist Party.[26]

Given the FBI's compilation during the 1980s of investigative files on at least a dozen Senators and Representatives who opposed President Reagan's policies in Nicaragua and El Salvador—some of which included material procured through electronic surveillance—it is difficult to accept the assertion in the 1989 report of the Senate Intelligence Committee that "there were no instructions given or requests for information made to FBI officials during the conduct of the CISPES investigation by anyone within the office of the White House or acting on behalf of the White House in an effort to influence their investigation."[27]

In the course of its operations against civil rights organizations, black political activists, anti-Vietnam War groups, the Free Speech Movement of university students, the American Indian Movement and the movement for Puerto Rican independence, the FBI opened hundreds of thousands of letters; wiretapped thousands of telephone conversations; conducted break-ins at hundreds of residences and offices; and surveilled untold numbers of groups and activists.

The Bureau, moreover, engaged in a number of disruptive tactics which the Church Committee called "indisputably degrading to a free society." These included attempts to have political activists fired from their jobs by anonymously informing their employees about their political beliefs—a tactic which was repeated in 1987 with the FBI's approach to employers of members of the TecNica organization.

It included, as well, anonymous letters to the spouses of FBI targets in order to destroy their marriages. One favored tactic of the FBI involved anonymously labeling political activists as FBI informants, thereby destroying their credibility and effectiveness as political organizers. It was this goal which apparently underlay Varelli's attempt to gain access to the printing press of Gene Lantz, the Texas-based activist.

The Bureau's anonymous provocations included, as well, anonymous letters to Black Panther Party members indicating they were on the "hit list" of other Panther activists and implying their wives or girlfriends were engaged in secret affairs with other Party members. One of the FBI's more notorious operations included providing Dr. King with a tape recording of his private activities, along with a note suggesting he commit suicide to avoid public humiliation.[28]

One of the FBI's most egregious actions involved the Bureau's engineering of the 1969 assassination of Panther leader Fred Hampton and Mark Clark in Chicago.[29]

In the following decade, between 1973 and 1976, the Bureau is said to have either provided assistance for or participated in the murder of nearly 70 members of the American Indian Movement and the violent attacks on another 300 Native Americans who had occupied the areas of Pine Ridge and Rosebud in South Dakota.[30]

Ten years later, the FBI's campaign against advocates of Puerto Rican independence peaked when more than 300 FBI agents and U.S. Marshalls conducted raids throughout Puerto Rico in 1985, trashing homes and offices and arresting scores of activists—two of whom were held without bail in pre-trial detention for more than two-and-a-half years.[31] The FBI's operations in Puerto Rico resulted in the creation of files on 74,000 individuals.[32]

Given the FBI's history of thinly rationalized political repression, it is very difficult to accept the conclusion of the Senate Intelligence Committee that: "The Committee does not believe the CISPES investigation reflected significant FBI political or ideological bias...."

Unfortunately, a review of the FBI's political operations also suggests that, with the exception of the Church and Pike Committee investigations in the mid-1970s, Congress has been unable or unwilling to exert the kind of control and oversight with which the public has entrusted it. In the case of the CISPES scandal, it is unclear whether the Senate report endorsed the FBI's cover-up because it was politically expedient or because the FBI withheld critical material from Congressional investigators. It seems that both factors played a significant role.

Concurrent with the history of documented FBI political abuses over the past 35 years, is an equally clear history of an institutionalized FBI practice of routinely lying about its activities. That history of lying to Congress has continued unabated from the 1960s to the end of the 1980s.

When the first set of FBI documents in 1988 indicated that the CISPES investigation was far more extensive than Congressional overseers had been led to believe, investigators on Capitol Hill said flatly that the FBI had lied to them in its previous briefings. Nor were the FBI's lies to Congress confined to the CISPES investigations.

The "DO NOT FILE" File

The Bureau, during the 1960s, maintained a set of files which were headed "DO NOT FILE." The files, which recorded FBI break-ins and thefts at civil rights and anti-war offices during the 1960s, were used to keep such activities away from public scrutiny. In the late 1970s and early 1980s, FBI officials swore under oath that they had discontinued the use of the "DO NOT FILE" caption, especially since the federal Freedom Of Information Act requires that the existence of all agency files be acknowledged, if not released, to requesters using the act.

But a "DO NOT FILE" file, provided to the author in 1988, indicates that the FBI has continued to maintain such records. The "DO NOT FILE" document, apparently unrelated to the FBI's campaign against Central America dissenters, was a 1985 communication from Revell to then-FBI Director William Webster. It cited a request from Henry Kissinger for a personal meeting with Webster about alleged harassment by members of the Lyndon LaRouche political organization. The document was titled "DO NOT FILE" apparently because Kissinger did not want any bureaucratic paper trail indicating his private meeting with Webster to discuss the LaRouche group.[33]

When Rep. Edwards questioned the FBI about the document, he was told simply that it was erroneously captioned. Despite Edwards' concern that "reinstituting 'Do Not File' files would emasculate the oversight process," Congress apparently accepted the Bureau's explanation that the file should have been captioned "Informal Advice—Not For Retention"—a freshly-minted FBI euphemism for "Do Not File."[34]

Then there is the matter of the Terrorist Photo Album. While Webster himself assured Rep. Patricia Schroeder, Sen. Christopher Dodd and others that they were not included in the FBI's Terrorist Photo Album and were not the subjects of FBI Central America-related investigations, an internal FBI memo, initialled by Webster, indicates that the Bureau deliberately lied to the legislators.

A reading of the Senate Intelligence Committee's CISPES reports indicates, as well, that the FBI withheld critical documents from the committee. In addition to concealing its retroactive alterations of Varelli's polygraph results, it is clear from the report that the FBI withheld other significant documents as well. As one example, the Senate report concluded that during his 1983 visit to Washington, "Mr. Varelli's report indicates that he never actually met any Washington members of CISPES or attended any of their meetings. He did report on several left-wing bookstores, however, as well as some churches..."[35]

However, the FBI's files contain a full debriefing of his infiltration of CISPES headquarters following the bombing of the Capitol—a document which was apparently withheld from the Committee to further discredit Varelli. The airtel sent from the FBI's Dallas Office to FBI headquarters, moreover, bears a handwritten notation, apparently from an FBI supervisor who wrote: "Good job. Thanks. I talked to (DELETED) who was very pleased. He sd the unit chief was impressed also."[36] The document substantiates Varelli's version of his visit to CISPES headquarters in Washington in December, 1983, following the bombing of the Capitol Building.

Again, when William Webster told the Congressional Iran-Contra Committee that he had disclosed all of the FBI's contacts with Oliver North, he neglected to mention a 14-month relationship between North and special agent David Beisner of the Washington Field Office—a relationship which was aimed at gathering intelligence on groups attempting to expose North's illegal contra-supply operations.

The findings of both the FBI and the Senate Intelligence Committee stand in stark contrast to those of U.S. District Executive Magistrate Judge Joan H. Lefkow, who ruled in February 1991 on a case involving Chicago-based Central America groups. In that ruling, the federal judge found that the FBI used infiltrators to penetrate the leadership of several groups. Moreover, the FBI's Chicago field office obtained copies of bank deposit slips, cancelled checks, and signature cards for CISPES members, as well as copies of the group's long-distance telephone records "to determine the identity of Chicago CISPES memberships and contacts."

"At the direction of Headquarters, the FBI conducted a photographic surveillance...of one Chicago CISPES leader and, on April 8, 1985, submitted his photograph and background data for inclusion in the Terrorist Photograph Album."

The judge found, moreover, that "In a sworn statement made on April 8, 1988 [three years after the original submission], the FBI case agent for the Chicago CISPES investigation, who submitted the photograph and data, admitted that he did not believe his investigation had established the Chicago CISPES leader to be a terrorist."

According to the decision, "The Chicago Field Office received and placed in its file articles attacking CISPES written by the political organizations Young Americas Foundation, Students for a Better America, Inc., and the Council for Inter-American Security. The FBI later, as a result of its internal inquiry, characterized these articles as 'conservative material.'"

The inadequacy of the Senate Intelligence Committee's findings was underscored by Judge Lefkow, who concluded: "The FBI has not shown that there is no reasonable expectation of recurrence against either the named petitioners or other[s]...Although the FBI has enacted new guidelines, they have also enacted guidelines in the past which were meant to prevent this type of investigation...The FBI's own regulations are, therefore, not sufficient to prevent violations. The regulations can also be repealed or modified in the future and do not, therefore, guarantee future compliance...Based on the FBI's past behavior, there is a reasonable likelihood of repetition."[37]

Criminal Penalties for Criminal Conduct

Clearly the FBI systematically uses distortion, disinformation and deliberate lies as official instruments of policy. Whether those lies are directed toward political adversaries, news reporters, other agencies of the executive branch or overseers in Congress charged with monitoring the Bureau's operations, the record of the FBI's counter-terrorism and counter-intelligence units demonstrates unequivocally that it is not to be trusted to tell the truth. With the acquiescence of the Congressional committees, the FBI has succeeded in lying its way out of a series of scandals whose casualties have been truth, the democratic process, and the First Amendment to the Constitution.

In the spring of 1990, Adm. John Poindexter, the former National Security Adviser to whom Oliver North reported, was sentenced to six months in prison for lying to Congress. At Poindexter's sentencing, U.S. District Court Judge Harold Greene said that, had Poindexter not served time in jail, "it would be tantamount to a statement that a scheme to lie to and obstruct Congress is of no great moment, and that even if the perpetrators are found out, the courts will treat their criminal acts as no more than minor infractions." Judge Greene held that Poindexter and North had acted "in violation of a principle fundamental to this constitutional republic—that those elected by and responsible to the people shall make the important policy decisions, and that their decisions may not be nullified by appointed officials who happen to be in positions that give them the ability to operate programs prohibited by law."[38]

It is perplexing that the appropriate officials of the FBI—Ronald Davenport, Oliver Revell, and William Webster— have not been held to the same standards as Poindexter and other federal employees who have been convicted of lying to Congress. The message inherent in the lack of such convictions is that the very agency empowered to enforce the federal laws of the country is, itself, beyond the reach of those laws.

Given the Bureau's tenacious adherence to illegal domestic operations in the face of public and Congressional criticism, given its unwillingness or inability to police its own actions in accordance with the requirements of free speech embedded in the Constitution, and given its time-tested proclivity to act, not as a guardian of the law but as a proprietary police force for the incumbent power structure, there seems no reason for advocates of civil liberties to accept, once again, another promise that the FBI will respect the basic rights of freedom and privacy of U.S. citizens.

The CISPES investigation, alone, involved 59 field offices, stretched from 1981 through mid-1985, generated thousands of pages of file material and resulted in not one conviction for illegal activities. (A 1990 report by the General Accounting Office found that between 1982 and 1988, the FBI used the "terrorism" excuse to open some 10,000 investigations of U.S. citizens, most of which were subsequently closed because no links between the subject of the investigation and terrorism could be found.)[39]

As Frank Wilkinson, a former minister who endured more than three decades of FBI surveillance and dirty tricks, has consistently pointed out, the only reliable remedy for illegal FBI activities is a Congressional charter that would remove the responsibility for overseeing the Bureau from the Bureau itself. Such a charter would mandate the so-called "criminal standard." Under its terms, the FBI would be prohibited from any investigation unless there were clear and present indications that a law had been broken or was about to be broken. Whether Wilkinson's organization, the National Committee Against Repressive Legislation, will be successful in its current efforts to promote such a charter remains to be seen. But short of completely abolishing the FBI, there seems no other solution that would be acceptable to the hundreds of thousands of law-abiding citizens who have been victimized by the zealotry of the Bureau.

A major accomplice of the unidentified individuals who coordinated, planned and executed the break-ins is a press corps which finds nothing extraordinary or ominous about a sustained campaign of political assault against law-abiding citizens who disagree with their president's foreign policies. That was the kind of activity that heralded the rise to power of Hitler. And, if the United States ever falls prey to demagoguery, zealotry or institutionalized intolerance, this is the way it will begin. And it will proceed with an assist from the press whose members who will most likely dismiss victims of political repression as "fringe types" as they turn away from uncomfortable clues of tyranny.

It was the press, after all, that was unconcerned that the FBI was permitted to enter tens of thousands of names of citizens into its terrorism files—records which can be used to deny them jobs, to savage their reputations, to subject them to arbitrary surveillance, and to make them criminal suspects the next time a bomb explodes in one of America's cities.

Caught in the grip of economic uncertainty and facing a future of environmental degradation and global political upheaval, much of the U.S. public has lost sight of the very civil liberties that distinguish the United States from other empires that were merely powerful and wealthy. If that forgetfulness persists, this country will have lost that which has made it an ideal for newly emerging "Pro-Democracy" regimes throughout Eastern Europe, that which has made it special in the light of history.

The notion of civil liberties—a major hallmark of the American Constitution—seems very elusive to many Americans in the 1990s and virtually irrelevant to others. But from both a societal and an individual point of view, it is critical to the survival of the country as we know it. Throughout U.S. history, solutions to problems have often come from oppositional political movements—most recently the Civil Rights movement, the Nuclear Freeze, the environmental movement, the women's movement—many of which began with small followings and marginal influence. But the existence of unpopular or dissenting groups provides a kind of intellectual wetlands, a spawning ground for new experiments, new ideas, new solutions to problems which are intractable to traditional approaches.

To wipe out those wetlands by means of censorship, intimidation or enforced silence is to undermine one of the richest resources of the country's public life. When new problems arise, there will be only old solutions. And both an important early warning system, as well as a source of innovation and ingenuity, will have been eliminated.

What we have learned about the operations of the FBI—not only against Central America activists, but also against opponents of nuclear weapons, civil rights groups, and environmental organizations—suggests that the Bureau sees its basic mandate as preventing the success of any significant movement for social change in America. From its mission as a national police force, dedicated to thwarting interstate and international crime, the FBI has become a guardian of the status quo, the incumbency, and the front line in the war against any set of citizens who oppose the policies of the country's leadership. That mission may have been appropriate in Stalin's Soviet Union or Deng's China or Pinochet's Chile. It is not appropriate to the laws of the United States.

From an individual point of view, the country was founded on the premise that each citizen has the political right and the moral obligation to develop his or her self and work to realize his or her potential as fully as possible.

Contrast that ideal with the hypothetical situation of a concerned individual in the 1980s—we will call her Jill—who is moved to action by her sympathy with Central American refugees she has seen on television or in the downtown area of the city she lives in. Or, perhaps, she found herself outraged at her government's support of a foreign regime which murders and incarcerates its citizens at will. Or, let's assume, she feels compelled to speak out against her government's attempts to undermine and destroy a democratically elected government in another part of the world.

Jill would probably be surveilled by FBI agents who enter her name in the Bureau's terrorism files. Her telephone could be tapped and her mail periodically opened and inspected. She might come home one night to find the house ransacked, files stolen and a death threat left in full view. She could spot her name in any one of a dozen publications published by extremist political groups and disseminated and financed by the State Department. She could, at the same time, be on a "watchlist" provided to the National Security Agency so that every international phone call she made was monitored and recorded. Her taxes could be audited by the Internal Revenue Service because of "questionable" political activities. Her landlord, employer and close friends could be interviewed by FBI agents who may well suggest that continued association with or employment of Jill could result in their own entry onto a government list. Because of her sincere convictions and her courage to act on them, she can find herself deprived of her rights to privacy, limited in her occupational opportunities, subject to physical attacks, and shunned by the society she thought she was working to improve.

All these things have happened to citizens who publicly opposed the Administration's policies in Central America and elsewhere.

They happened in the 1980s with barely a notice in the mainstream press and with hardly a protest from the public at large.

And, unless American citizens are able to remember why this country was founded and what made it unique in the sight of history, it will, no doubt, happen again.

Notes

Preface

1. NSDD-22:Jan. 29, 1982: *Designation of Intelligence Officials Authorized to Request FBI Collection of Foreign Intelligence.*
2. Numerous portions of documents contained in both the FBI's CISPES files and its file on Varelli were withheld from requesters on the basis that they involved a "third agency" which can be assumed in most cases to be the Central Intelligence Agency.
3. The practice of talking to a journalist "on background"—normally used by government officials to impart authoritative but unattributed information to reporters—was used in this case to conceal the identity of specific FBI officials in their efforts to discredit Varelli.

Chapter 1

1. *Mandate for Leadership: Policy Management in a Conservative Administration.* The Heritage Foundation, 1980, Washington, D.C. Section on intelligence policy edited by Samuel Francis.
2. *New York Times,* March 12, 1981.
3. *Mandate for Leadership.,* Heritage Foundation.
4. *Boston Globe,* Jan. 22, 1984.
5. *Keeping America Uninformed: Government Secrecy in the 1980s,* by Donna A. Demac, The Pilgrim Press, New York, 1984.
6. *Boston Globe,* April 20, 1986.
7. *Veil,* Bob Woodward, Pocket Books, New York, 1987, p. 110.
8. Ibid., p. 111.
9. Executive Order 12333, Dec. 4, 1981, United States Intelligence Activities.
10. *Veil,* p. 171; also: *Soviet Active Measures,* Hearings before the Permanent Select Committee on Intelligence, House of Representatives, July 13-14, 1982.
11. Executive Order 12333, Dec. 4, 1981, United States Intelligence Activities.

Chapter 2

1. *Boston Globe,* March 26, 1985.
2. FBI Document: CISPES Headquarters file 199-8848—Section 6: Number 254.
3. Author's interview with Joe Roos, Editor of *Sojourners* magazine, 1984.
4. *Boston Globe,* Dec. 30, 1984.
5. Author's interview with Edward Haase, 1989.
6. *Boston Globe,*Dec. 9, 1985; also author's interview with Sara Murray.
7. Author's 1989 interview with Francisco Cavazos. Additional investigator's notes provided to the author by Phoenix journalist Don Devereux.
8. *Boston Globe,* Jan. 6, 1987; also author's 1987 interview with Rev. Victor Carpenter and Margaret Hasbrouck, administrator of the Arlington Street Church.
9. Author's interview with Rev. Timothy Limburg, January, 1987.
10. Author's 1987 interviews with Catherine Suitor and Glynnis Golden.
11. *Boston Globe,* April 7, 1987.
12. Author's 1987 interview with Beverly Truemann of NICA.
13. *Boston Globe,* July 12 and Nov. 7, 1987; also author's interview with Yanira Corea and investigating Los Angeles police officers. Letter from Los Angeles physician attesting to Corea's wounds in author's possession.
14. *Boston Globe,* July 14, 1987; text of letter in author's possesion.
15. Ibid.
16. *Los Angeles Times,* July 19, 1987.
17. Author's 1987 interview with Kathy Engel of Madre.
18. *Boston Globe,* Nov. 7, 1987.

Chapter 3

1. Article in *Diario de Hoy* in FBI Dallas office file on Frank Varelli: Folder on El Salvadoran Terrorism.
2. Author's 1988 interview with Col. Agustin Martinez Varela.
3. FBI Dallas Field Office file on Frank Varelli: Volume 2, Document 160.
4. Author's 1988 interview with Col. Agustin Martinez Varela.
5. *Veil,* p. 117.
6. Opening Statement by Oliver B. Revell, executive assistant director, Federal Bureau of Investigation, before an open session of the Select Committee on Intelligence, United States Senate, Washington, D.C., Feb 23, 1988.
7. *The FBI and CISPES,* Report of the Select Committee on Intelligence, United States Senate, July 14, 1989, p.97.
8. Author's 1989 interview with Beth Perry.
9. Author's 1989 interview with Michael Lent.

10. The Congressional staff member requested anonymity as a condition of the interview.
11. *Review of the News,* April 8, 1981, vol. 17, no. 14.
12. Western Goals fund-raising letter [undated] in possession of author.
13. *The FBI and CISPES,* Report of the Select Committee on Intelligence, United States Senate, July 14, 1989, p.97.
14. FBI Headquarters file on Frank Varelli; Dallas Cross References, Volume 3, Document 6.

Chapter 4

1. Author's interview with Frank Varelli.
2. Letter from Vides Casanova to Agustin Martinez Varela in author's possession.
3. *The Central American Crisis Reader,* edited by Robert S. Leiken and Barry Rubin, Summit Books, New York, 1987, p.546.
4. Narrative version of Frank Varelli.
5. Ibid.
6. List of materials offered by Villacorta et al. in author's possession.
7. *Political and Military Strategy Against Communist Subversion in Latin America,* 1980. Report in author's possession.
8. Author's interview with Frank Varelli.
9. Ibid.
10. Lists in author's possession; See also *Break-Ins At Sanctuary Churches and Organizations Opposed to Administration Policy in Central America.*Hearings before the Subcommittee On Civil and Constitutional Rights of the Committee on the Judiciary, House of Representatives, February 19 and 20, 1987.
11. Samples of CESPDES material in author's possession.

Chapter 5

1. Tape recordings of telephone conversations between"Gilberto Mendoza" and CISPES members in author's possession.
2. Tape recordings of phone conversations between Frank Varelli and Antonio Villacorta in author's possession.
3. Narrative of FBI's detention of Ana Estela Guevara Flores from Frank Varelli. Elements of Varelli narrative of Ana Estela Guevara Flores are also corroborated in Opinion of Judge John R. Brown, U.S. Court of Appeals for the Fifth Circuit: Case of Ana Estela Guevara Flores vs. Immigration and Naturalization Service, April 11, 1986.
4. National Guard of El Salvador Report: To Director General; From: Chief of Section II; RE: Information regarding G.A.R.; copy in author's possession [author's italics].

5. Department of Defense Intelligence Information Report No. 6 829 5052 81, dated July, 1981. (Translation of National Guard document in Defense Intelligence report reads:"The GAR"allegedly receives assistance from Catholic organizations, unions, gay power groups, pro-abortion groups and other organizations in the U.S."

Chapter 6

1. Executive Order 12333, Dec. 1981.
2. *Inside the League,* Jon Lee Anderson and Scott Anderson, Dodd, Mead and Co., New York, 1986.
3. Ibid.
4. FBI documents involving activities of the CARP organization of the Rev. Sun Myung Moon's group were released under a Freedom of Information Act request to Lawrence Zilliox of the Cult Awareness Network in New York. Documents in author's possession.
5. Ibid.
6. Author's interview with Frank Varelli. Varelli said his recollection of the Moon-group members being paid by Flanagan was reinforced in 1984, after Flanagan was forced to leave the FBI, partly because it was learned he had withheld funds from several FBI sources, including Varelli. Varelli recalled that Special Agent Jim Evans went to the Moon group to find out whether or not Flanagan had withheld any money from them.
7. FBI Washington Field Office CISPES File 199-1397. Document 89:"Cispes: A Guerrilla Propaganda Network," by J. Michael Waller.
8. Copies of Waller's contracts with the Office of Latin Public Diplomacy of the US Department of State have been released under a Freedom of Information request.
9. Western Goals literature in author's possession.
10. Author's interview with John Rees, March, 1987.
11. Author's 1987 interviews with two former staff members of Western Goals who asked not to be publicly identified.
12. IPS v. John Mitchell et al., U.S. District Court for the District of Columbia, July 20, 1977.
13. Internal FBI memo from Alex Rosen to Cartha DeLoach, Sept. 27, 1968. In author's possession.
14. Ibid.
15. Ibid.
16. Author's 1987 interview with John Rees.
17. *Newark News,* July 12, 1968.
18. Internal FBI memo from Alex Rosen to Cartha DeLoach, September 27, 1968. In author's possession.
19. Author's 1987 interview with John Rees.

20. *Report to the Standing Committee on Governmental Operations of the New York State Assembly,* June 8, 1976. Copy in author's possession.
21. Letter of April 27, 1976, from Rep. Larry P. McDonald to Assemblyman Mark Siegel of the New York State Assembly. Copy in author's possession.
22. *Report to the Standing Committee on Governmental Operations of the New York State Assembly,* June 8, 1976. Copy in author's possession.
23. Notes of Nov. 10, 1983, interview of Richard K. Miller by Detective Wealer and Sgt. Szymanski of the Internal Affairs Division of the Los Angeles Police Department. Portions of the Internal Affairs report in author's possession.
24. Statement Pursuant to Rule 3(g), Notice of Motion for Partial Summary Judgment, National Lawyers Guild, et. al. v. Attorney General of the United States, United States District Court, Southern District of New York, Jan. 15, 1982. Copy in author's possession.
25. Transcript of series on "Private Spies," broadcast Nov. 10, 11 and 12, 1987, KRON-TV, San Francisco, produced by Jonathan Dann.
26. Letter of June 7, 1988, from FBI Director William S. Sessions to Rep. Don Edwards, Chairman, Subcommittee on Civil and Constitutional Rights, Committee of the Judiciary, House of Representatives. Copy in author's possession.
27. Ibid.

Chapter 7

1. FBI Dallas Office Frank Varelli file #199-4441, Volume 2, Doc. #160.
2. Author's interview with Frank Varelli.
3. *Veil,* by Bob Woodward, Pocket Books, New York, 1987.
4. Opening Statement of Sen. Jeremiah Denton before the Subcommittee on Security and Terrorism, June 24, 1982.
5. Author's italics.
6. Author's italics.
7. *Soviet Active Measures,* Hearings before the Permanent Select Committee on Intelligence, House of Representatives, July 13-14, 1982.
8. Ibid.
9. *The Nation:* Nov. 6, 1982, "But Will They Come? The Campaign to Smear the Nuclear Freeze Movement," by Frank Donner.
10. Ibid.
11. Ibid.
12. Author's interview with Frank Varelli.
13. *New York Times,* March 9, 1981.
14. *Soviet Active Measures,* Hearings before the Permanent Select Committee on Intelligence, House of Representatives, July 13, 14 1982.
15. Ibid.
16. Ibid.

17. Tape recording of John Rees address to The Conservative Caucus, titled:"The Geo-Strategic Crisis: What is to be Done? Soviet Active Measures in America" April 9, 1983. Recording in author's possession.

Chapter 8

1. Frank Varelli, testimony before the House Judiciary Subcommittee on Civil and Constitutional Rights, February 19-20, 1987. Also: Author's interview with Frank Varelli.
2. Author's interview with Frank Varelli.
3. Copy of Terrorist Photo Album entry in possession of author. See also: *Break-Ins at Sanctuary Churches and Organizations Opposed to Administration Policy in Central America,* Hearings before the Subcommittee on Civil and Constitutional Rights of the Commttee on the Judiciary, House of Representatives, Feb. 19 and 20, 1987.
4. Ibid.
5. Ibid.
6. Ibid.
7. Letter from FBI Director William Webster to Rep. Patricia Schroeder, April 3, 1987.
8. FBI Dallas Field Office Frank Varelli File: 199-4441: Volume A I: Document A-58.
9. Letter from William Webster to Sen. Christopher Dodd, March 24, 1987, retained in FBI Headquarters file on Frank Varelli 199-4441, Vol. 2, Document 76.
10. Ibid.
11. Author's italics.
12. Internal FBI memo to FBI Director William Webster, Executive Assistant Director Oliver Revell, and FBI chief of Congressional and Public Affairs William Baker, retained in FBI Headquarters file on Frank Varelli 199-4441, Vol.2, Document 76.
13. *Sanctuary: A Story of American Conscience and Law in Collision,* by Ann Crittenden, Weidenfeld & Nicholson, 1988. Pp. 95-96.
14. *Report on Human Rights in El Salvador,* Compiled by Americas Watch Committee and the American Civil Liberties Union, Vintage Books, 1982.
15. Author's interview with Frank Varelli.
16. Author's interview with Frank Varelli. See also:"The Death Squads Hit Home," by Vience Bielski, Cindy Forster and Dennis Bernstein, *The Progressive,* Oct. 16, 1987. Also reports in several FBI documents, released to the Center for Constitutional Rights, which detailed speeches and activities of visiting Salvadorans in Florida bore the code numbers of right-wing Salvadorans who were used as assets by the FBI's Miami Office, according to Varelli.
17. Author's interview with Frank Varelli.

Chapter 9

1. Senate Judiciary Subcommittee on Security and Terrorism, March, 1981, statement of Sen. Jeremiah Denton.
2. *AlternativeMedia,* "The Big Liars are Back in Town," Chip Berlet, Fall, 1981.
3. Copy provided to the author by Margaret Ratner of the Center for Constitutional Rights.
4. *Alternative Media,* "The Big Liars are Back in Town," Chip Berlet.
5. Author's interviews with Chip Berlet, Margaret Ratner and Michael Ratner.
6. Complaint 82-1824, United States District Court for the District of Columbia, June 30, 1982.
7. FBI Headquarters CISPES file 199-8848-254.
8. Movement Support Network Incident Reports.
9. Author's interview with Frank Varelli.
10. Various charts, reports, etc. compiled by Varelli for the FBI, in author's possession. FBI San Antonio Field Office document: 199-768-5, March 30, 1983.
11. The map indicated new CISPES chapters in Seattle, Portland, Sacramento, Oakland, Los Gatos, San Francisco, San Jose, Fresno, Los Angeles, Santa Ana, San Diego, Phoenix, Tucson, Denver, Santa Fe, El Paso, Harlingen (TX), San Antonio, Austin, Houston, Fort Worth and Dallas, Oklahoma City, New Orleans, Jackson, Selma, Little Rock, Kansas City, St. Louis, Nashville, Atlanta, Tampa, Miami, Coral Gables, Columbia, Winston-Salem, Greensboro, Washington (DC.), Baltimore, Philadelphia, New York, Nutley (NJ), Boston, Manchester (NH), Hanover (NH), Syracuse, Buffalo, Pittsburgh, Cleveland, Detroit, Grand Rapids, South Bend, Indianapolis, Chicago, Milwaukee, Minneapolis, and San Juan.
12. Author's interview with Frank Varelli.
13. Selected CESPDES publications in author's possession.
14. Author's interview with Frank Varelli.
15. *Inside the League,* Jon Lee Anderson and Scott Anderson, Dodd, Mead and Co., New York, 1986.
16. Ibid.
17. Copies of *Replica* in author's possession.
18. FBI Dallas Field Office file on Frank Varelli, Document 1A137.
19. *The FBI and CISPES,* Report of the Select Committee on Intelligence, United States Senate, July 14, 1989, pp. 26 and 27.
20. Ibid., p. 27.
21. Ibid., p. 29.
22. Ibid., p. 30.
23. FBI Headquarters CISPES File Document: 199-8848-105, Oct. 28, 1983.
24. Author's interview with Dr. Ann Mari Buitrago.

Chapter 10

1. *State Department and Intelligence Community Involvement in Domestic Activities Related to the Iran-Contra Affair,* Committee on Foreign Affairs, U.S. House of Representatives, Sept. 7, 1988.

2. "Iran-Contra's Untold Story," By Robert Parry and Peter Kornbluh, *Foreign Policy Magazine,* Winter, 1988.

3. *Boston Globe,* Oct. 4, 1988.

4. *Miami Herald,* Oct. 13, 1986.

5. "Iran Contra's Untold Story," by Robert Parry and Peter Kornbluh, *Foreign Policy Magazine,* Winter, 1988.

6. Ibid.

7. Memo to: Mr. Pat Buchanan, Assistant to the President, Director of Communications, The White House; From: S/LPD—Jonathan S. Miller; Subject:"White Propaganda" Operation, May 13, 1985. Copy in author's possession.

8. "Iran Contra's Untold Story," by Robert Parry and Peter Kornbluh, *Foreign Policy Magazine,* Winter, 1988.

9. *Boston Globe,* Oct. 4, 1988.

10. Waller's contracts with the State Department's Office for Latin Public Diplomacy were released through a Freedom of Information request.

11. Memorandum for the Honorable William J. Casey, The Director of Central Intelligence: Subject: Central American Public diplomacy, Aug. 7, 1986. Copy in author's possession.

12. "Iran Contra's Untold Story," by Robert Parry and Peter Kornbluh, *Foreign Policy Magazine,* Winter, 1988.

13. Author's interview with Frank Varelli.

14. Ibid.

15. FBI Dallas Field Office file on Frank Varelli, 199-4441 - Document A-48.

16. FBI Dallas Field Office file on Frank Varelli, 199-795 - A:48: 6/30/83.

17. Author's interview with Frank Varelli.

18. Ibid.

19. Ibid.

20. Letter from Gene Lantz to"Gilberto Mendoza," June 29, 1983 in FBI Dallas Field Office File on El Salvadoran Terrorism, Not Numbered.

21. FBI Dallas Field Office File on Frank Varelli, Sub A, Document A-40; also: FBI Dallas Field Office File on Frank Varelli, Document 1A65.

22. FBI Headquarters Frank Varelli file: 199-4441-94.

23. Author's interview with Frank Varelli; also: FBI Dallas Field Office File on Frank Varelli, 199-4441-1A75.

24. Author's interview with Frank Varelli.

25. ACLU FUND of the National Capital Area: Political Asylum Project, Sept. 5, 1984.

26. Author's interview with Frank Varelli.

Chapter 11

1. *Washington Post,* Nov. 8, 1983.
2. In May, 1982, a bomb was discovered in the Air Canada cargo area at Los Angeles airport. Police arrested three members of ASALA, an Armenian political group. On September 20, 1982, a bomb damaged the building of the Bankers Trust Co. in New York. The Puerto Rican FALN claimed credit for the bombing. In December, 1982, bombs exploded almost simultaneously at IBM in Harrison, New York, and the South African airline office in Manhattan. The United Freedom Fighters claimed responsibility. On New Year's Eve, 1982, four bombs exploded within a 90 minute period in New York, at police headquarters, a federal building, a metropolitan correctional facility and the U.S. District Court building. Responsibility was claimed by callers who said they represented the FALN and the Palestine Liberation Organization. In January, 1983, a bomb exploded at a federal building in Staten Island New York. A group calling itself the Revolutionary Fighting Group claimed responsibility. In April, 1983, a bomb exploded at the National War College at Fort McNair, Maryland. The Armed Resistance Unit claimed responsibility. In August, 1983, a bomb damaged the outside of a building at the Washington, D.C. Navy Yard. The ARU claimed responsibility and asserted that it had acted on behalf of the Salvadoran FMLN.
3. The "secret" chain of command of the FBI's Global Counter-Terrorism Unit, as it was called, which by-passed director Webster, ran from Special Agent Daniel Flanagan in Dallas, to Special Supervisory Agent Ron Davenport, who was in charge of the FBI's Salvadoran Terrorism investigation in Washington, to Oliver "Buck" Revell, the FBI's executive assistant director, according to an affidavit filed in the Washington D.C. Federal Claims Court by Frank Varelli in 1987. See: United States Claims Court, In the Matter of: Frank Varelli v. The United States of America, Docket No. 393-87C.
4. Author's interview with Frank Varelli.
5. FBI Los Angeles Field Office CISPES file: Document 142. Also: FBI Headquarters CISPES File, document (unnumbered) after 144X: "Investigation in several recent bombings believed to be perpetrated by the May 19th Coalition has indicated a possible connection between May 19th Coalition and CISPES membership and/or leadership. Recipients ensure that all pertinent info in this inv. is furnished to Dallas and FBIHQ. NOTE: The above forwarded…also requests information to determine what, if any connection may exist between CISPES and the May 19th Coalition. This concern will be coordinated between the domestic unit and ITU-II." Dec. 22, 1983.

6. Associated Press, Sept. 7, 1990, "Three Leftists Plead Guilty to Bombing the U.S. Capitol."

7. Author's 1989 interview with Ruth Fitzpatrick.

8. FBI Washington Field Office CISPES File Document 199-1397-104.

9. Author's interview with Frank Varelli.

10. FBI Washington Field Office CISPES Document 199-1397-66.

11. Author's interview with Frank Varelli.

12. FBI Dallas Field Office file on Frank Varelli 199-795-309. The introduction to this airtel notes: "Bureau [Headquarters] requested Dallas to provide additional details regarding implied threats to the President and other government officials as contained in newspaper issued by C.E.S.F.M., Nosotros," March 3, 1984.

13. FBI Headquarters CISPES files: Document 128X.

14. FBI Headquarters CISPES files: Document 128X1.

15. FBI Headquarters CISPES files: Document 155.

16. FBI Headquarters CISPES files: Document 134X.

17. FBI Headquarters CISPES files: Document 157.

18. FBI Headquarters CISPES files: Document 300X3.

19. FBI Headquarters CISPES files: Document 436.

20. FBI Headquarters CISPES files: Document 548.

21. FBI Headquarters CISPES files: Document 483.

22. FBI Headquarters CISPES files: Document 510.

23. FBI Headquarters CISPES files: Document 543.

24. FBI Headquarters Frank Varelli file: Vol 1,Document 54, April 14, 1983.

25. Author's 1989 interview with David Lindorff.

Chapter 12

1. FBI Washington Field Office File on Frank Varelli, 199-795-192, indicates authorization for Flanagan and Varelli to travel to Washington on Dec. 11, 1983, and for Flanagan to stay at the Twin Bridges Marriott hotel.

2. Account of task force meeting from author's interview with Frank Varelli.

3. The source of this quote, a former FBI official, has requested anonymity.

4. Account of task force meeting from author's interview with Frank Varelli.

5. Regarding the electronic surveillance of Congressmen and women, Varelli has insisted under repeated questioning that he did read file entries on the legislators marked ELSUR (the FBI's acronym for electronic surveillance, i.e., wiretapping.) But it is unclear whether the FBI actually tapped the legislators' phones, or whether the electronic surveillance material was gathered through phone calls from legislators to, for example, the Nicaraguan Embassy or the Washington office of the Salvadoran FDR, which were legitimate targets for wiretapping under the FBI's foreign counter-intelligence guidelines.

6. Varelli has repeated this conversation in testimony before Congress, as well as to numerous journalists, including the author.

7. Varelli has insisted repeatedly that Flanagan and others knew he carried a gun into the CISPES office, despite the fact that it would appear to violate FBI guidelines for this type of operation.

8. While Varelli's account of his visit to the CISPES headquarters in Washington is recounted in detail in FBI files, the Senate Intelligence Committee inexplicably noted in their report that:"Mr. Varelli's report on that trip indicates that he never actually met any Washington members of CISPES or attended any of their meetings. He did report on several left-wing bookstores, however, as well as some churches that he suspected of harboring illegal aliens...He was more successful in visiting the headquarters of Western Goals, where he obtained more right-wing literature..." *The FBI and CISPES,* Report of the Select Committee on Intelligence, United States Senate, July 14, 1989, p.75. However, Varelli's account of his meeting with CISPES officials, as well as his other activities in Washington, are recounted in an extensive, highly detailed 16-page FBI Dallas Field Office File on Frank Varelli, document 199C-795-218X. The cover page of the document contains the following handwritten notes:"Good job (blank) Thanks. I talked to (blank) who was pleased. He said the unit chief was impressed also." The note bears the initials TK. At the time, Thomas Kelley was the Special Agent in Charge of the Dallas FBI office.

9. Author's interview with Frank Varelli.

10. FBI Dallas Field Office file on Frank Varelli file, Dallas Cross-References: 199C-795-218X.

11. Copy of *El Salvador Alert* which Varelli used for entries into the FBI's terrorism files in author's possession.

12. Account of Flanagan's mysterious ride from author's interview with Frank Varelli. Flanagan has, on repeated occasions, declined to talk to the author.

13. Varelli's visit to Western Goals is confirmed on page 75 of the Senate Intelligence Committee report on the FBI and CISPES.

14. Account of the Varelli-Flanagan conversation from author's interview with Frank Varelli.

15. It is unclear whether Varelli's account of his misgivings were reconstructed accurately in interviews with the author or whether Varelli decided, at a later date, to put forth these misgivings in order to cast himself and his actions in a different light for the author.

16. Author's 1987 interviews with officials at CISPES and the Institute for Policy Studies.

17. Author's 1987 interviews with members of Old Cambridge Baptist Church. Break-in at Honduran Information Center was reported to the Movement Support Network.

18. Author's 1986 interview with Esmerelda Brown.

Chapter 13

1. *Los Angeles Times,* running stories from the summer of 1983 to October 1985.

2. Many details of the Jay Paul - Western Goals operation are cited in a secret Los Angeles Police Department Internal Affairs investigation of the incident conducted in 1983 and 1984. Portions of the unreleased Internal Affairs report in the author's possession.

3. *Los Angeles Times,* April 19, 1984.

4. Internal Affairs report of L.A.P.D., in author's possession.

5. Ibid.

6. Western Goals documents in author's possession. Also: *Boston Globe,* March 15, 1988.

7. Hearings of the Select Committee to investigate the Iran-Contra Affair, May 31, 1987.

8. Author's interviews with two former staff members of Western Goals. The former staffers have requested anonymity.

9. Statement Pursuant to Rule 3(g), Notice of Motion for Partial Summary Judgment, National Lawyers Guild, et. al. v. Attorney General of the United States, United States District Court, Southern District of New York, Jan. 15, 1982. Copy in author's possession.

10. Copy of *Information Digest* in author's possession.

11. Young Americas Foundation document: FBI Headquarters CISPES FILE: Document unnumbered, after number 423.

12. Under a Freedom of Information Request, the State Department in 1989 released copies of four contracts to Waller from the Office of Latin Public Diplomacy to produce studies, material from which later turned up in FBI files. Also, Waller confirmed in an interview with the author that he prepared material under contract for the State Department.

13. *Dallas Morning News,* April 6, 1986, "The Informant Left Out in the Cold," by Christi Harlan. The article details, with confirmations by sources in the intelligence community, Flanagan's security breach and loss of documents.

14. Varelli's account of the Flanagan security breach and subsequent events is contained in a sworn, 16-page summary Varelli wrote at the request of Thomas Kelly, at the time Special Agent in Charge of the Dallas Field Office. The statement concludes: "Under penalty of perjury, I state that this statement is true to the best of my knowledge. Dallas, Texas, May 15, 1984, Frank Varelli." Copy in author's possession.

15. Testimony by Oliver B. Revell, executive assistant director, Federal Bureau of Investigation, before an open session of the Select Committee on Intelligence, United States Senate, Washington, D.C., Feb 23, 1988.

16. United States Claims Court, Washington, D.C., Docket No. 393-87C, Frank Varelli v. United States of America.

17. Documents on the Institute for the Study of the Americas and the book commissioned by the State Department's Office for Latin Public Diplomacy were released to the author by the State Department in 1988 under a Freedom of Information Request.

18. Author's interview with Frank Varelli.

19. Copy of the manuscript is in the author's possession.

20. Ibid.

21. The source, who was close to Oliver North during the period of time in question, has requested anonymity.

22. Special Agent Daniel Flanagan declined several requests for an interview with the author. In January 1989, while in the Dallas area, the author left a note in Flanagan's mailbox, asking for an interview and leaving the phone number of his motel room. During the night, the author received a number of phone calls at the motel in which the caller hung up without speaking. The following morning, both the author and Frank Varelli noticed a man with binoculars in a van outside the rear of the motel surveilling the author's motel room.

23. Varelli's sworn statement to Thomas Kelly, at the time Special Agent in Charge of the Dallas Office. Copy in author's possession.

24. Ibid.

25. Author's interview with Frank Varelli.

26. Varelli's account confirmed by notes and conclusions of polygraph examiner which were released by the FBI to Frank Varelli under a Freedom of Information lawsuit. The examiner's notes and conclusions are contained in FBI Headquarters file on Frank Varelli: Document 1A143.

27. Author's interview with Frank Varelli.

28. FBI Headquarters file on Frank Varelli: Document 1A143, dated June 7, 1984:"It is the opinion of the examiner that the recorded responses to Series I and Series II [dealing with Varelli's FBI activities] reflect no apparent deception. The responses to Series III [dealing with the Duarte conversations] indicate deception."

29. FBI Memorandum in Headquarters file on Frank Varelli: Document number 148, dated July 19, 1984.

30. Tape recording of Varelli's interview with Secret Service agent Jerry Kluber in the summer of 1984, in which Varelli explained his concerns that the President might be in danger from an attack of a terrorist who might infiltrate CISPES, is in the possession of the author.

31. FBI Headquarters CISPES file: Document 381 and others.

32. FBI Memorandum in Headquarters file on Frank Varelli: Document not numbered, dated April 24, 1987."A technical review of the polygraph examination documents pertaining to the examination of Frank Varelli on 6/7/84 in response to an inquiry regarding this matter has been completed by (blank) FBIHQ. This review disclosed that the responses indicate that the examinee was deceptive. It was noted during this review that the

report erroneously concluded the examinee truthful to the first two series of questions. This was an error in the report and should be disregarded." The document bears the following handwritten note from an official in the Dallas Field Office:"Pls prepare AT [airtel] to HQ suggesting they consider review of [Varelli] file pursuant to (blank) FCIM and corrective action be taken by HQ if appropriate inasmuch as they have had the file for years and Dallas cannot assess the significance of this [illegible word] without the file."

33. *Boston Globe*, December 29, 1988.

34. Several Congressional sources told the author to be cautious with Varelli since he had failed his polygraph examination.

Chapter 14

1. *Miami Herald*, July 5, 1987, by Alfonse Chardy.

2. Author's 1989 interview with researcher Diana Reynolds.

3. Hearings of the Select Committee to Investigate the Iran-Contra Affair, Summer, 1987.

4. Author's 1989 interview with researcher Diana Reynolds.

5. Mabry has provided the author with a note from Fawn Hall, dated April 18, 1985, as well as a letter from Edwin Meese, dated Nov. 15, 1983.

6. Copies of Mabry's phone logs in author's possession.

7. *Boston Globe,* Feb. 29, 1988.

8. Mabry's letter to Webster in author's possession.

9. Revell's response to Mabry in author's possession.

10. Author's interview with Philip Mabry.

11. Photocopy of check in author's possession.

12. Copies of Mabry's list of organizations to monitor as well as of several photographs of Fort Worth-area activists are in author's possession.

13. Note from Fawn Hall to Mabry and Pearce in author's possession.

14. Oliver Revell interview with staff members of the Iran-Contra Committee: *Report of the Congressional Committees Investigating the Iran-Contra Affair,* Appendix B: Volume 27, Washington, D.C., 1988.

15. Copy of Watson notebook entry in author's possession.

16. The CIA veteran has been interviewed extensively by writer Jeffrey McConnell, who has graciously shared the information with the author.

17. *Boston Globe Magazine,* May 13, 1990: "Coups, Wars and the CIA" by Jeffrey McConnell.

18. Ibid.

19. William Webster, at Congressional Confirmation Hearings as director of CIA, Knight-Ridder Newspapers, May 1, 1987.

20. Motion to Supplement Previously Filed Selective Prosecution Motion, United States of America v. Jack Terrell, et al.: United States District Court, Southern District of Florida, Case No. 88-6097, Jan. 18, 1989.

21. Oliver Revell interview with staff members of the Iran-Contra Committee: *Report of the Congressional Committees Investigating the Iran-Contra Affair,* Appendix B: Volume 22; Washington, D.C., 1988.

22. Entries from North's notebooks and calendar, indicating his relationship with Special Agent David Beisner, provided to the author by writer Jeffrey McConnell.

23. William Webster, at Congressional Confirmation Hearings as director of CIA, Knight-Ridder Newspapers, May 1, 1987.

24. *Boston Globe,* July 27, 1988 and August 10, 1988.

25. Memo in possession of author: "MEMORANDUM FOR THE PRESIDENT: FROM: JOHN M. POINDEXTER. Subject: Terrorist Threat: Terrell: Issue: Anti-Contra and anti-U.S. activities by U.S. Citizen, Jack Terrell."

26. *Report of the Congressional Committees Investigating the Iran-Contra Affair,* Appendix A, Volume 1: pp. 862-863.

27. *Boston Globe,* March 24, 1988.

28. *Wall Street Journal,* Dec. 7, 1987.

29. *Report of the Congressional Committees Investigating the Iran-Contra Affair,* Washington, D.C., November, 1987. Additional Views of Honorable Peter W. Rodino, Jr., Honorable Dante B. Fascell, Vice Chairman, Honorable Jack Brooks, and Honorable Louis Stokes, pp. 643-650.

30. *Boston Globe Magazine,* "Coups, Wars and the CIA," by Jeffrey McConnell, May 13, 1990.

31. Revell made the comment to Daniel Noyes, managing editor of the Center for Investigative Reporting.

32. Author's 1987 interview with Lindsay Mattison, executive director of the International Center for Development Policy. The break-in was also reported in the *Washington Post* and the *Boston Globe,* Dec. 1, 1986.

33. Author's 1987 interview with Jeffrey Heimers.

34. Testimony by Lindsay Mattison before the House Judiciary Subcommittee on Civil and Constitutional Rights, *Break-ins at Sanctuary Churches and Organizations Opposed to Administration Policy in Central America,* Feb. 19-20, 1987.

Chapter 15

1. Author's 1987 and 1989 interviews with Rev. Donovan Cook.

2. *Break-Ins At Sanctuary Churches and Organizations Opposed to Administration Policy in Central America.* Hearings before the Subcommittee On Civil and Constitutional Rights of the Committee on the Judiciary, House of Representatives, February 19-20, 1987.

3. Movement Support Network. Confirmation from officials of Amnesty International.

4. Movement Support Network incident log.

5. Movement Support Network incident log.

6. Testimony by Michael Lent before the House Judiciary Subcommittee on Civil and Constitutional Rights, Feb. 19, 1987.
7. Movement Support Network incident log. Also, author's interview with Hugh Byrne of CISPES.
8. Author's 1989 intervew with Rev. James Flynn.
9. Movement Support Network incident log.
10. Author's interviews with Moser and Weiss, reported in the *Boston Globe,* April 25, 1986.
11. Testimony by Martha Doggett of NACLA before the House Judiciary Subcommittee on Civil and Constitutional Rights, Feb. 19, 1987.
12. Movement Support Network incident log. Investigator's notes provided to the author by free-lance journalist Don Devereux. Author's 1989 interview with Mary Kay Espinoza.
13. Movement Support Network incident log.
14. Author's 1987 interviews with David Cunningham and Robert Mandel.
15. Author's 1987 interview with Catherine Burke.
16. Author's interview with Hugh Byrne.
17. Author's interview with Victor Rios. Reports of car break-ins and other harassments in the Los Angeles area in the spring of 1987 were discussed by the author with Mark Rosenbaum of the American Civil Liberties Union in Los Angeles, who confirmed them with investigating police.
18. Movement Support Network.
19. Author's 1987 interview with David Reed.
20. Author's 1988 interview with Beverly Truemann of NICA.
21. Author's 1989 interview with Alicia Fernandes.
22. Author's interview with Sean Conway, November, 1989.
23. *Boston Globe,* Dec. 15, 1989.
24. Ibid.
25. Associated Press, March 29, 1990.
26. Author's interview with David Lerner and Jinsoo Kim of the Center for Constitutional Rights, 1990.
27. Author's interviews with Anne Wright and Thomas Donnebrink of NECAN, 1990.

Chapter 16

1. Tape recording of Varelli discussion with Secret Service agent Jerry Kluber is in author's possession.
2. FBI Director William Sessions testimony before the Select Committee on Intelligence of the United States Senate, Sept. 14, 1988.
3. *The Dallas Morning News,* April 6, 1986,"The Informant Left Out in the Cold," by Christi Harlan. Also: Author's 1988 conversation with Harlan.

4. United States Claims Court, Docket No. 393-87C: In the Matter of: Frank Varelli v. The United States of America, 1989.
5. *The FBI and CISPES,* Report of the Select Committee on Intelligence, United States Senate, July 14, 1989, Pp.24 and 25.
6. FBI Headquarters CISPES Document, 199-8848-105, 10/28/83, initialled"OBR" .
7. *The FBI and CISPES,* Report of the Select Committee on Intelligence, United States Senate, July 14, 1989, P.23.
8. *Veil,* p.220.
9. NSDD-22:Jan. 29, 1982: "Designation of Intelligence Officials Authorized to Request FBI Collection of Foreign intelligence". Copy in author's possession.
10. *Soviet Influence Activities: A Report on Active Measures and Propaganda, 1987-1988,* U.S. Department of State, August 1989.
11. ACLU Fund of the National Capital Area: Political Asylum Project, Sept. 5, 1984.
12. "The Unsolved Break-Ins," by Don Edwards, 1987. A copy of a typed version of this article is in the author's possession.
13. Report to the House Committee on the Judiciary by the U.S. General Accounting Office, Feb. 24, 1976.
14. *Intelligence Activities and the Rights of Americans,* Book[s] II & III: Final Report of the Select Committee to Study Governmental Operations with respect to Intelligence Activities, United States Senate, April 26, 1976, pp. 7-18.
15. Ibid.
16. Ibid.
17. Ibid.
18. Ibid.
19. *Can We Take Our Freedoms for Granted?* By Richard L. Criley, Bill of Rights Foundation, Chicago, Ill., 1985.
20. *Intelligence Activies and the Rights of Americans,* Book[s] II & III: Final Report of the Select Committee to Study Governmental Operations with respect to Intelligence Activities, United States Senate, April 26, 1976.
21. Ibid.
22. Ibid.
23. Ibid.
24. Ibid.
25. Ibid.
26. Ibid.
27. *The FBI and CISPES,* Report of the Select Committee on Intelligence, United States Senate, July 14, 1989, p.127.

28. *The Cointelpro Papers: Documents from the FBI's Secret Wars Against Dissent in the United States,* Ward Churchill and Jim Vander Wall, South End Press, Boston, 1990: pp. 98-99.

29. *Racial Matters: The FBI's Secret File on Black America, 1960-1972,* by Kenneth O'Reilly, The Free Press, New York, 1989, pp. 303-316.

30. *Agents of Repression,* Ward Churchill and Jim Vander Wall, South End Press, Boston, 1988, p.175.

31. *The Cointelpro Papers: Documents from the FBI's Secret Wars Against Dissent in the United States,* Ward Churchill and Jim Vander Wall, South End Press, Boston, 1990, pp. 86-88.

32. *Agents of Repression,* Ward Churchill and Jim Vander Wall, South End Press, Boston, 1988, pp. 368-370.

33. "DO NOT FILE" File in possession of author. See also *Boston Globe,* June 29, 1988.

34. Letter from William Webster to Rep. Don Edwards, Aug. 19, 1988.

35. *The FBI and CISPES,* Report of the Select Committee on Intelligence, United States Senate, July 14, 1989, p.75.

36. FBI Headquarters file on Frank Varelli, 199C-795-218X #0025.

37. Report of Executive Magistrate Judge Joan Humphrey Lefkow to the Honorable Ann C. Williams, U.S. District Court, Chicago, Feb. 4, 1991. Copy in author's possession.

38. *Boston Globe,* June 12, 1990.

39. *New York Times,* Oct. 9, 1990.

Index

A

Abrams, Eliot, Asst. Secretary of State, 125
Active Measures, 14, 21, 87-95, 147, 216-218
Alcorn, Daniel, 211
American Civil Liberties Union, 105, 170
American Civil Liberties Union Fund, Political Asylum Project of, 133, 218-219
American Friends Service Committee, 29, 177
American Indian Movement, 223
Americans for Human Rights and Social Justice, 186
Amnesty International, Los Angeles office of, 198
Ansbach, Susan, 187
Ansesal, 54
Arceo, Msgr. Sergio Mendez, 98
Arlington Street Church of Boston, 30
Armed Resistance Unit, 141
Atthowe, Patricia, 82
Avirgan, Tony, 190-2

B

Barnes, Rep. Michael, 98, 124, 151
Baruch, Bernard, 223
Beisner, Special Agent David, 191-4, 226
Berkman, Alan, 138
Berlet, Chip, 105, 107-9, 117-8
Blunk, Timothy, 138
Boone, Special Agent Randall, 189
Boyle, Fr. Greg, 206
Brannon, Stephen, 200

Brooks, Rep. Jack, 184-5
Brown, Esmerelda, 118
Buchanan, Patrick, 124
Buck, Marilyn, 138
Buitrago, Dr. Ann Mari, 105, 109, 118-20
Bumpers, Sen. Dale, 89
Burke, Catherine, 201
Bush, George, 183
Byrne, Hugh, 201-2

C

Capelle, Ruth, 206
Capitol Bombing, 135-8, 140-2
Capuchin Religious Order, 102
CARP (Collegiate Association for the Research of Principles), 75-7
Carpenter, Rev. Victor, 30
Carranza, Col. Nicolas, 103
CASA (Central America Solidarity Association), 27
Casa Oscar Romero, 187
Casanova, Eugenio Vides, 36, 47-51, 71
Casey, William, 14, 16, 19-21, 40, 74, 87, 121-4, 171, 176, 183, 216-8
Casolo, Audrey, 206
Casolo, Jennifer, 205-6
Catholic Charities Refugee Halfway House, Houston, Texas, 131
CAUSA (Confederations of Associations for the Unity of the Societies of America), 187
Cavazos, Francesca, 29-30
Center for Constitutional Rights, 6, 23, 28, 105, 119, 138, 202-4, 207, 209, 211

Central America Peace Campaign, 187

CESPDES (Center for Socio-Political Studies of El Salvador), 56, 98, 112-13

Chan, Tina, 202

Chardy, Alfonse, *Miami Herald,* 123, 184

Christian Reformed Church of Washington, D.C., 30-1

Christic Institute, 187, 190

Church Committee (of U.S. Senate), 221-3

CIA, 41, 68, 121-5, 183-4, 189, 193, 213, 216-8, 219-20

CISPES (Committee In Solidarity with the People of El Salvador), 21, 31; car break-ins, 32, 33; beginnings of, 41-6; Dallas chapter, 61-5; 110-1; 148, 152; FBI infiltration of Washington office, 154-9; 168, 179, 187, 194, 199, 201, 215-7, 221, 226, 228

Clark, Special Agent Drew, 178

Clark, Mark, 224

Clark, William, National Security Adviser, 122

Clarke, Special Agent Floyd, 189

Coalition Against U.S. Intervention in Central America and the Caribbean, 177

Coalition for a New Foreign and Military Policy, 66, 202-3

Committee of Concern for Central America, 187

Contragate Action Committee, 201

Conservative Caucus, 93-4

Conway, Sean, 205-6

Conyers, Rep. John, 151

Cook, Rev. Donovan, 179-80

COPREFA (Salvadoran military information agency), 150

Corea, Yanira, 32-4, 203

Covert Action Information Bulletin, 107

Council for Inter-American Security, 22, 76-7, 171

CPUSA (Communist Party of the USA) 42, 177

CRECEN (Central American Refugee Center) of Los Angeles, 206

Crockett, Rep. George, 152

Cuban Intelligence Agency (DGI), 116, 137

Cubias, Daisy, 25

Cunningham, David, 201

Customs Service, 27, 108-9

D

Dailey, Peter, 123

Dallas Morning News, 119, 211

Daniel, Sean, 186

Dann, Jonathan, 83-4

D'Aubuisson, Maj. Roberto, 54-5, 103, 171

Davenport, Supervisory Special Agent Ronald, 8, 117, 126, 136, 143, 149-50, 152-3, 214, 228

Defense Intelligence Agency, 72

de Graffenreid, Kenneth, 217

Dellums, Rep. Ronald, 42, 151

Denton, Sen. Jeremiah, 87-90, 106-7

Dodd, Sen. Christopher, 98, 101-2, 151

Dominican Religious Order, 102

"Do Not File" Files, 225

Donnebrink, Thomas, 207

Douglas, Michael, 186

Douglas, William O., 223

Duarte, Jose Napoleon, 38-41, 75, 180, 213

Duke, Elizabeth, 138

Durenberger, Sen. David, 193

Dymally, Rep. Mervin, 152

E

Edwards, Rep. Don, 32, 83, 151, 205, 220, 225

Eisenhower, Dwight, 223

El Salvador 19-20; recent history 37-41

El Salvador Alert, 156, 161-3

Epica, 152
Escobedo, Special Agent Sal, 174, 178
Espinoza, Mary Kay, 200
Evans, Special Agent Jim, 36, 86, 97, 110, 173-4
Evans, Linda, 138
Executive Order 12333, 17, 21, 73, 94

F
FALN (Armed Forces of National Liberation [Puerto Rico]), 135
FARA (Foreign Agents Registration Act), 21, 42, 85-6, 108
FBI (Federal Bureau of Investigation), restoration of powers by President Reagan, 16-17, 20-1; recruitment of Varelli, 36-7; beginning of CISPES probe, 44-6; 59-66; adoption of "active measures" doctrine, 85-9; compilation of Terrorist Photo Album, 97-102; 1983 terrorism conference at FBI Academy, Quantico, Va., 115-7; infiltration of Dallas Anti-Klan coalition, 125-130; infiltration of Taca Airline, 132-4; activities following 1983 Capitol Bombing, 135-8, 140-2, 149-53; confusion in FBI field offices, 144-7; infiltration of CISPES headquarters, 154-9; security breach of CISPES investigation, 173-6; links to Oliver North, 186-7, 189-94; scapegoating of Varelli, 210-6; involvement with deported Salvadoran refugees, 218-9; history of political abuses, 221-5; dissembling to Congress, 225-7.
FBI Field Offices: Chicago, Ill., 146, 226-7; Dallas, Tex., 37, 46, 62, 85-6, 100, 110-1, 127, 147, 173-5, 226; Denver, Colo., 141; Houston, Tex., 134, 212; Los Angeles, Calif., 132; Louisville, Ky., 145-6; Miami, Fla., 28; Milwaukee, Wisc., 25-6; Mobile, Ala., 145; New Orleans, La., 144, 146; Phoenix, Ariz., 144; San Antonio, Tex., 178; San Juan, Puerto Rico, 69; Washington, D.C., 76, 100, 140, 142, 149, 152, 154, 159, 165, 166, 191
FDR (Democratic Revolutionary Front [El Salvador]), 40, 59-60
Federal Emergency Management Agency (FEMA), 184
Fernandes, Alicia, 203-4
Fiers, Alan, 125
Fife, Rev. John, 102
Finkelstein, Ellen, 32
Fitzpatrick, Ruth, 139-40
Flanagan, Special Agent Daniel, 36-7, 49, 67-70, 76, 85-6, 97, 110, 117, 136, 140-3, 149-50, 155, 159, 161, 164, 166-7, 173-5, 178-9, 211, 214
Flores, Ana Estela Guevara, 67-71
Flynn, Rev. James, 199, 206
FMLN (Farabundo Marti Front for National Liberation [El Salvador]), 19, 21, 35-6, 40, 48, 58-9, 98, 143
Ford Foundation, 115
Fort Worth Nuclear Freeze Campaign, 187
Fort Worth TCU Students for a Democratic South Africa, 187
Free Speech Movement, 223
Freedom of Information Act, 17, 118-120

G
GAO (Government Accounting Office) 124, 228
GAR (Armed Revolutionary Group [El Salvador]) 52, 71-2
Giersbach, Susan, 199
Gorson, Arthur, 186
Golden, Glynnis, 31

Greene, Harold, U.S. District Judge, 227-8
Guatemala News and Information Center, 26
Guell, Linda, 165, 187
Guilmartin, John, 124

H
Haase, Edward, 27
Hajek, Sr. Linda, 127
Hall, Fawn, 186, 188
Hall, Wilma, 186
Hamilton, Rep. Lee, 193
Hampton, Fred, 224
Handal, Farid, 42, 216
Handal, Jorge Shafik, 42
Harkin, Sen. Thomas, 152
Harlan, Christi, *Dallas Morning News*, 211
Hasenfus, Eugene, 188
Haverly, Ferd, 206
Healy, Sr. Peggy, 98-9
Hearst Newspapers, 124
Heimers, Jeffrey, 195
Hemmings, Allan Bruce, 189
Heritage Foundation, 16-7
Holy Ghost Catholic Church, Houston, Texas, 131
Honduran Information Center, 162, 168
Honey, Martha, 190-2
Houston Human Rights League, 131

I
Immigration and Naturalization Service, 102
Information Digest, 78, 80-2, 170-2
Inouye, Sen. Daniel, 185
Institute for Policy Studies, 42, 106, 134, 152, 160, 168, 177
Interfaith Peace Coalition, 201
Internal Revenue Service, 25
International Center for Development Policy, 152, 187, 191, 193-5
Inter-Religious Task Force on Central America, 110, 187
Iran-Contra scandal, 2, 18

Iran-Contra Committee, 184-5, 188-9, 194, 226

J
Jackson, Jesse, 162
Jagger, Bianca, 151
John Birch Society, 45
John Brown Anti-Klan Committee, 126
Johnson, Lyndon, 223
Johnson, Special Agent Manny, 149

K
Kasten, Sen. Robert, 26
Kelly, Special Agent in Charge Thomas, 175, 178-9
Kennedy, Fr. Michael, 206
Kennedy, Robert, 222
Kerry, Sen. John, 191-3
King, Jr., Martin Luther, 222-3
Kissinger, Henry, 225
Koenig, Robert L., *St. Louis Post Dispatch*, 162
Kramarsic, Special Agent James, 190-1
Kuhn, Dee, 186

L
Lantz, Elaine, 126, 187
Lantz, Gene, 126-130, 187, 224
Latin American Studies Association (LASA), 115
Lefkow, Joan, U.S. District Magistrate Judge, 226-7
Leland, Rep. Mickey, 152
Lent, Michael, 43, 119
Levison, Stanley, 222
Lewis, Flora, *New York Times*, 91
Limburg, Rev. Timothy, 30-1
Linder, Benjamin, 32
Lindorff, David, 147-8
Lopez, Ana Maria, 33
Los Angeles Police Dept., internal affairs report, 169-171
Lutheran Refugee Services, Houston, Texas, 131
Lyndon LaRouche organization, 225

M

Mabry, Philip, 185-9,
MacFarlane, Robert, National
    Security Adviser, 184, 190
MADRE, 34, 187
Magic Fingers, 34
Maitre, Joachim, 122, 124
Mandel, Robert, 201
Mattes, John, 190
Mattison, Lindsay, 195
May 19th Communist Organization,
    137-8
Mayorga Quiroz, Roman, 59
Mazzoli, Rep. Romano, 94
McConnell, Jeffrey, 91
McDonald, Rep. Larry, 22, 45, 77,
    84, 170-2
McGee, Vonetta, 187
McMahon, John, 88-9
McMahon, Marilyn, 32
McMichael, David, 193
Meese, Edwin, 82, 184-6
"Mendoza, Gilberto," 60-5, 127-30,
    156; also see Varelli, Frank
MICAH (Michigan Interfaith Com-
    mittee on Central American
    Human Rights), 28-9
Miller, Rep. George, 152
Miller, Jonathan, 124
Mirelles, Special Agent Edmundo,
    149, 154, 159, 165
Moon organization, Rev. Sun
    Myung, 22, 74-7, 82, 171, 173,
    187
Moser, Dana, 200
Mother Jones, 60-1, 106
Movement Support Network, 109
Murdoch, Rupert, 122
Murray, Sara, 28
Myers, Rev. David, 198

N

NAACP (National Association for
    the Advancement of
    Colored People), 222

NACLA (North American Confer-
    ence on Latin America), 106,
    134, 177, 200
National Association of Religious
    Women, 140
National City Christian Church,
    Washington, D.C., 160-1
National Committee Against Repres-
    sive Legislation (NCARL), 228
National Guard of El Salvador, 14-5,
    23, 37, 41, 47-55, 65-71, 98, 103-
    4, 111, 130, 132-4, 213-4, 218-9
National Network in Solidarity with
    the Nicaraguan People, 186-7
National Security Agency, 26, 65,
    134, 141
National Security Council, 123, 125,
    153, 175-8, 215, 217-8
New El Salvador Today (NEST), 187
New England Central America
    Network (NECAN), 207
New Institute of Central America
    (NICA), 32, 203
New York Daily News, 147-8
New York Times, 90-1, 124
Newsweek, 124
Nicaragua Exchange Office, 186
Nicaragua Network, 187
North, Lt. Col. Oliver, 14, 45, 74,
    171, 178, 183-8, 190-4, 199
Nosotros, 143
Nuclear Freeze Campaign of
    Houston, Texas, 131
Nuclear Freeze movement, 20, 72,
    88-90

O

O'Dell, James, 162
Office of Public Diplomacy (See
    State Department)
Old Cambridge Baptist Church, 1,
    26-7, 32, 203
Olivares, Fr. Luis, 33, 206
O'Malley, Edward J., FBI director of
    intelligence, 88, 91, 94
O'Neill, Thomas P. "Tip", 124

Ostertag, Bob, 156-9
Our Lady of Guadelupe Church, Houston, Texas, 131
Oxfam America, 177

P

Palestine Liberation Organization, 116
Paul, Jay, Los Angeles Police Dept. 169-72
Peace Links, 89-90
Pearce, Randy, 186
Peccorini, Alfredo, 56, 102
Pedrosa, Manuel, 156-9
Pell, Sen. Claiborne, 98
Peoples Anti-War Movement, 126
Permanent Charities Fund of Boston, 115
Perry, Beth, 43
Perry, William, 176-8
Pico Rivera Methodist Church, 199
Pike Committee of the House of Representatives, 224
Poindexter, John, National Security Adviser, 122, 227
Pollack, Sandy, 42

Q

Quantico, FBI Academy at, 7, 115-7

R

Ratner, Margaret, 105-7, 209
Ratner, Michael, 105, 108-9
Raymond, Jr., Walter, 14, 122-4, 176-8
Reagan, Ronald, 16-18, 20, 24, 73, 82, 183
Reed, David, 202-3
Rees, John, 22, 45, 77-84, 94, 95, 98, 165, 170-2; New York State Assembly report on, 80-82
Reich, Otto, 122, 150
Replica, 98, 113-5
Revell, Oliver "Buck", FBI executive assistant director, 8, 101, 121, 134, 136, 175, 187, 188-90, 193-4, 210, 215-6, 220, 225, 228
Review of the News, 45

Rex 84, 184-5
Reynolds, Diana, 185
Richardson, Ed, 26
Ricks, Special Agent Bob, 189
Ridgeley, Sr. Patricia, 127
Rios, Victor, 201-2
Ripley House, Houston, Texas, 131
Rivera, Marta Alicia, 33
Robinette, Glenn, 193-4, 220
Rockefeller, David, 122
Rockefeller Foundation, 115
Romero, Carlos, 35, 39, 213
Romero, Msgr. Oscar Arnulfo, 40
Roos, Joe, 26
Roosevelt, Eleanor, 223
Roosevelt, Franklin, 223
Rosenberg, Susan, 38

S

Saint Phillips Presbyterian Church, 187
Salcedo Press, 117
SALPRESS, Information office of FDR-FMLN, 163
Salvadoran Ecumenical Aid Council, 68
Sanctuary movement, 19, 37, 98, 200
Sarandon, Susan, 187
Sarbanes, Sen. Paul, 171
Schaeffer, Dr. Steven, 145
Schroeder, Rep. Patricia, 98-9
Schultz, Rev. Gustav, 198
Scripps-Howard Newspapers, 124
Senate Select Committee on Intelligence, 43, 45-6, 210, 216-7, 223, 226
Senate Subcommittee on Security and Terrorism (SST), 105-7
Sensenbrenner, Rep. James, 209
Sessions, William, FBI director, 8, 181, 205, 210-13
Sheen, Martin, 187
Sheridan, Special Agent Jack, 130, 134, 162
Singlaub, Maj. Gen. John K., 74, 77, 171

Sisters of Mercy, 102
Slade, Stephen, 202
Smith, William French, Attorney
    General, 184
Socialist Workers Party, 222
Sojourners, 26
Solarz, Rep. Stephen, 151-2
State Department, 41, 77, 83-4, 90-1,
    218; Office of Latin American
    Public Diplomacy (OPD) of, 22,
    122-5, 150, 173, 176-8, 184, 188
Stearns, Assistant Special Agent in
    Charge Parks, 36, 127, 179
Studds, Rep. Gerry, 152
Students for a Better America, 22
Students for a Democratic Society,
    222
Suitor, Catherine, 31

T
Taca, 71, 102, 132-4
Tarver, Heidi, 157-9
TecNica, 31-2, 223
Tecos, 98, 113
Terrell, Jack, 183, 190-3
Terrorist Photo Album, 96-102, 225-7
Thatcher, Allen, 202
Tower Commission, 186
Trips Out Travel, 202
Tucson Committee for Human
    Rights in Latin America, 144
Tucson Ecumenical Council, 102

U
Unitarian Universalist Committee,
    102

U.S. Peace Council, 42
USA Today, 124

V
Valley Religious Task Force on Cen-
    tral America of Phoenix, Ariz., 206
Varela, Col. Agustin Martinez, 6, 36,
    39, 47-8, 213
Varelli, Frank, 3-4, 6-11, 23, 35-7,
    46, return to El Salvador, 47-60;
    97-102, 104, 110-2; at Quantico,

115-7; 125- 34, 140-4, 149-67,
    173-6, 178-81; polygraph of,
    180-1; 209-16
Villacorta, Antonio, 47, 51-5, 65-7,
    69-70, 113

W
Wall Street Journal, 123
Waller, J. Michael, 77, 125, 173, 187
War Resisters League, 126
Washington Office on Latin America
    (WOLA), 42, 134
Washington Post, 124
Weber, Special Agent Tim, 149, 154,
    165
Webster, William, FBI Director, 83,
    100-1, 135-6, 186, 189, 194, 210,
    217, 225-6, 228
Weiss, Rachel, 200
Weiss, Rep. Ted, 152
Western Airlines, 102
Western Goals Foundation, 22, 45,
    77-8, 83-4, 98, 165, 170-2, 187
Western States Legal Foundation,
    200
White, Robert, 39, 50, 98-9, 152, 191
Whitehorn, Laura, 138
Wick, Charles, 122
Wilkinson, Frank, 228
Willes, Bury, 202
Women's International League for
    Peace and Freedom (WILPF),
    83-4
Woodrow Wilson International
    Center, 115
Woodward, Bob, 217
World Anti-Communist League
    (WACL), 73-4, 84, 113-4, 171
Wright, Anne, 207
Wright, Rep. Jim, 187

Y
Young Americas Foundation, 22, 227

About South End Press

South End Press is a nonprofit, collectively-run book publisher with over 150 titles in print. Since our founding in 1977, we have tried to meet the needs of readers who are exploring, or are already committed to, the politics of radical social change.

Our goal is to publish books that encourage critical thinking and constructive action on the key political, cultural, social, economic, and ecological issues shaping life in the United States and in the world. In this way, we hope to give expression to a wide diversity of democratic social movements and to provide an alternative to the products of corporate publishing.

If you would like a free catalog of South End Press books or information about our membership program—which offers two free books and a 40% discount on all titles—please write us at South End Press, 116 Saint Botolph Street, Boston, MA 02115.

Other titles of interest from South End Press:

The COINTELPRO Papers: Documents from the FBI's Secret Wars Against Dissent in the United States
Ward Churchill and Jim Vander Wall

Agents of Repression: The FBI's Secret War Against the American Indian Movement and the Black Panther Party
Ward Churchill and Jim Vander Wall

War at Home: Covert Action Against U.S. Activists and What We Can Do About It
Brian Glick

Freedom Under Fire: U.S. Civil Liberties in Times of War
Michael Linfield

Necessary Illusions: Thought Control in Democratic Societies
Noam Chomsky

Washington's War on Nicaragua
Holly Sklar

Rules of the Game: American Politics and the Central America Movement
Joshua Cohen and Joel Rogers